The Word of
Cardinal Bernardin

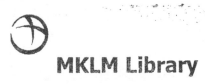

To Maria Simion,
mother of Joseph Cardinal Bernardin

The Word of
Cardinal Bernardin

by
Paolo Magagnotti

© 1996
Center for Migration Studies
New York

The Center for Migration Studies is an educational, nonprofit institute founded in New York in 1964 to encourage and facilitate the study of sociological, demographic, historical, legislative and pastoral aspects of human migration movements and ethnic group relations. The opinions expressed in this work are those of the author.

The Word of Cardinal Bernardin

First Edition
Copyright © 1996 by
The Center for Migration Studies of New York, Inc.

Center for Migration Studies
209 Flagg Place
Staten Island, New York 10304-1199

Library of Congress Cataloging-in-Publication Data

ISBN 1-57703-000-1

Printed in the United States of America

Contents

Preface

Joseph Bernardin's words – both as a Bishop and as a cardinal – have always stirred up deep emotions and a great interest in me. The message they carried out was a strong one and deserved my careful reflection. For this reason I have nurtured myself by reading and studying with utmost desire and attention the works and addresses of this rare and extraordinary man since the early '80s. Our sharing of a common homeland – the Trent region, in the Italian Alps – increased my desire to know and understand his thought. The present work is my way of inviting other readers to give a close look at Cardinal Bernardin's words and to meditate upon them.

In assembling the chapters of this book, my main task has been to collect Bernardin's words and disseminate them. Therefore, I ask the readers to approach my attempt with the same spirit that guided me while I was editing the numerous sources the Cardinal graciously made available to me. The cuts, paraphrases, slight modifications, and summaries of original speeches, manuscripts, tapes, and conversations are only meant to draw attention to the core of his thought on contemporary society. Where my own words have been added, it was only in order to link one source to the next and make contextual references easier to understand. I hope that my interventions never modified the true sense of the original sources.

I started this work some years ago, and the manuscript of the first 27 chapters was submitted to the Cardinal for his approval. On May 4, 1993, he returned the revised texts to me with some notes and indications that I precisely followed. After that point I began preparing other texts, but for personal reasons I had some delay. The death of the Cardinal has moved me to conclude the work sooner and offer this book to the public. Compared to the first draft approved in 1993, a few paragraphs have been added to chapters 7 and 26. The new paragraphs have been taken from Cardinal Bernardin's speech at Georgetown University on September 9, 1996. Chapters 28 to 30 have been added following other addresses given by the Cardinal after he had been told of having a cancer.

Chapters dating back to 1993 were deliberately left untouched. In reading them today, I feel that their deep meaning shows the farsightedness of the Cardinal's thought and intuitions, and the impact of his message on the Church and society is even more enhanced and clarified.

The general introduction on his life is just a tiny help to better know the life of this remarkable great man who has taught the world how to live and how to die. Some of the first parts are an abridged version of the biography *Cardinal Bernardin*, by Eugene Kennedy (Bonus Books Inc., Chicago, 1989). My thanks to the editor for granting me permission to quote from it. My deep gratitude may reach Cardinal Bernardin for his generous help and availability, for his encouragement and closeness, for his constant presence during the writing of this volume, although he was miles away from me.

Special thanks also go to Fr. Alphonse Spilly, C.PP.S., member of the staff of the Cardinal that worked with him on his speeches and writings since 1984. He was of great help both before and after the cardinal's death.

For research and editing I owe many thanks to Father Bonifacio Bolognani, O.F.M., Father Efrem Trettel, O.F.M., Megan McConville, Patricia and Eugene Pellegrini. A special thank to Erminia Minnie Santangelo whose linguistic assistance was precious to me.

I also thank the Center for Migration Studies and particularly its Executive Director, Fr. Lydio Tomasi,C.S., for their prompt availability to publish this volume. Special thanks go Jacqueline Williams, Anastasia Mather, and Mary Brown of CMS for producing this book "under pressure."

Last but not least, let me express my warm thanks to my wife Luigina and my daughter Serena for their patience and support.

I hope that those who will read these pages may experience the same joy I felt in preparing them.

introduction

A Man of Encompassing Stature

I
t was August 30, 1983. The Italian community of Chicago originating from the Italian Province of Trent, at the Austrian border, was gathering in the Lido Restaurant of the American metropolis. They wanted to welcome the newly-made Cardinal Joseph Bernardin, whose parents emigrated to America from a small village of that area four month before his birth in Colombia, South Carolina, on April 2, 1928.

After hearing of the gathering, I felt I should be there. It was my deep desire to celebrate the event with other friends and with a cardinal who shared my same origins and came from the region where the Catholic Church organized the Council of Trent over 450 years ago. A very happy Cardinal Bernardin was at the party with his mother, Maria. We spoke about our common origins and some traditions of our land. He was very proud of his Italian heritage and of the values that his parents, especially his mother (his father Joseph, a stonecutter, died when the boy was only six) instilled in him through words and examples. He thankfully recalled this fact throughout his whole life, even when he became prince of the Church.

On February 2, 1983, eighteen bishops from all continents were lined up in the Paul VI Hall. They were waiting for Pope John Paul II to arrive and complete the installation of the new cardinals. Joseph Louis Bernardin, Archbishop of Chicago, was the sole American among the eighteen whom the Pope would shortly invest as princes of the Church. His long journey

3

from South Carolina to Chicago and then to Rome, from the seminary to his first parish, and his ordination to the bishopric, had gone another step forward, and the 55-year-old bishop was now waiting to wear the scarlet cloth that would put him among the churchmen appointed to maintain the organizational integrity and unity of the teachings and traditions of the Church. His choice as future cardinal also reflected a generalized change in the attitude of the Church towards the new world. Until then, American Catholicism had been seen as a superpower church in a superpower country. Everybody knew of the rise and fall of Bernardin's predecessor as Archbishop of Chicago, John Patrick Cody, who was immersed in media stories related to financial dealings and personal relations.

A Mother's Voice in the Vatican's Rooms

Now, waiting to receive the red hat of a cardinal from the hands of the Pope, in the silent majesty of the ancient pillars and towers of the Vatican, Bernardin thought of his mother watching this special moment of her son's life on television from the Little Sisters retreat house in Chicago and of the advice she had given him prior to his ordination to the bishopric seventeen years before: "Walk straight, and try not to look too pleased with yourself." His mother's common sense – the one she learned in her small Italian village of Trentino and kept with her during her life in America – reached him even then.

His childhood had been shadowed by the specter of the Great Depression and by the phantom of illness and hospitals, culminating in the death of his father. On that Candlemas morning of 1983, the son of Italian immigrants was about to be the first Italian American to become a prince of the Church, after being a mediating leader in the post-conciliar American Catholicism. He also had another record: hardly more than a hundred days had elapsed between his becoming Chicago's Archbishop and his being named a cardinal. This was without parallel in American Catholic history. It had happened perhaps because the Vatican needed to select an extraordinary bishop of unimpeachable integrity as a replacement for the embattled Cody. And Bernardin, who experienced the full weight of a church and world greatly changed for both Catholics and cardinals, was the chairman of a committee of American Catholic bishops charged with drawing up a pastoral letter on the morality of nuclear war.

In becoming a cardinal, the southern gentleman had combined with the modest, practical pastor in him and had discouraged friends and pilgrims from the States to come to Rome to attend the event and to organize gala festivities at home. Instead, he asked that a special collection for the poor be taken up.

Parish Priest in Charleston

After a year of pre-med studies at the University of South Carolina, Joseph Louis Bernardin entered the seminary and studied at St. Mary's College in Kentucky, St. Mary's Seminar in Maryland, and at the Catholic University of America in Washington. He was ordained a priest of the Diocese of Charleston on April 26, 1952.

The year of 1958 marked a turning point in the life and career of Joseph L. Bernardin. He was then a parish priest in Charleston, South Carolina, and embodied the classic, dutiful, unquestioning priest of the period, with little time for anything but work. Yet, American Catholicism was on the verge of great transformations and Bernardin's life would be permanently transformed with it. That same year the 47-year-old Paul Hallinan, a priest from Cleveland, was named bishop of Charleston by Pope John XXIII. Hallinan soon recognized that the quiet and reserved Bernardin was not only bright and efficient but also a gentleman of good manners who knew how to get things done and could contribute much to the Church. Hallinan chose him as his assistant. "He was a man of great faith and optimism," Cardinal Bernardin would later say while recalling their years of work together and acknowledging the lessons of unswerving devotion and pastoral realism he had learned from Bishop Hallinan, his first important mentor. These lessons would not be lost but rather inspire him to follow his instinct and serve the Church and its people in the same way. In 1962 Hallinan was appointed as archbishop of Atlanta and petitioned Rome to have Bernardin, whom he had come to know and esteem, as his auxiliary bishop.

His request was fulfilled and on April 26, 1966, Joseph L. Bernardin, just turned 38, was ordained as titular bishop of Ligura and auxiliary bishop of Atlanta, becoming the youngest bishop in the country. The two men could continue to work together and commit themselves to the drawing up of a local pastoral letter on war and peace during the Vietnam war. The letter would become the basis for the one to be issued by the entire National Conference of Bishops – whose title was eventually, "Peace in Vietnam" – released on November 18, 1966.

By that time, Hallinan was seriously ill with a hepatitis infection and eventually died in 1968. Before dying, he asked his auxiliary to arrange a party that he meant to be a "going away party." In pajamas and bathrobe and unable to eat, Hallinan welcomed the members of the chancery staff with calmness, courage, and generosity of spirit, as Bernardin would later recall. The man, who first received the Reverend Martin Luther King Jr. when he returned from Oslo with the Nobel Prize for Peace in December 1964, and who organized a civic banquet for him, thus vigorously contributing to the lessening of racial problems, died in January 1968. Bishop Bernardin preached at his funeral, and looked down at the first pew, where the segregationist Governor Lester Maddox and the Reverend Martin Luther King Jr. sat next to each other. Bernardin understood that only the great effort of mediation made by the late Bishop Hallinan had brought the two foes together. He also understood that his apprenticeship and novitiate were over. A new phase in his extraordinary ecclesiastical education was about to begin.

General Secretary of the National Conference of U.S. Catholic Bishops

Shortly before Hallinan died, Bernardin accepted the appointment as general secretary of the National Conference of Bishops and moved to Washington. He found in Archbishop Dearden a new guide. Dearden was chosen in 1966 as the first president of the National Conference of Catholic Bishops after Vatican II and wanted to develop it into a conference where the bishops could learn to work together and reach an effective expression of collegiality. In the past, the previous aggregation of bishops, the national Catholic Welfare Council, had been suspected of being subversive of Roman authority and in 1922, the Consistorial Congregation – the Roman department responsible for the world's bishops – decreed that the Council should no longer meet. The task now became to develop a conference of bishops who could be completely loyal to the Holy See and the Pope. John Dearden was pleased that Bernardin had accepted the appointment for which his training, experience, and disposition fit him so well.

The year 1968 saw the assassinations of Reverend Martin Luther King Jr. and Senator Robert F. Kennedy, as well as riots and demonstrations against the Vietnam war in the nation's largest cities. In this wave of burning protests, the Catholic Church, rocked with its own parallel convulsions, was likewise torn between old models and mentalities and the new ideas ushered in by Vatican II, of which Bernardin attended the fourth session sitting among the expert consultants. Archbishop Dearden had ordered a multidisciplinary study of the American clergy, with the conviction that in investigating the priesthood, the Church would better understand itself and the great transformation through which it was passing. That same year, Bishop Bernardin was about to take over his office at the National Conference of Catholic Bishops.

Most of the staff had expected Msgr. Francis Hurley – a priest who had been working as the conference administration for some years – to become its general secretary and were disappointed when the one chosen fell to be a man they considered an outsider. But Dearden wanted someone new at the conference, a general secretary who had not only been previously involved with the long-time staff members, but also a person free of friendship or other commitments that might hamper his freedom in overseeing changes.

Bernardin tried to be on good terms with Hurley and visited him to express that he had refused the job twice and didn't want it at the price of Hurley's being hurt. Bernardin's determination – although he changed the world with which they were familiar – never to hurt bishops and staff members' feelings soon gained him the esteem of the whole conference.

Facing the Turmoil in the Church Hierarchy

The doctrine of papal infallibility spread out by the Vatican I had contributed to the centralization of all authority in Rome, reducing that of the world's bishops. Vatican II had renovated the basic theological principle of the Pope's primacy but had also recognized that bishops possessed – in virtue of their ordination – authority over their own Church. This acknowledgment had caused and changed forever the unquestioning attitude towards the central authority.

At the same time, America was facing one of its most difficult moments. The assassination of Reverend Martin Luther King Jr. hadn't stopped the Poor People's March, a demonstration to take place in Washington, D.C., and aimed at racial justice and a better national grasp of the problem of poverty. Bernardin, aware of racial problems from his own South Carolina upbringing and his work with Hallinan in supporting the black cause in Atlanta, was anxious to provide something more concrete than just moral support. A program, the Campaign for Human Development, grew under his guidance to provide monetary grants for deserving projects aimed at alleviating poverty and obtained full approval by the whole body of bishops. In the way he handled the problem and put the program into action, Bernardin's mode of combining his roles as a pastor and a manager became fully apparent.

Becoming Familiar with the Vatican

Archbishop Dearden thought it necessary that Bernardin come to know the leaders of the various Roman departments with whom he would be dealing and asked John Cardinal Cody of Chicago to accompany and introduce Bernardin to the curial officials in Rome. Cody, who loved Rome and had visited it more than a hundred times, was happy to carry out the task. He went to Rome with Bernardin and was a helpful companion for the man who, fourteen years later, had to succeed him as archbishop of Chicago. In Rome, Msgr. Giovanni Benelli, Vice-Secretary of State, met Bernardin and decided that the American bishop was a man whose opinions could be trusted. Besides, Bernardin, being an Italian American, needed no education in the subtleties and nuances of Vatican communications.

Meanwhile in the American homeland, the priests' understandable post-Vatican II interest in greater participation in the decisionmaking process had established the National Federation of Priests' Council. New turmoil was to be expected. The spark that ignited the situation was the encyclical letter on birth control, *Humanae Vitae*, issued in 1968 by Pope Paul VI. The Catholic world, and the world in general, split into two different parties, one supporting the orthodox view stated also by the encyclical and the other assessing the primacy of the individual conscience in the choice of birth-control means. Incidents happened here and there inside the church.

In 1967, the *American National Catholic Reporter* had published a text in which the traditional primacy of conscience for Catholics in their moral decision was highlighted. A year later, the archbishop of Washington, Patrick Cardinal O'Boyle – a staunch defender of traditional teachings – distributed a letter to his priests demanding total compliance with the encyclical. The dissenting priests were suspended and never reinstated, although groups of their parishioners sent petitions to Cardinal O'Boyle.

Mediator of the Pope

In the autumn of 1968, Bernadin was asked by Pope Paul VI – through Secretary of State Cicognani – to mediate the dispute between Cardinal O'Boyle and the priests. Bernardin was forbidden to disclose that he had received the assignment from the Holy See and was supposed to act as though he had been invited to intervene by Cardinal O'Boyle. He accepted the impossible assignment, but his mission of arbitration did not succeed. Bernardin had no real authority, but he worked very hard at the problem, trying as usual not to hurt anyone. The American bishops repeatedly pledged their loyalty to the Pope but dealt with birth control, as they do still, as a pastoral rather than a disciplinary matter.

In that period of tumult, however, Bernardin himself also made sure that the multidisciplinary study of the American priesthood went forward. In

1970 he recruited Father James Rausch from Minnesota to work with him as associate general secretary. Two years later father Rausch succeeded Bernardin as general secretary when the latter became archbishop of Cincinnati. During that stormy year, Joseph Bernardin had undergone an extraordinary test of his faith and convictions, experienced the scrutiny of Rome authorities, his fellow bishops, and American priests without being diminished in the sight of any of them. His arbitration had failed, but he had not. He emerged from his baptism by immersion in the international Church believing more firmly than ever in the importance of process over personality in resolving disputed issues within it.

In the Middle of New Church Challenges

It was a time of great identity crisis, and the priesthood faced its own. Many clergymen came openly to express their doubts about their relevance in society and about other formerly unquestioned disciplines of their calling, such as celibacy. Priests and nuns withdrew in large number and married. In the mid-1960s reports said that in the United States more than 700 priests had left to get married whereas more than 10,000 worldwide had requested dispensation for the same reason. Bishop Bernardin thought that these events were making more and more urgent his primary task of reorganizing the bishops' conference and completing the inquiry on priesthood. Also in this case, Bernardin showed great discretion – never violated a confidence, told others only as much as they needed to know, and displayed a strenuous impartiality. This gained him a reputation not only in the United States but also among the Roman congregations.

Bernardin, aware that a genuine crisis existed in the American priesthood, wanted the study to succeed. In convincing men as different as John Cardinal Krol and Father Andrew Greeley to work together for the good end of the project, he was attempting to manage a major cultural change in ecclesiastical Catholicism and was moving between an old generation of largely Irish bishops, truculent and traditional, and a new generation of progressive and impatient Vatican II priests. The most crucial issue was priest sexuality. Krol opposed his firm intention to investigate it. Bernardin respected the priesthood as deeply as Krol but he also understood the need to look at the areas of sexuality and spirituality about which many priests were expressing conflicts. In this instance, as in many others, the future cardinal displayed the Italian gift for earthy realism that balanced and sweetened his obsessive bureaucratic dedication.

In the summer of 1969, auxiliary bishop James V. Shannon of Minneapolis had resigned and married. In so doing, he had removed himself from the top of the list for preferment in ecclesiastical assignments. Bernardin moved up on the line of prospective leaders of the Church in the United States. From these events and crucial decisions, Bernardin understood that progress in helping the Church to grow organically demanded the maintenance of a difficult balance between institutional expectations and personal convictions and integrity. In the fall of 1970, he was negotiating the successful conclusion of the priesthood studies. The bishops were hesitant about a public affirmation of the Church's teaching on celibacy, but quite open to learning the truth about clerical problems and discontents shown in the completed research.

Leader in the Synod of Bishops

Rome began to signal its confidence in Bernardin. In 1969, he was asked to be an associate secretary of that year's Synod of Bishops, and from 1974 on he would have an important position at every Synod. The National Conference of American Bishops had to gather to elect its new president. As the meeting approached, Bernardin continued his involvement with the bishops of Canada and South America, which ultimately led to the Inter-American Bishops Meeting. One of the results of this new association was Bernardin's becoming well known and trusted by churchmen throughout the hemisphere. The Conference elected Krol as its new president, but Bernardin received 94 votes. In electing Krol – as it was expected – the bishops were not traversing much ground, but with the votes to Bernardin they were planning a more significant transit in the future.

Archbishop in Cincinnati Challenging the White House

Meanwhile providence was helping Bernardin advance in the ranks of Church hierarchy. The seat of Cincinnati was made vacant by the death of Archbishop Leibold. In November 1972, Archbishop Luigi Raimondi, the apostolic delegate, announced the appointment of Joseph Louis Bernardin to become archbishop of Cincinnati. Raimondi was recalled to Rome and named a cardinal the following year. He was succeeded by Jean Jadot as apostolic delegate in the United States.

It was clear from the very beginning that Bernardin would never be regarded only as the archbishop of a mid-western archdiocese, for he was already perceived as a man whose substantial influence in the ranges of Catholicism could only increase. His first Christmas sermon as archbishop startled his listeners and drew wide attention in the media. He complained of the bombing in Vietnam and spoke directly to the Nixon Administration, whose maneuvers he had closely observed during the years. His was not the cry of an emotional antiwar activist. Bernardin was not only condemning this new flare of warfare but making it clear that the Catholic Church was not a silent and malleable force that Nixon could use as he wished for political advantage. Bernardin's words in that Christmas mass challenged the government policies in Vietnam and offered a prophecy of the position that the entire conference of bishops would take against nuclear war a decade later in the pastoral letter, "The Challenge of Peace." The chairman of the committee of bishops who drafted it would be Joseph L. Bernardin.

In response to his Christmas sermon, Bernardin was asked to preach at the White House on the Sunday immediately following Nixon's second inauguration. Evangelist Billy Graham and Rabbi Edgar Magnin would have the same task for their respective religious communities. After a long and careful examination of the invitation, Bernardin decided to accept it and represent the Catholic Church at the event. Nonetheless, he could read the manipulative message hidden in the invitation. Bernardin delivered a talk that was appropriate for the occasion. It was not full praise for Nixon or his programs. He delivered a message both about Catholic values and about the manipulation-resistant character of the Church. President Nixon was forcefully smiling as he handed Bernardin an autographed Bible and bade him farewell.

The Pro-Life Project

To better know his archdiocese, Bernardin planned a series of pastoral visitations which started on January 22, 1973, the same day in which the U.S. Supreme Court issued its first ruling on a moral acceptability of abortion. Archbishop Bernardin immediately took a position against abortion. Ten years later, after he had become a cardinal, he would assume the chairmanship of the Pro-Life Committee of the National Conference of Catholic Bishops. In his ruling of the archdiocese, he offered masses at homes and centers for the aged and poor in Cincinnati and later elsewhere. He also initiated a Christmas mass at the Cincinnati Workhouse for prisoners, something no previous archbishop had done. In his contacts with the priests and nuns of his diocese, he was quick to understand and avoid embarrassing others for the errors they committed.

Priests and people began to think that they had never met anyone quite like him. Gradually, Bernardin modified the structures of his archdiocese, achieving what he wanted through his patient evocation of the cooperation of others, fruit of a constant consultation with his assistants and priests. His loyalty to the Vatican was such that he could never approve arrangements that did not match ecclesiastical legislation, but neither would he ever administer his territory in concrete literalistic fashion. He wanted to organize the archdiocese, trim and simplify its plans, consolidate its offices, and bring its practices into harmony with the official regulation of the Church.

President of the Conference of the U.S. Bishops

The National Conference of Catholic Bishops had been set on firm foundations and was now functioning well. The solid, developing sense of cooperation among the members of this organization was the fruit of the collaboration of John Dearden and Joseph Bernardin. Yet, the conference was now entering a crucial phase of its maturation process. It could become a truly collegial body or it might, under hesitant or passive leadership, stall and never achieve its full development. Krol's presidency would be up in the fall of 1974 and a successor had to be chosen soon.

America's history was going on rapidly. In August 1974, vexed by pressure about Watergate, President Nixon resigned. On the Catholic front, Cardinal Cody was more and more isolated. Bernardin was not only mentioned as the likely successor to Krol as president of the American bishops but also as possible successor some day to John Cardinal Cody in Chicago. In the fall of 1974, the bishops elected Bernardin for a three-year presidency of the conference. Providence was on his side as ever, and Cardinal Dearden smiled pleased that his "Joe" could move on.

Reference Point Both for Vatican and U.S. Bishops

Cardinal Dearden had asked Bernardin to handle Roman business when Bernardin was general secretary. Now that he had been elected president of the National Conference, he felt that the presidency should have regular relationships with the dicasteries and department of the Roman Church. His aim in that was to solidify the character of the conference and institutionalize as many aspects of its functioning as possible. As a consequence, Rome witnessed regular visits by the president and vice-president, as well as other relevant officers, of the National Conference of American Catholic Bishops. In Bernardin's judgement, these structural visits would carry out sound policies and procedure that would outlast the personalities who had established them.

The result of Bernardin being known more and more in the Roman environment was that he was consulted on most appointments of bishops in the United States and was a member of the congregation in Rome. His intention was to seek out the best men possible, through as much consultation as possible, to be bishops of the country. Thus, through a quiet but carefully shepherded consultation, Bernardin began the collaboration with the apostolic delegate that brought dozens of moderate, pastoral, Vatican II bishops into the American Church.

The historical moment was one in which people were confronted with moral dilemmas. The conference was giving the bishops a forum to discuss internal Church problems and voice the Catholic opinion on questions of general interest to society. The conference, however, was not yet enough at ease structurally to mediate in an effective collegial way on the moral dilemmas of the day. The Catholic people had to pay a deep reflection to their own beliefs and practices. More work had to be done to achieve the new goal, but Bernardin had a clear insight of what had to be done.

Facing New Turmoil Again

In 1975 the American bishops planned a series of public hearings across the country to listen to both Catholic and non-Catholic Americans on the great issues of the time. For the time being, they felt, the conference, barely ten years old, was not affecting the general culture very much and was not bringing about sufficient response or follow-through from its own communicant. The problem was complex. The bishops had not only to take strong leadership roles. They had to encourage those Catholics with a real interest in the church, but, at the same time, they could not and would not support the pressures brought by the dedicated people for optional celibacy, women priests, and other remedies for the Church's problems that the latter considered urgent. Bernardin believed in strengthening the Pope and the institutional Church, but he was also dedicated to the people who wanted that very Church to reform its bureaucracy once and for all. His personal concern, his capacity to understand and not indict human failings, his own commitment to a reinvigorated Catholicism, his gentleness and self-effacing manners won him the respect of friends and foes, as a leader of great integrity and trustfulness. Nineteen seventy six was an election year and the Catholic vote – the ethnical vote that Nixon had so prized – was seen as vital to the eventual success of either Jimmy Carter or Gerald Ford.

The two candidates decided to meet the Conference of Bishops to explain their positions. The general secretary of the bishop, Father James Rausch, proposed that the Executive Committee of the bishops, which included Bernardin, would meet with the presidential candidates in the late summer. Bernardin didn't want to meet the candidates. He felt that the meeting was *"haud opportune,"* by no means opportune. The meeting happened at the

Mayflower hotel in Washington, D.C., on August 31. As president of he conference, Bernardin pointed out that the Church does not "involve itself in partisan politics; it does not endorse or oppose particular parties or candidates." Anyway, the bishops were disappointed with Carter's position on abortion. Their sentiments encouraged Ford's position. The media made a case of this and attacked the conference and Bernardin. The latter, however, in a situation in which he could not control the interpretations of the press, felt he had acted with complete integrity. The Executive Board of the bishops issued a unanimous declaration of support for Bernardin and his committee. Nonetheless, Bernardin described the period as "one of the most difficult of my life." He was sure that there had to be a better way for the bishops to address the moral concerns of the nation and to express Catholic convictions on matters of social policy.

Owing nothing to the Catholic bishops, Jimmy Carter defeated Ford and became President. Bernardin took it indifferently. He had concern enough for other more relevant matters. American canon lawyers had been pioneers in applying the insights of social science and medicine into the Church court procedures, but the Vatican had criticized the "American Norms" for the dissolution of marriages by annulment. Besides, some abuse of the norms occurred. Bernardin, as president of the bishops, had to support and explain these new experimental norms in Rome in a lengthy personal interview with Pope Paul VI. Other matters were on the eye of the Roman Church. In some American dioceses general absolution was practiced in some circumstances instead of individual confession. Once again, Bernardin was called upon to work out a solution that would preserve the integrity of the Church teaching while doing as little damage as possible to pastoral intentions. In his visit to Rome, he stood on firm ground in managing the problems. As always, he would never go against what the Church asked of him, but he would not sacrifice a pastorally beneficial project; the Roman authorities had to understand that.

Back in the United States, Bernardin realized how much he was immersed in national and international activities, and decided to stop for a while in order to examine the state of his own soul. The social commitment, he was persuaded, had to be paralleled by the same amount of spiritual involvement. "I decided," he explained later, "to give God the first hour of my day, no matter what." He thus started a personal journey into an uncharted desert of reflection, from which he returned with both his own humility and his appreciation of the problems of others deepened. His trip abroad brought him to Poland and Hungary in 1976.

In the homeland, Greeley was desperately active against Cardinal Cody. He recorded on some tapes, his message to the other bishops to substitute

Cody with Bernardin, so that the latter could influence the imminent election of a new Pope. When Paul VI died, however, Bernardin was not yet a cardinal and did not take part in the conclave. His friend and mentor, Cardinal Dearden was there, but no information was exchanged between the two. The burning tapes with Greeley's declarations fell in the hands of the media and Bernardin's name with them. They nicknamed him "Deep Purple" and clearly hinted at his plotting to manipulate the conclave. Bernardin, however, was completely extraneous to the fact and eventually succeeded in putting an end to any notion that he had participated in the chimera of conclave manipulation.

The Challenge of Nuclear War

The bishops gathered again in November 1980 to study the Reagan agenda, which differed greatly from their own, especially on social issues. On that occasion, the bishops voted the proposal for two pastoral letters on economy and nuclear weapons. The development of the first was given to Archbishop Weackland of Milwaukee. The second, on nuclear weapons, was entrusted to Archbishop Bernardin. The decision marked a turning point in the history of American bishops. For the first time they began to examine the morality of the country's posture of defense and the economic system that undergirded it. The two letters were not at all what government officials expected or wanted from the Catholic bishops. Reagan and his many Catholic appointees were hardly enthusiastic about the bishops' examining and criticizing their policies. Bernardin was aware of these reaction and of the pressure that the government was prepared to exert on the bishops.

Archbishop of Chicago

At the same time, Cody's case fostered by Greeley was intensely followed in the press. Roman authorities knew well that Bernardin was innocent of any involvement in papal conclave machinations. The same charges Greeley affirmed were only fantasies, but pressure and phone calls by journalists forced Bernardin to pronounce an official statement. "Father Greeley has said that these are fantasies and that is what they are," was the only public statement Bernardin would ever make about the matter. In 1982 Cardinal Cody died. In light of the tumult that had been set off in Chicago, his successor would have to have a personality and a record that could stand an investigation worthy of the KGB. Pope John Paul II summoned Bernardin in Rome. Here he told him that he was his choice. The appointment was officially announced on July 10, 1982. One long chapter in the history of Bernardin's life and in the history of Chicago had come to a close. The new archbishop immediately began to bring healing and reconciliation to that local Church. He set the tone of his first meeting with his priests, telling them "I am Joseph your brother," working hard to restore unity and confidence in the archdiocese.

As new archbishop of Chicago, Bernardin attended a party given by the mayor of Chicago, Mrs. Jane Byrne. Bernardin was gracious but cautious about being photographed with her or with any other of her politicians. He had learned a bitter lesson about press manipulation of events. In his first words as archbishop on the day of his installation, he stated a position of civic independence and declared himself a religious leader who would not allow the power of his spiritual office to be co-opted by any power center. Meanwhile, his work in the bishops's conference went on.

The first version of the pastoral letter on nuclear weapons had been completed in June 1982. The core issues of the proposed document were: questions about the morality of first-strike use of nuclear weapons; a halt to the development of nuclear arms, and a careful examination of the government's stated targeting policy in regard to civilian populations. By the second week of October a second draft had been completed and distributed to the bishops. The letter remained a document in progress, and another round of comments was solicited in mid-December so that a third draft could be prepared late in winter. The final version's main conclusion stated that a) nuclear war was a morally unacceptable means and was not justified; b) the innocent killing of civilians was always wrong; c) nuclear weapons constituted an unjustifiable moral risk; d) the bishops supported immediate agreement to curb the testing, production, and development of new nuclear weapons.

The bishops approved the document on May 2, 1983 – Archbishop Bernardin was already Cardinal – during a convention held at the Palmer House in Chicago, and it became matter of attention and discussion all over the world. A later survey revealed that the pastoral letter had influenced the thinking of Catholics in a very significant way. The letter was entitled, "The Challenge of Peace: God's Promise and Our Response." The aim was to develop, define and apply a consistent ethic of life to those issues that emerged from the widely shared convictions about the indefensible moral character of nuclear war. The question was: In a time when we can do anything technologically, how do we decide morally what we never should do? Bernardin received the 1983 Albert Einstein Peace Prize and accepted it in the name of the conference of bishops. At this point, Cardinal

Dearden's dream of a national conference that could mediate relevant moral issues had come fully to age.

As we already know, during the Consistory of February 2, 1983, the Holy Father made Bernardin a cardinal with the titular Church of Jesus the Divine Worker in Rome. In an address at Fordham University later that year, Cardinal Bernardin, then chair of the bishops' Pro-Life Activities Committee, articulated the need for a "Consistent Ethic of Life," a concept that he continued to develop through the years. Acknowledging that each of the "life-issues" affecting human life from conception to natural death – and in all its circumstances – is distinct, Bernardin also demonstrated continuously a linkage among such issues as abortion and assisted suicide, poverty and healthcare. The U.S. episcopal conference adopted the Consistent Ethic of Life as the basis for its Respect Life Program from 1985 onward.

Revitalizing the Course of the Church

Now Bernardin wanted the bishops develop the pro-life position and broaden their horizon by putting all the pro-life issues together. The defense of the life of the unborn had to be joined by the defense of life whenever its value was threatened in the culture. Bernardin succeeded in a threefold manner. He made the church personnel rethink their positions on questions in which the sanctity of life was at risk. He disturbed the country's liberal left by connecting it to issues – such as capital punishment – they had long championed. He stimulated the militant right – which had emphasized only antiabortion issues – to examine other categories. Issues such genetics, abortion, capital punishment, modern warfare and the care of the terminally ill were put together. The cardinal was aware that these burning problems needed individual treatment and responses. But his purpose was to highlight the way in which new technological challenges in each one of these areas were faced. From now on, the right to life had to be considered together with the quality of life. Bernardin set the Church on a revitalized course through a presentation that perhaps was the most significant address given by any archbishop in the history of American Catholicism

However, the cardinal had also to deal with the archdiocese of Chicago and its needed changes, among which were the closing or consolidation of parishes and schools and racial problems. Bernardin's practiced collegiality settled the problems in the least painful way possible. In the meanwhile the two archbishops of New York and Boston had died. The new ones were chosen without Bernardin's consultation. They were both of Irish heritage and initiated personal terms of service in which their individual actions and statements tended to overshadow the function of the conference.

On the other hand, the media were always interested in the conflictual aspects of the relationship between Catholic officials and Catholic bishops. This time, during a speech delivered on October 24, 1984, Bernardin raised the question of how – in the objective order of law and politics – to determine which issues were public moral questions and which were best defined as private moral questions. By doing that, he supported the bishops' position but gave Catholic officials a breathing space and allowed the Church to be present in national life in a more restrained and balanced manner.

In 1988 Bernardin and his brother bishops went to Rome for their *"ad limina"* visit. He reviewed with Pope John Paul II all the matters connected with the archdiocese of Chicago. The problems of communication and the misunderstanding between the American bishops and the Holy See – thanks to Bernardin and the collegial process he had established and defended – had now been largely solved.

The Pope and Bernardin, the Cardinal of Chicago, were alone in the Pope's office. "Thank you," the Pope said to Bernardin. "Thank you for the examples of real collegiality, of brother helping brother."

Perhaps no phrase could better sum up the meaning of Joseph Bernardin's life and career. He left the room feeling that he had only done his duty. He had only done what the Church he loved had asked of him. Amid conflicts and controversies, however, the cardinal who had learned not to be "too pleased with himself," had placed a unique, indelible mark on the U.S. Church.

Faith and Courage till Death

Joseph Bernardin, known as the Cardinal of Chicago *par excellence*, has left a deep mark with his thoughts and his actions in the life of the Church, not only in the United States, but also overseas. Always very respectful of the distinction between religion and politics, he never hesitated to challenge the authority of issues, behaviors, and programs that may have been lacking in coherence with the teaching of the Gospel – a Gospel he always preached and witnessed with vigor. The numerous honorary doctorates received from colleges and universities in the United States and Europe and other high acknowledgments are eloquent confirmations of the esteem he enjoyed.

Joseph Bernardin – as priest, archbishop or cardinal – always molded his life and his pastoral commitments with the principle of being one of "those who serve," giving full priority to the people and recognizing the dignity of every human being. And it's exactly on the principle and the demands of the dignity of man, seen as a child of God, that Bernardin started all his activities in defense of human rights. He was a man of exceptional intelligence, great courage, and extraordinary capacity in reading "the signs of the times." He never avoided the challenges that life threw at him as a man and as a minister of God, but he faced them with utter honesty. With an inexhaustable energy fed by a profound unshakable faith, he never failed to act with decision, which left a deep mark in the final part of our century.

As an eloquent speaker, he always suceeded in engaging an intimate personal dialogue with large crowds gathered both in churches and in open spaces, and faithfully spoke with enthusiasm of projects and programs aimed at defending the dignity of the person. His tone never changed: whatever he said was always calm, gentle, and soft spoken. Joseph Bernardin surprised many with uncommon, courageous initiatives and behaviors. His personality grew above ordinary limits and brought him to become an intimate part in human and spiritual events, especially during the last three years of his life.

Cardinal Bernardin was widely recognized as a man of prayer and deep faith. His integrity, honesty, equanimity, and courage in the face of adversities became increasingly clear. Despite the fact that he became a leader in the Catholic Church's response to clerical sexual misconduct, in November 1993, Cardinal Bernardin was falsely accused of sexual misconduct by Steven Cook – a young man with AIDS who had been a seminarian in Cincinnati while Bernardin was archbishop there. The humiliating charges were immediately broadcast throughout the world. The cardinal didn't look for a cover up, but called for a press meeting to affirm his innocence. The media jumped all over him, and the whole world became aware of the charges made against the cardinal, who can be considered the first martyr of global communication.

Shortly after Steven Cook accused him, Bernardin wrote him a personal letter – which never arrived to the recipient – requesting that they meet so they could pray together. The following springtime, Cook withdrew his accusations: they were a product of his imagination. The cardinal answered with his usual generosity, with goodness and understanding, offering brotherly help. On December 30, 1994, the cardinal flew to Philadelphia to meet Steven, spending two hours with him and celebrating Mass. "Never in my 43 years as a priest have I witnessed a more profound reconciliation," the cardinal later wrote.

In June 1995, the cardinal faced another tremendous challenge. Dr. Warren Furey, his personal physician, discovered that he had pancreatic cancer. Once more, Bernardin showed his courage and his sense of reality. He summoned a press meeting, and announced that he would undergo surgery. The resulting surgery and treatment slowed him down but did not bring to a halt his pastoral ministry, which he resumed as quickly and as fully as possible. He never even stopped traveling. Among others, he came to Rome, and visited his village of origin in the Italian Alps. Late in 1995, he began to experience severe constant pain in his back because of two spinal conditions unrelated to the cancer.

Being "At Home"

In the meantime, he counseled the cancer patients with whom he was in touch, "to place themselves entirely in the hands of the Lord." Following his instinct and always strong desire to bring people together, to create human relations, and to encourage friendship in every field, in mid-August 1996, he announced the establishment of a Catholic Common Ground Project designed to engage Catholics in dialogue about various topics of disagreement within the Church but within the boundaries of ecclesial teaching. He was enthusiastic of and fully dedicated to this project, and was already thinking of future ones. But, once again, a new challenge confronted him.

On August 28, Loyola Medical Center's examinations indicated that the cancer had returned, this time in the liver. The prognosis was without hope: the cancer was diagnosed as a terminal one and the cardinal's life expectancy was one year or less. In a statement given on August 30, the cardinal wrote: "We can look at death as an enemy or a friend. If we see it as an enemy, death causes anxiety and fear. We tend to go into a state of denial. But if we see it as a friend, our attitude is truly different. As a person of faith, I see death as a friend, as the transition from earthly life to life eternal." And here, how can we not think about his pastoral letter, "A Sign of Hope," published on October 7, 1995, just a few months after he was diagnosed with cancer: "My initial experience was of disorientation, isolation, a feeling of not being 'at home' anymore!" In that same August statement he added: "In the coming months I will continue to serve the archdiocese in the way I have in the past."

With his unbelievable generosity and goodness the cardinal, now withstanding the growing weakness caused by the chemotherapy, continued his ministry in his beloved archdiocese, performing impossible tasks. With great faith and heroic generosity he intensified his visits to the terminally ill and those condemmed to death, bringing them comfort, praying with them in the heart of the night, till the very last moment of death. Nor did he interrupt his frequent presence at public meetings and conferences.

On September 9, ten days after receiving the news of his terminal cancer, Cardinal Bernardin went to the White House to receive the "Medal of Freedom," the highest U.S. civilian honor, conferred to him by the President of the United States. Soon afterward, he addressed the students of Georgetown University on very important social and religious themes.

"I now face a very different horizon," he said to the students. And added: "As my life now ebbs away, as my temporal destiny becomes clearer each hour and each day, I am not anxious, but rather reconfirmed in my conviction about the wonder of human life." Once again, in a very clear way, he has made his point.

After a few weeks of chemotherapy, he realized that the treatment was not very effective and was draining him of the energy he needed for his work in the archdiocese. He decided to terminate the treatment, with the hope of being able to commit himself to his pastoral ministry a little more. The dying Cardinal continued until his last breath to promote the principles and values of the Gospel that had motivated the service of his entire life, and in a letter reflecting his impending death, Cardinal Bernardin told the U.S. Supreme Court justices that there "can be no such thing as a 'right to assisted suicide.'"

In his statement of August 30, 1996, he said: "I will keep a full schedule for as long as I can. Moreover, as appropriate, I will keep everyone informed of my health."

It wasn't long after that other people had to speak for him. On Thursday, November 14, 1996, the announcement was: " Joseph Cardinal Bernardin died at 1:33 this morning."

"Cardinal, Eminence" – said Rev. Kenneth Velo, in his Homily in the Holy Name Cathedral, remembering his 'beautiful ride' – you're home." I was there too, with millions of the Cardinal's "brothers and sisters" in prayer, both in the church and all over the world watching television and listening to the radio. I, too, had responded to his call and was there, in great acknowledgment of all he taught and did, even while dying. I, too, am an heir of his legacy of love. From the bottom of my heart, I could say again, "Thank You, Cardinal."

1

The Ten Commandments and Human Rights

Cardinal Bernardin implores us all to lead "a consistent ethical life," and calls on the youth of this world to examine the increasingly evident moral dilemmas that technological development has introduced into our society.

Governments and young people of good will must work together to build a peaceful world. Our youth are called to make those decisions that will affect family life and the life of nations in the years to come. As a result, they must seek the common good of all mankind and work for diminishing the threat of nuclear war, fighting hunger, setting free all those who are politically and spiritually oppressed. Living in peace, harmony and unity is the fulfillment of all expectations linked to human rights. As the Archbishop of Chicago often pointed out, this is the basis of the Ten Commandments and the main challenge that confronts the youth of today.

Cardinal Bernardin's religious view of the world is genuine and in accordance with the problems of contemporary society. His insistence on developing a comprehensive moral vision – what he calls "a consistent ethic of life" – has shaped many of his ideas and given strength and unity to his addresses. Among these, the one delivered to young people at St. Thomas of Villanova University, Miami,

Florida, in 1985 is particularly significant. He stated it is the "boredom" of the Yuppie generation to which he denies any justifiable grounds.

The Moral Problems of Technological Development

His argument is: look at the incredible amount of problems – "a qualitatively new range of moral problems" – that technological development has brought about. In a time when we can do almost anything technologically, we are faced with a new set of moral questions. The technological challenge, he argues, "cries out for a consistent ethic of life." And what about peace in this context?

Following Pope John Paul II's argument, he continues by saying that peace cannot be left in the hands of governments alone: it must be built by "the resolute determination of all people of good will." He concludes: "If we are to have hope in the task before us of building a peaceful world, we must have confidence in the God-given genius of the human spirit." He then addresses his audience directly, with the following words:

> My young brothers and sisters, you will make decisions which will affect family life in the next decade. You will make decisions which will affect the life of nations into the next century. Will you work for the common good of all? Will you work for peace? Will you work to diminish the threat of nuclear war, to combat hunger and malnutrition, to preserve the environment, to provide employment, to free those oppressed politically and spiritually? Remember the challenge of Pope John Paul II to you: "The future far into the next century lies in your hands. The future of peace lies in your hearts."

> This is International Youth Year. I clearly prefer to think of it in this way rather than as the "Year of the Yuppie." I'm not suggesting that you shun excellence in your careers or that you avoid making money. I'm offering an alternative to being bored, an option to being merely trendy. The world in which we live – the times in which we live – are challenging! The are exciting!

The challenge, therefore, is to live in peace, harmony, and unity. In order to do so, we must live in proper relationships. As Cardinal Bernardin has said in another place: "We need the Ten Commandments to show us how to do this."

The Values of the Commandments for the Present Society

In 1985, in The Chicago Catholic, the archdiocesan newspaper, Cardinal Bernardin wrote a series of articles in which he discussed the value and significance of the commandments for society today. He points out that it is precisely because "the goal of human life is harmony, peace and unity that we need to follow the Ten Commandments, which provide the guidelines for establishing and maintaining proper relationships." What is most significant is that Bernardin interprets the commandments as "a divinely inspired chart of basic human rights."

The First Commandment, "I am the Lord your God. You shall not have other gods besides me," guarantees us the right to give God first place in our lives. God must come before all the other "gods" of contemporary society – wealth, material success, comfort, pleasure – in order to safeguard the liberty of human beings to live as they should.

The Second Commandment, not to take God's name in vain, "affirms and defends the basic human right to cultivate and maintain an attitude of reverence toward God, of respect for what is holy, of awe toward the transcendent other who is our origin and our destiny." Cardinal Bernardin observes how basic a right it is to recognize that God exists – it gives meaning and purpose to life.

The Third Commandment, "Remember to keep holy the sabbath day," states a fundamental human right – the right to sabbath rest. He insists that to live in peace, harmony and unity, we must invest quality time in rest.

The Fourth Commandment, "Honor your father and your mother," must not be understood as restricted to young children. In fact, the Cardinal points out, it refers to the basic human right to family life, which we are invited to cherish and foster.

The Fifth Commandment, "You shall not kill," shows better than any of the others the strict relationship between commands and rights. Liberty without rules necessarily infringes on somebody else's rights. The statement that human life is both sacred and social, the Cardinal observes, leads us to foster and protect it in all circumstances. For this reason, since 1972 the United States bishops' Respect Life Program has invited the Catholic community to focus its concerns on "the sanctity of human life and the many threats to human life in the modern world, including war, violence, hunger and poverty."

The Sixth Commandment, "You shall not commit adultery," rules out, by extension, any misuse of sexuality. It points to the right of marital fidelity and to the obligation of responsible sexuality.

The Seventh Commandment, "You shall not steal," shows clearly, one more time, the relation between obligation and right. In fact, not to steal means respecting others' rights to possess and enjoy what one is entitled to by one's labor "or simply by the fact of one's humanity"; most importantly, it means also that no nation can steal from other nations. Industrialized nations of the North are not supposed to exploit the underdeveloped countries of the South; especially, they shouldn't spend vast amounts of money on armaments, when there is poverty and human suffering in the rest of the globe.

The Eighth Commandment, "You shall not bear false witness against your neighbor," shows the dire consequences of lying. The Cardinal insists that "everyone has an obligation to be truthful," in particular governments, whose "systematic lying" is perpetrated "for the sake of controlling and manipulating people." Equally blameful is the behavior of those who censor and distort history as well as the news. In this regard, Cardinal Bernardin reminds us that "truth will set us free. In commanding truth, the Eighth Commandment protects what is essential to freedom."

The Ninth Commandment tells us not to covet a neighbor's spouse. Bernardin shows the implications of this command by analyzing the meaning of "coveting": it is not simply desiring; it is wanting something to which one has no right. "Covetousness debases the one who covets," he observes, because it enhances disharmony over peace in one's soul. Society today encourages people to indulge in their passions, but this licence has not made the world a happier place. Rather, it has led to alienation, pain, and even despair for some.

The Tenth Commandment, not to covet our neighbor's possessions, reiterates the danger of falling into painful disruptions in relationships between human beings. This commandment asks us to be just in our relationships with others, including groups, social classes, and nations.

This schematic summary of Cardinal Bernardin's interpretation and actualization of the Ten Commandments clearly shows the interconnection between rights and obligations, and the essential role played by the teaching of God in organizing our social life on the principle of human rights. They affect not only expected areas of moral life but the entire social structure. The ten commandments are perennial pillars which mark the course of changing times.

2

How Catholics
Read the Bible

*A correct reading of the Bible is, for Cardinal Bernardin, an impor-
tant responsibility and pleasure for Catholics, who are called to accept the fullness of the message that they find in the Scriptures
and incorporate it into their daily life. Considering that both on
the street and in the workplace, it is not difficult to encounter fundamentalist Christians arguing on Biblical interpretations and underlining how past Catholics had a reputation for ignoring the
biblical books, The Cardinal helps to resolve confusions and motivate reading of the Scriptures, offering several valid points. Questions are also raised about some Catholic beliefs and actions that
are not explicitly found in the Scriptures. Cardinal Bernardin underlines the fact that the authors of the Bible should be understood in terms of their relationship with the teaching authority of
the Church, which was founded prior to the development of the
biblical books, also called the New Testament.*

*Furthermore, the Cardinal adds that the apostles, in their
teaching and preaching, handed down oral traditions about the
life of Jesus and His message to the world. He also casts light
on the fact that Catholics esteem Scripture as part of their tradition and consider the Bible as a source of divine revelation.*

*In addition to that we must look for an authentic interpreta-
tion of Scripture by asking how the community of believers understood biblical texts through the centuries. In this context it
is very important to recognize the interpretation of the apostolic generation and the fidelity evident in its apostolic teach-*

ing, which was a point reiterated by the Second Vatican Council.

Cardinal Bernardin analyzes not only the differences between the Catholic Bible and those of other religious sects, but also the meanings of the different interpretations. The Archbishop of Chicago concludes, underlining that regular use of the Bible is a point of departure for guidance and nourishment.

To present a detailed analysis of the role of the Scripture in the development of Church teaching is a constant commitment of Cardinal Bernardin. The reputation for neglecting the Bible that the Catholic Church earned seems to have changed rapidly in the past three or four decades. In the dark days of World War II, Pope Pius XII gave new impetus to the study of the Scriptures in the Catholic Church. With the encouragement of his successors, extensive biblical research was undertaken and had a significant impact on the Second Vatican Council.

As individuals and as a Church, Catholics have experienced the challenge to live in accordance with the Gospel; especially today, there are many concrete reasons for identifying the Catholic Church as a "Church of the Bible." Cardinal Bernardin mentions three main reasons as examples to support this point: there is much greater stress on the word of God in our preaching, the Bible being the point of departure in all our religious education; the U.S. bishops urge Catholics to turn to the Scriptures in order to confront the challenges of today's life. The Bible is having a significant impact on the lives of individual Catholics. Cardinal Bernardin himself recognizes the importance of a careful study of God's word in order to be an effective teacher of the Gospel. He summarizes this point by using St. Jerome's words: "Ignorance of the Scriptures is ignorance of Christ."

A Challenge

The fruit of this study and prayerful reflection on the Bible is guidance and nourishment, but it is also a challenge. What we are called to do, in fact, is to accept the fullness of the message that we find in the Scriptures and to incorporate it into our daily lives.

The renewal of interest in the Bible has had a great impact on the Church and its members, but this new emphasis in the Church's life and practice raises a new set of pastoral questions and challenges. Using a variety of approaches to the Bible, Catholics join study or prayer groups, in which they can share their faith and insights, thereby enriching one another's lives and providing support and solidarity to their brothers.

Questions arise regarding the meaning of a particular biblical passage, and such questions involve deeper concerns about the authority of the Scripture. In addition, Catholics sometimes feel inferior to Bible-quoting

Christians who seem to have a precise verse to fit each occasion, not to mention their ability to cite its specific chapters and verses as well! These are issues that Cardinal Bernardin discusses with devoted insight and bright argumentation.

The Truth of the Sacred Scripture

In other contexts of daily life, similar issues arise. In the workplace and marketplace, Catholics often encounter fundamentalist Christians who challenge the beliefs, teachings, and practices of the Catholic Church. Some evangelical groups are aggressively trying to "convert" Catholics, and in recent years some Protestant and Evangelical publishers seem to target a specifically Catholic market for their books and publications, the Cardinal adds. TV evangelists also have a serious impact on their viewers as they seek to persuade people to agree with their way of thinking. Pastors frequently encounter the subsequent confusion which arises in the minds of Catholics, especially those who feel they are not equipped to explain adequately the Catholic approach to the Bible or those who begin to have doubts about this approach.

To help resolve this confusion, Cardinal Bernardin devotes himself to addressing Catholics and helping them appreciate more clearly and deeply an authentically Catholic approach to the Bible. He underlines how in the past Catholics had a reputation for ignoring the Bible, and observes that it is true that Catholics do not memorize Scripture passages as readily as others do or that they often cannot tell you the precise chapter and verse where certain passages are found.

But Cardinal Bernardin stresses the fact that Catholics do know the Bible much more than they give themselves credit for. He emphasizes that most Catholics will recall the passages regarding the parable of the Prodigal Son or the marriage feast at Cana. But he also observes that the Catholic Church has officially approved more than one translation, and therefore it is problematic nowadays to memorize a specific passage. The issue is thus shown to be of secondary importance.

On the contrary, the most significant question Cardinal Bernardin poses regards the problem of what Catholics understand as the authority of the Sacred Scripture. The question may be phrased in more than one way. Some people ask: Why do Catholics believe things that are not explicitly found in the Scriptures? Why do they do things which are not explicitly mentioned in the Bible?

The underlying assumption of these questions is that any religious doctrine or practice which cannot be found clearly and explicitly in the Sacred Scripture is either not true or should be regarded with great skepticism. Cardinal Bernardin understands the authority of the Bible in terms of its relationship to the Church, its relationship with the tradition and the teaching authority of the Church. And this is an important point indeed in the controversy.

The Church's Relationship to the Biblical Books

Jesus Christ gathered a community of disciples around him and, after his ascension to the Father, sent the Holy Spirit to guide the growth and development of such a community of believers. Therefore, the Church was prior to the development of the biblical books which are called the New Testament; it received also the influence of the Jewish heritage, through the Old or First Testament. Moreover, from the apostles and the earliest disciples it also collected numerous oral traditions concerning Jesus.

These facts are brought forward by the Cardinal as evidence that for Catholics, Christianity is not merely a "religion of the book"; the special relationship that exists between God and the disciples or followers of Jesus constitutes the core of Christianity for Catholics.

Cardinal Bernardin's emphasis on the fact that the story of the Church begins before the writing of the New Testament clearly shows that what is important is to be aware of how the books of the New Testament developed within the early communities of believers.

In their teaching and preaching the apostles handed on oral traditions about the life of Jesus and His message, and during the early decades of the Church's formation some of these were set down in writing because of the rapid spread of the Christian Way. St. Paul explicitly refers to both kinds of tradition – oral and written – in one of the earliest books of the New Testament: "Hold fast to the traditions you received from us, either by our word or by letter" (II Thess. 2:15).

We see how the books of the New Testament were written under divine inspiration by believers for believers – a fact which Cardinal Bernardin constantly reminds us of. In addition, we should not forget that it was also the early Christian Church that decided which books of both Testaments were inspired and, therefore, were to be included in the canon of Scripture.

Cardinal Bernardin also casts light on the fact that Catholics esteem Scripture as part of their tradition and consider the Bible as a source – although not the full source – of divine revelation.

Both Scripture and tradition "are bound closely together. . . . They flow from the same divine well-spring and . . . move towards the same goal" (*Dei Verbum* 9). That is also why "both Scripture and tradition must be accepted and honored with equal feelings of devotion and reverence" (*Dei Verbum* 9). Cardinal Bernardin underlines the fact that the task of authentically interpreting Scripture and tradition has been entrusted to the official teachers of the Church, the bishops in union with the bishop of Rome.

Another problem arises because of the existence of many translations of the biblical text and disagreements about which books belong to the canon of Scripture. In this regard, the Cardinal points out that seven books found in the Old Testament section of Catholic Bibles do not appear in Protestant Bibles. These are the Books of First and Second Maccabees, Sirach, the Wisdom of Solomon, Tobit, Judith, Baruch, as well as parts of Daniel and Esther. This difference of canons affects the discussion between Catholics and Protestants on issues like purgatory. Catholics consider a passage in Second Maccabees (12:42–46) as a biblical source for the Church's teaching on purgatory, but Protestants do not accept the canonical authority of the Books of Maccabees.

This aspect raises some basic questions, as the Cardinal observes; for instance, who decides which books are really inspired and to be included in the canon of Scripture?

Local Churches and the Teaching Role of the Bishops

The Cardinal points out that the Bible is for everybody, and it contains stories of faith providing guidance and support for our lives. But each of us approaches the biblical text with certain presuppositions, and each of us reads the Bible selectively. Cardinal Bernardin recognizes in this the possible danger of subjectivity in which the believer assumes from the biblical text anything he or she needs for support and comfort. There is obviously the danger of hermeneutical subjectivity, whereby the believer assumes that the biblical text means anything he or she thinks it means. This question is addressed by the Cardinal, who points out the importance of the local assembly as a critical element in the process of interpreting the Bible. In fact, he reminds us of the collective wisdom of groups. The New Testament itself presents a picture of the larger Church as a network of local communities under the leadership of the apostles and their successors.

We must look for an authentic interpretation of Scripture by asking how the community of believers understood biblical texts through the centuries, the Cardinal emphasizes. Those who exercise authority have an official teaching role, especially in regard to the interpretation of the record of revelation in Scripture and historical tradition.

Recently, Pope John Paul II spoke about the relationship between Scripture and the teaching office of the Church. Approaching the Bible from the context of the "living tradition of the Church" enables teachers to resist the temptation of imposing their personal interpretation on God's word; the bishops of the Church in union with the Pope have the ultimate responsibility for interpreting God's word. It is in obedience to these words that Cardinal Bernardin examines the teaching role of the bishops "in union" with the Pope.

The accurate passing on of tradition by the community of the faithful was a serious concern of St. Paul. In addressing the Corinthians, he makes this clear by observing: "I received from the Lord what I handed on to you" (I Cor. 11:23). Among all the Scriptures, The Acts of the Apostles is the one that gives us the most revealing insights into how the apostles carried out this mandate of the risen Lord.

It is Cardinal Bernardin's aim to illuminate the writings of the early Fathers of the Church. More specifically, it is in St. Ignatius of Antioch's letters that he recognizes a clear distinction of Church offices: bishops, presbyters, and deacons. The same message he finds in St. Irenaeus of Lyons, who noted that it was possible to list the names of those appointed by the apostles to serve as bishops as well as of their successors to his own day.

The Second Vatican Council

But Cardinal Bernardin's primary aim is to recognize the importance of the apostolic generation and fidelity to its apostolic teaching. This traditional understanding was reiterated by the Second Vatican Council in its Dogmatic Constitution on Divine Revelation (*Dei Verbum*). It acknowledges that, "the holy Scriptures themselves are more thoroughly actualized in the Church" (*Dei Verbum* 8). It concludes from this that "it is for the bishops, with whom the apostolic doctrine resides, suitably to instruct the faithful entrusted to them in the correct use of the divine books" (*Dei Verbum* 25).

Cardinal Bernardin's focus then shifts to a further hermeneutical question: How do we interpret the Bible? When we read something written by another, he observes, the clues are fewer and more subtle since the written sentence can convey several possible meanings or express many different sentiments. The problem especially arises when we do not have access to the authors, when we are reading ancient documents like the books of the Bible. The issue of biblical exegesis is ongoing.

Human Authors Wrote under Divine Inspiration

After having described the difference between a Catholic and a Protestant Bible, the Archbishop of Chicago discusses the problem of translations, which themselves are exercises of interpretation. The original languages used in the composition of the biblical books were Hebrew, Aramaic, and Greek, and the meanings of certain words or phrases still elude us. Moreover, some translators judge that a paraphrase of the original text expresses its meaning better than a literal translation.

In this regard, the Cardinal stresses the significance of new research, which is aimed at the renewal and enrichment of translations and interpretation studies, and which take into serious account the fact that the ancient manuscripts on which we must rely present many readings that vary from one another. More than a thousand of them in New Testament manuscripts are important for translation and interpretation, but only twenty or so involve doctrinal questions.

Once these factors have been acknowledged, where do we begin as we try to discover the meaning of the biblical text? Cardinal Bernardin emphasizes this serious matter, while underlining that God shares his own words with us through the Scriptures; He speaks to us today through words written by human authors, under divine inspiration, many centuries ago. That is why it is important to ask God for help in understanding His word with open minds and hearts. What is the most important factor in interpreting and understanding the Bible? The Archbishop of Chicago has no doubt – it is faith.

The Bible is essential, and to use it regularly is a point of departure for guidance and nourishment. It is relevant for our time and culture. Listening to God's word through the Bible is Cardinal Bernardin's suggestion for pursuing a life of joy, hope, and understanding in our times.

3

Justice, Peace, and Public Morality

The Gospel, the Archbishop underlines, calls people to social justice. Furthermore, it is the Church's responsibility to provide people with a framework that prepares them to encounter moral decisions and dilemmas on a daily basis. All Catholics have the responsibility to bring social justice issues to the attention of the public. In addition, priests must provide examples through their behavior and must practice what they preach.

Peace is another fundamental issue of importance for the Cardinal. He believes that it can be maintained by defending religious freedom but risks disruption when religious freedom is lost. Law, he says, must serve the family in such a way that it defends and protects those values which enhance human life and dignity. Moreover, conflicts arise between law and morality, namely how the two should interrelate, and how inadequate laws should be changed.

Although this is not its only message, the Gospel calls every Christian to social justice, states Cardinal Bernardin in no uncertain terms. In addition, he says that, if Christians are really committed to implementing the Gospel message in today's world, then there is no way they can avoid issues of social justice. Furthermore, one of the Church's basic responsibilities is to provide its people with a moral framework to make their own analysis of the various issues they are daily called to face in contemporary society.

We do not exist only for ourselves. The task of Church leaders is not to engage in partisan politics, however; it is rather to adopt a moral stance, which obviously has an impact upon the social and the practical order. Thus, Cardinal Bernardin asserts that, even if justice and peace can be challenging – indeed frightening – goals, Church leaders must convince people of the validity and logical consistency of their arguments. In fact, today it is no longer possible to force people to accept things simply on the basis of authority – i.e., simply because one is a bishop, as is his own case. Cardinal Bernardin concludes with the observation that today many people are well educated, and therefore the bishops must make sure that they understand whatever topic they are dealing with and provide good arguments to support their positions.

According to Cardinal Bernardin, the real challenge U.S. Catholics have to face is that of reconciling the radical call of the Gospel with the realities of contemporary life. Indeed, this is a demanding challenge, the more so if we consider the message of the Gospel and a consumer-oriented society in which "more is better." Christians have the important task of remembering that they do not exist only for themselves.

Of course, they must take care their own needs, but at the same time they must be concerned with the needs of others. The Cardinal firmly believes that all Catholics have a role to play in bringing social justice issues to the attention of the public.

Nevertheless, he makes a distinction between the role of the laity and that of the clergy. In fact, he says that the laity have the responsibility of doing whatever is needed in order to shape a just and compassionate society – they do have such responsibility simply by virtue of the fact that they are in the world. He emphasizes that it is his responsibility, just as it is of all the priests, to keep in focus the moral dimension of each issue and to provide the laity with encouragement and motivation. In addition, he underlines that priests must also provide an example: they must practice what they preach. Indeed, we should mark Cardinal Bernardin's effective, conclusive words: if priests do not practice what they preach, they can be considered as "phonies" and people are justified in not taking them seriously. The ultimate result of such behavior ends in a loss of credibility for the Church as a whole.

Religious Freedom is a Condition for Peace

The best source of learning about Cardinal Bernardin's convictions regarding the issue of peace may be extrapolated from the pastoral letter on war and peace approved by the National Conference of Catholic Bishops in 1983. The Cardinal chaired the committee which drafted the pastoral letter, which better than anywhere else defines the arms race as one of the greatest curses on the human race, as a danger and a folly. These powerful words will suffice to show the Cardinal's and his fellow bishops' passionate commitment to such vital and fundamental issues for humanity.

Peace can be safeguarded by defending religious freedom. In fact, Cardinal Bernardin – in complete agreement with Pope John Paul II's proposal to reflect upon the theme "Religious Freedom: A Condition for Peace," an offer which was made on the occasion of the World Day for Peace in 1988 – notes that the loss of religious freedom is both a cause of tension and discontent and a violation of a fundamental human right. The loss of religious freedom can thus be the cause for the disruption of peace. To support his position, the Cardinal provides a list of countries where religious freedom has been violated, such as is the case in some of the Islamic countries.

The Law Must Protect Values Promoting and Enhancing Human Life and Dignity

As for the administration of justice and the task of correctly interpreting the civil law, Cardinal Bernardin believes that the latter must be at the service of the human family. The main purpose of the law must be the defense and protection of those values which are needed to promote and enhance human life and dignity. At the same time, however, the Cardinal underlines that the law is a human instrument – hence, it is both finite and imperfect. Consequently, not all legislation is good, not all legal interpretations are of equal value or validity. At times conflicts arise between a given law and one's own conscience, and one may have to strive to change a law that has become inadequate or is based on faulty premises.

In order to resolve conflicts between conscience and law, Cardinal Bernardin suggests that we draw certain distinctions. The first concerns the differentiation between morality and law. He correctly points out that, although the premises of law are grounded on moral principles, the scope of law is more limited and its purpose is not the moralization of society. In fact, moral principles govern personal and social human conduct and cover interior acts and motivations as well, whereas civil statutes and laws govern public order and concern only external acts and values that are formally social. Consequently, it is not the function of law to enjoin or to prohibit everything that moral principles enjoin or prohibit.

The reason for ensuring that the restraints against the claims of freedom caused by the law are valid is that the limitation of freedom has many consequences. A possible one is the risk of damaging freedom in other domains, with the consequence of increasing the dangers for the community as a whole. Cardinal Bernardin concludes by saying that the conflict between law and morality may be resolved by recognizing the presumption in favor of freedom and by ensuring that the advocacy of constraint is, indeed, convincing.

But the Cardinal's argument goes even further. He observes how there are other distinctions to be drawn in order to resolve possible conflicts between law and morality. First, we must determine which issues are public moral questions as opposed to private moral questions; second, we must consider how public officials should relate their personal convictions about religious and moral truths to the fulfillment of their public duty.

As for the distinction between public and private morality, the Cardinal bases his convictions upon the writings of Father John Courtney Murray, S.J., a respected authority on Church-State matters. For Murray, an issue is one of public morality if it affects the public order of society – the public order including public peace, essential protection of human rights, and commonly accepted standards of moral behavior within a community. With reference to this discussion, Cardinal Bernardin relates two cases in order to exemplify the way in which the United States has struggled to take public morality into account in the past.

The first case he cites is the issue of Prohibition. (The 18th Amendment to the U.S. Constitution, ratified in 1919, prohibited the manufacture, sale, or transportation of intoxicating liquors. It was repealed by the 21st Amendment in 1933.) The Cardinal regards Prohibition as the attempt to legislate behavior in an area ultimately beyond the reach of civil law, and not sufficiently public in nature to affect public order. The second case he brings into the argument is the U.S. struggle for civil rights during the 1960's. This fight turned out to be so central to public order, particularly in areas such as housing, education, employment, voting, and access to public facilities, that the State, at a certain point in history, could no longer remain neutral on the question.

Cardinal Bernardin's enlightening analysis concludes by showing how today in the United States there is a consensus in law and public policy that clearly defines civil rights as issues of public morality, and the decision to drink alcoholic beverages as one of private morality. The history of these two cases simplifies and clarifies the theoretical issue concerning the distinction between the public and the private.

Moral Analysis in the Public Policy

Cardinal Bernardin's reflections and writings have also confronted the dilemma which is at times caused by the conflict between personal conviction and public duty. In this regard, he states that the central question is not whether the deepest convictions of judges, attorneys, or government officials should influence their individual public decisions. Rather, the basic question is how the two should be related. As a consequence, the next question is how imperfect laws should be changed. This is a fine argument indeed, and Joseph Bernardin addresses it by stressing firmly the necessity of moral analysis in the public policy debate, a necessity due to the character of the issues we all face nowadays. In fact, he points out that the major issues of our time are fundamental questions whose moral dimension is a pervasive and persistent factor. Hence, to ignore the moral dimension of public policy is to forsake the constitutional heritage of the United States, itself a bearer of moral values.

Moreover, the purpose of the separation of Church and State in the United States is not to exclude the voice of religion from the public debate. On the contrary, it is meant to provide a context for religious freedom where the insights of each religious tradition can be set forth and tested. The very testing of the religious voice opens the public debate to assessment by moral criteria. Therefore, Cardinal Bernardin affirms that to ignore the moral dimension of public policy is also to forsake the religious heritage of the United States.

To the question "Who should participate in public policy discussions?" the Cardinal responds that developing and implementing a moral vision for the United States is a task for all citizens, and it is through the force and influence of public opinion that the citizens make their own voices heard.

Public opinion, however, is not always wise, nor is it well-formed politically or ethically. These are the reasons why Cardinal Bernardin goes on to observe that the task of trying to shape a well-formed public opinion is central to the role of the Church in public affairs, because the Church must never be separate from society, even if it is separate from the State.

More specifically, the churches should be considered as voluntary associations with a disciplined capacity to analyze the moral-religious significance of public issues. It is with this insightful analysis that Cardinal Bernardin defines the place of the churches in public policy debates. His lucid argument is conversant with the most practical political issues and cannot be ignored by anybody who wishes to lead a Christian life in today's society.

4

Prayer
Spending Time With God

Prayer and spirituality must constitute a life plan for Catholics. This spiritual foundation comes to us through participation in Holy Mass, Communion, personal prayer, repentance of sins, and spiritual texts and the Scriptures, together integrated to maintain and nurture a deep relationship with God.

The Mass is the center of our lives as Christians. It provides both an organizing principle of everyday life and a forum for communication and spiritual union between Christians and Christ, through the Holy Eucharist. As a result, Christians should attend Mass daily, if possible, or at least frequently and regularly.

Prayer is another important component of a spiritual program. This form of conversation with God is indispensable to establish and maintain a relationship with Our Lord. The Archbishop of Chicago distinguishes between two different kinds of prayer : 1) vocal prayer constituted by words and formulas, i.e., the Rosary with its Mysteries, and 2) mental prayer that comes from the heart. In mental prayer, we express our most inner sentiments to God by relaxing and focusing on His presence.

Repentance and conscience examination must be regular activities in our lives as Christians. Repentance is the sacrament in which we meet Christ in order to receive forgiveness for our

sins and find strength for future efforts. Conscience examina-
tion, rather, demands deep self-reflection and better under-
standing of ourselves.

The Apostolate is the continuation of the mission of Christ in
our world. In light of this goal, Cardinal Bernardin advises us to
view our relationship with Christ as all encompassing, and not
isolated from other relationships in our lives. A Christian must
reach out to his neighbors and experience their joys and sor-
rows as his own. He urges us to let God be part of our lives, to
find time for Him – a few minutes or days – according to the
choice and disposition of our soul. Prayer, he emphasizes, can
be a great help in dealing with the challenges of one's life.

Cardinal Bernardin clearly expresses his beliefs and convictions about prayer and spiritual life in a series of fundamental writings, in which he outlines a program or plan of life for Catholics who want to experience spiritual growth. He acknowledges that some people may find the idea of having a "plan" for their interior life strange, even unappealing. Yet, he observes, this may be true only at first. The Cardinal is convinced that a person who is serious about his or her own spiritual life recognizes the need for a strategy – for "a game plan", as he likes to call it – within which each person can bring his or her own creativity to bear on the process of spiritual growth.

It is illuminating to borrow Joseph Bernardin's metaphor to understand this point fully. He reminds us that, just as every building needs a solid foundation, so our spiritual edifice needs the foundation that is provided by a plan of life. The Cardinal has made it his task to offer a few reminders concerning the main elements of a plan of life for Catholics who want to make spiritual progress.

The Mass

Among the major elements of such a plan are Mass and Communion, personal prayer, Penance (both reception of the Sacrament and penitential practices), the Scriptures, and spiritual reading. It should be clear that a plan of life must include several "activities," as the Archbishop of Chicago insists. In order for such activities to have the maximum benefit, however, it is important that they do not remain isolated, individual practices. On the contrary, they must be integrated and oriented towards an overall purpose – of establishing, maintaining, and constantly deepening our relationship with God.

Naturally, in every spiritual plan the Mass must be given a central place. The Cardinal sees the basic fact about the Mass to be that it is here that Christ renews the act by which He redeemed us and thus it is the Mass which makes it possible for us to share in that act. The Mass is indeed the center of our lives as Christians, since it is an organizing principle of Christian life. Why this is so can be explained by several reasons. For one thing, it is necessary for us to live authentic Christian lives in order to celebrate the Mass well. Without this condition, our lives would not be in harmony with what we propose to express through participation in the Mass, and this, in turn, will scarcely result in a rewarding experience for us.

In fact, there are people who complain that they do not get much out of Mass. Cardinal Bernardin shows understanding for such people and explains that there may be various reasons for their reaction. However, he insists, a possible reason is that these people do not prepare for Mass by leading lives which are authentic expressions of what the Mass proclaims and celebrates. On the contrary, for those who do strive to live authentic Christian lives, the Mass is a genuine organizing principle of everyday life. In the course of each day, these people prepare the material, as it were, which they will bring with them to join in Christ's offering to the Father, during Mass. This material is simply the content of their lives.

Although the reasoning illustrated here is rich in arguments, Cardinal Bernardin is well aware that there is still more to it than that. At Mass, in fact, Christians are strengthened by receiving the Eucharist – that is, by being united with Christ Himself.

In his writings and preaching, the Cardinal addresses a further question: "How often should Christians go to Mass?" His answer is very simple and direct: "as often as possible – daily if that can be done, but in any case frequently and regularly." As we can also see, this point is treated with the usual open-mindedness and flexibility which is the richness and originality of the Cardinal's thought.

Vocal and Mental Prayer

In every spiritual program or plan of life, another very important, necessary role is played by prayer. Cardinal Bernardin states that there are two classic definitions of prayer: the first considers it as a lifting of the mind and heart to God; the second, as a conversation with God. Of these two definitions, the Cardinal finds the latter perhaps the more enlightening since it is prayer as conversation with God which makes absolutely clear the functional role of prayer in general. In fact, if the purpose of the spiritual life is to establish, maintain, and strengthen a relationship with God, then a conversation with God – i.e., a prayer – is unquestionably indispensable.

Cardinal Bernardin distinguishes two kinds of prayer. One is vocal prayer – the prayer of words and formulas: the Our Father, the Hail Mary, and so on. The other is mental prayer, which is a form of praying that should be engaged in regularly by everybody. As a matter of fact, the very words "mental prayer" sound forbidding, in that they are associated with mystics, and we Christians are led to assume that such experience is not part of our tradition. According to Bernardin, this is a serious mistake because the activity of mental prayer is an effort that everyone should make. Given this situation, the natural question is then, "How to begin?"

According to Cardinal Bernardin, there are numerous techniques for mental prayer. Nevertheless, he warns beginners against becoming too burdened with excessive theory and method. He underlines, on the contrary, that mental prayer must come from the heart and that we may use words only if we wish to, since words are not essential to this act. What is essential, instead, is that we open ourselves up to God, that we express what we really feel in our hearts, in order to seek His light and help. Cardinal Bernardin suggests only one method, which is accessible to everyone. This is the method called "Centering Prayer." In this form of prayer, we simply try to relax, set aside distractions, and concentrate on God's presence and His goodness, responding to Him with loving gratitude for all He is and does for us. In such prayer, we only spend time with God. This unstructured time, as it were this "wasting of time," is nevertheless an extremely rewarding experience of spiritual refreshment. The Cardinal places great emphasis on the positive value of such "wasting of time."

However, he also recognizes the difficulties which are inherent in mental prayer. These difficulties are such, he acknowledges, that sooner or later anyone who makes the effort to pray will encounter them. One of the most common of these is dryness, by which the Cardinal means the absence of consolation, the feeling that one is merely going through the motions without accomplishing anything. However, he hastens to point out, dryness is by no means a sign of failure. On the contrary, it is God's way of simultaneously testing us and encouraging us to persevere; the sense of His absence – paradoxically – is an incentive to continue seeking Him. The Cardinal's insight into this thorny issue is fascinating as well as illuminating.

While mental prayer requires time set aside every day for this purpose, continues the Cardinal, vocal prayer is possible in many different circumstances. He considers the Rosary one of the best vocal prayers of all. In fact, its "mysteries" provide the subjects for short meditations through which it is in turn possible to grow in understanding and appreciation of central episodes in the lives of Jesus, Mary, and Joseph. It also deepens our devotion to the Blessed Virgin.

Penance

As for penance and the examination of conscience, the Cardinal sees them as a joint issue. Examination of conscience should not be an occasional activity only; it should be a regular, daily part of our plan of life. The point of all this, the Cardinal teaches us, is precisely to be as realistic and accurate as we can about our spiritual selves. For its part, Penance is the sacramental action in which we directly encounter Christ for the specific purpose of receiving forgiveness for our sins and strength for our future efforts. Actually, sin and weakness are part of the reality of everyone's life. There is no better way of coping with our frailty and of receiving Christ's pardon and encouragement than through this Sacrament.

Joseph Bernardin affirms also that the practice called "particular examination" is very useful. This traditional spiritual exercise is an examination in that it requires us to reflect on ourselves and to come to a better knowledge of ourselves. The main point of this exercise is to concentrate on one area in which improvement is needed, and subsequently to adopt a very specific method in achieving our task. For instance – as the Cardinal notes – a husband, determined to be kinder to his wife, might decide during his particular examination that he will wash the family's dishes every day.

Hence, examination of conscience, Penance, and the particular examination are all of the utmost importance: each in its own way helps us to overcome our weaknesses and to grow in the life of the spirit.

Apostolate

In conclusion to his reflection on the spiritual life and its growth, Cardinal Bernardin states that all these practices are useful, even essential for our progress in interior life. But what is also crucial is to realize that our relationship with God cannot be seen as isolated from our relationships with other people. This is where we can clearly appreciate the Cardinal's comprehensive vision of the spiritual life. The ultimate test of how well we have loved the Lord, he emphasizes, will be how well we have loved other human beings.

One useful way for expressing this is to refer to the concept of the "apostolate." The Cardinal states that every Christian is called to the apostolate. It is important to understand in detail what the Cardinal means when he speaks of the "apostolate." Fundamentally, the word refers to the continuation of the mission of Christ in our world. The apostolate should begin with friendship. Christians who want to live apostolically must get to know other people, become part of their lives, share their sorrows and their joys, constantly look for new ways to extend to them the human encouragement and support that help them cope with their manifold needs and challenges. This is why the apostolate is a necessary part of a plan of life for seriously engaged Christians.

Personal and Spiritual Experience in Prayer

In his reflections about spiritual life and prayer, with a few insightful remarks, Cardinal Bernardin reports his personal experience. This is a clear indication of the originality and depth of his thought. He tells of the time when he was ordained, when he was working hard at pursuing his ideals and he was keeping himself so busy that he didn't make enough time to develop a deep spirituality. It seemed to him then that the work he was doing always had to take priority over prayer. It was only a number of years later and when he had already become a bishop, that he began to realize that he was counseling people to do things that he himself was not doing. He was calling them to spirituality and to a way of life that were situated far beyond the point at which he was conducting his own life. This is why he decided to make the development of his spirituality a priority in his life and the foundation for his ministry to people. He decided that from that moment on he would give the first hour of every day to God, no matter what his schedule might be. He decided then that he would get up early enough to spend the first hour of every single day of his life in prayer. The Cardinal's teaching of the importance of a determined way of conducting our lives is very effective because he opens up his heart to us in a very touching way.

But Cardinal Bernardin's self-examination does not stop here. He goes further by offering us some of the most compassionate pages in his entire writing when he relates more details of his personal spiritual experiences. He says that one of the best things came from his sharing his experience with other people. In fact, he maintains that, when people go to him, they tend to take it for granted that he has, so to say, everything "put together," that he has never himself experienced the problems they are experiencing. It is therefore when he has the opportunity to tell them that he has gone through the same troubles that he can offer them a great deal of encouragement – a big boost.

One thing that has changed his life and enriched his spirituality, the Cardinal adds, is that he no longer sees God as someone who is very detached, very far away from us. He thinks more in terms of God as being part of our lives, now that he is able to cultivate his spiritual life. He observes how we encounter Him in prayer in the same ways as we also encounter Him in our relatives, our friends, as well as many other people whose lives we touch in one way or another.

Also praying with the Rosary has acquired a different significance for him since he has changed his attitude towards spirituality. In fact, it gives him an opportunity to reflect on the Lord and the specific events in His life, which have so much importance for the Church and for his own personal life.

Spending Time with God

As for other people, Cardinal Bernardin believes that individuals need to find those ways of praying that best fit them. Again, he humbly does not think he can provide any rule about this important act. There is no right amount of prayer, as well as there is no right or wrong way to pray, he emphatically adds. In the final analysis, he concludes, what is really important is to spend time with God. Whether this takes a few minutes or days, it is left to everyone's individual choice and disposition of soul.

However, part of prayer is simply reflecting on what has been happening to us, on the ways in which God talks to us through our life experiences, through things that other people have done or said. Therefore prayer is not only talking – it is listening, too. This interpretation of the concept shows the depth of the development of the Cardinal's reflection on prayer.

He affirms that prayer can be of great help in discerning the direction one should take in order to solve his or her problems, or in dealing with the challenges of one's life. But he also asserts that prayer should not be considered primarily as a problem-solving tool. Consequently, he claims that he much prefers to avoid praying for specific reasons or outcomes; rather, when he prays, he tries to pray that there will be simply a good outcome, whatever that might be.

One difficulty of prayer is that sometimes we place all the burden on God, forgetting that we have to do our share. Cardinal Bernardin sees prayer as helpful in the necessary collaboration between human beings and God. But it is important to keep in mind – he wisely warns us – that the burden cannot be totally shifted away from us.

By personalizing his teaching to the extent illustrated above, the Cardinal offers a refreshing view and a stimulating perspective on these classical issues for all Christians.

The Third Millennium and the Unity of the Church

In the upcoming third millennium, it is crucial to reflect upon the unity of the Church. Christians must examine a wide host of issues and concerns, including ecumenism, which implies that Christians professing a common faith in Jesus Christ cannot live and serve God in separate ways, but rather in communion with one another.

The Church's inner life and ministry, for example, is an area where many concerns have been raised. Cardinal Bernardin addresses the strained atmosphere between local churches and the Universal Church, as well as the tensions caused by conflicting approaches to liturgy. Unity, attainable only through Faith, must be at the core of the Church's existence in order to ensure a healthy future.

Unity can be achieved in the Church, which is considered both a place of intimate union with God and a forum for unity among all people. Furthermore, Cardinal Bernardin underlines the idea of unity as a present reality in our lives and a promise sought for the future. In this day and age, Christians of different denominations must see themselves as pilgrims who are journeying towards a common goal. Unity is a gift from God which requires our acceptance, much like the gift of Faith. It grows within the Church, thanks to mutual knowledge and reciprocal love, the inner life of both the Holy Trinity and the Church. The Church's unity is a luminous hope that present division or alienation cannot dim.

A s the Church prepares to face the third millennium of its history, the urge to analyze exhaustively and to reflect seriously upon the unity of the Church and on its future is deeply felt by Cardinal Bernardin.

The question of the unity of the Church embraces a broad range of issues and concerns which can be gathered under the rubrics of ecumenism, intraecclesiastical matters, and the Church's relationship to the world. The Cardinal stresses the importance of identifying such issues and concerns because it is only by considering them together that they can provide a fruitful context for our reflection on the unity of the Church, as well as a solid background for our prayer in favor of its realization and in support of our action as Christians aimed at favoring its emergence.

Ecumenical Concerns

Ecumenical concerns are real concerns. Consistent with his beliefs, the Cardinal states that, as long as we Christians profess our common faith in Jesus Christ while at the same time living, worshipping, and serving God separately from one another, we live in such a way that he defines as "scandalous."

Recalling the root of the Greek word *skandalon*, Cardinal Bernardin defines us as a stumbling block, and adds that ecumenical efforts are not merely a luxury for idle and otherwise self-satisfied Christians. He emphasizes that they are, in no uncertain terms, a Gospel imperative.

Intraecclesiastical Concerns

Beside ecumenical issues which cross denominational lines, under the topic "The Unity of the Church" the Cardinal includes also intraecclesiastical concerns – i.e., matters related to the Church's inner life and ministry. Actually, there are many issues in Roman Catholicism today which are rooted in concerns having to do with the unity of the Church. Among these, the Cardinal cites the example of the tension, real or perceived, between the local churches and the universal Church – such tension raises the issue of unity. For instance, in the United States, this seems evident in the relationship between the Catholic institutions of higher education and the Holy See. There are, however, other issues which might be considered even more critical for the Church's unity: for example, the Cardinal specifies the tensions generated by different approaches to liturgy, which are often characterized, for want of better terms, as conservative or liberal.

Another example of intraecclesiastical concerns is the propensity of some to indulge in a Catholicism which the Cardinal defines, appropriately, as being "cafeteria style"; he employs this expression to define a Catholicism that picks and chooses, taking one thing and discarding another as if religion were akin to shopping in a supermarket. In addition, there are those divisions and separations determined by lines of sexism, racism, or economic disparity among members of the Church. The Cardinal has demonstrated his deep preoccupation with these issues through his numerous interventions.

The Church and the World

There is also a third level of concern about the unity of the Church, defined vis à vis the relationship of the Church to the world. Cardinal Bernardin recalls that some time shortly after the promulgation of the Second Vatican Council's Dogmatic Constitution on the Church, the famous French theologian and ecclesiologist Yves Congar wrote his article entitled, "The Church: Seed of Unity and Hope for the Human Race." As the title suggests, what is of fundamental importance for Christians is to be vigilant in order to prevent the confinement of their concern for the unity of the Church to matters which are solely ecumenical or intraecclesiastical. In Bernardin's effective image, their embrace is to be as wide as the world they serve.

In such a world, he identifies a number of issues and concerns which he lists under the rubric of unity. In ways that are both creative and practical, the Church must be the seed of unity and hope. And this thought is well explained in Congar's article. The issues of unity engaging the larger world include the following: global interdependence and its implications for world justice and peace; the relationship between men and women; the scandals of racism and the lack of care for the poor and most vulnerable in contemporary society. Relating his analysis to his archdiocese, Cardinal Bernardin observes that the city of Chicago and its metropolitan area faces serious threats to its unity. "We are confronted with the particular challenge of bringing together so many who are so different – racially, ethnically, economically, educationally, religiously, culturally," highlights the Archbishop of Chicago. The same is true for the Church.

But we should ask why the unity issues are considered of so much importance. They are indeed important because the opposite of unity is fragmentation, and beyond fragmentation – observes the Cardinal – there is conflict; worse than that, beyond conflict there is destruction. On the contrary, he underlines, unity is life. The more we move away from unity, or – more simply – the less we struggle to achieve it, the more we move towards death. That is why the unity issues of our time must be considered matters of life and death.

Cardinal Bernardin's fine thought on this topic is further developed in his numerous other writings. In order to suggest a general understanding of the nature of the unity of the Church, he asserts that such unity cannot be understood except in faith. This is not to dismiss altogether the disciplines of sociology, psychology, and anthropology. The Cardinal deems them all useful to a certain extent, but he also emphasizes their limitations when it comes to providing the grounds for understanding the unity of the Church.

In his view, the core of unity is nothing other than a matter of faith. Quoting from a section of the Second Vatican Council's Dogmatic Constitution on the Church, Cardinal Bernardin elaborates his position and adds that, "By her relationship with Christ, the Church is a kind of sacrament or sign of intimate union with God, and of the unity of all people. She is also an instrument for the achievement of such union and unity."

We must therefore accept that our essential understanding of the Church and of its unity can only be grasped in faith. These are the necessary conditions to begin identifying the full dimension of the mystery of the unity of the Church.

The Unity of the Church: Three Descriptions

It is with these premises that the Cardinal proposes three descriptions of the Church's unity. Each description he provides is framed in a polarity.

First, the unity of the Church is at the same time a present reality and a promised future. It is a present reality in that it is alive and at work because of God's grace and thanks to the response of God's people. In other words, we already have the gift of unity. However, at the same time, this unity is also a gift which we do not yet have – it lies ahead of us; it is something already started but which is still to be realized in all its fullness. As St. Paul wrote, God has given us the wisdom to realize His plan, "namely, to bring all things in the heavens and on earth into one under Christ's leadership" (Eph. 1:9–10).

With this explanation, therefore, it should not surprise us that the unity of the Church is a present reality and a promised future. As Joseph Bernardin says, we are a pilgrim people who have begun a journey that has still to be completed.

That is why the Cardinal describes the unity of the Church as both a gift of God and a task of God's believing people. This is a nodal thought in Cardinal Bernardin's elaboration on this question. In fact, it implies that we cannot envision the unity of the Church as a gift imposed from above, as something given and achieved without any human involvement. At the same time, the Cardinal emphasizes that we cannot claim the unity of the Church as solely our task or accomplishment, nor as a measure of our own success. As it was stressed above, it is crucial to keep in mind at all times that the unity of the Church is both a gift of God and a task given to God's believing people.

Second, Cardinal Bernardin stresses how this thought coincides with a real restatement of the best aspects of the Catholic theology of grace. Indeed, believing in the primacy of God's gift is equal to believing in His grace; at the same time, we affirm that the very same God who created us free "in His image and likeness" does not force His grace upon us.

The third and final elaboration of this complex argument entails the recognition that the unity of the Church is both something proclaimed and something prayed for. In the context of worship, we find the nature of the Church's unity in proclamation and in prayer. In John's Gospel we can find instructive words apropos of this point: these are the words of Jesus to His disciples in His farewell discourse. In Chapter 15, Jesus proclaims the unity of His disciples in Him in an exhaustingly rich image: "I am the vine, you are the branches" (15:5). This is a proclamation, since it is given in the indicative mode. But a short while later we hear Jesus' great prayer: I pray also for those who will believe in me through their word, that all may be one as you Father, are in me, and I in you: I pray that they may be one in us, that the world may believe that you sent me. (17:20–21)

The pattern of Jesus, which concludes this wonderful piece of textual exegesis that Cardinal Bernardin offers to our attention, is also the pattern of the Church. For, as often as we both proclaim and pray for it, we acknowledge that the Church's unity is both a present reality and a promised future, that it is both a gift of God and a task of believers.

Free Response and Mutual Dialogue

From these descriptions of the unity of the Church it is possible to draw a main conclusion, which the Cardinal sums up in the following: 1) there is unity; 2) it is imperfect; 3) we are growing in this unity principally by God's gift but also by our ongoing response to that gift; 4) in the end, unity will be fully given to us as a gift.

What we are called to deal with – Cardinal Bernardin sharply observes – is a situation of tension, because polarities are by no means reducible to one side or the other: the unity is given, yet to come; it is a gift, yet a task; it is proclaimed, yet prayed for. The Cardinal insists that we can only recognize this in faith, accept it in hope, and work for it in love. As soon as we realize this condition, he reflects, we begin to appreciate that the deepest religious attitudes are at play when we stand before the issue of the Church's unity.

The tension in this understanding of the Church's unity positions us in a particular stance in contrast and, at times, in opposition to other options and especially in opposition to ideology, which tries to establish unity reductively, seeking to explain everything under a single, univocal rubric; to every strategy, which tries to impose unity in the Church by using power plays at the cost of free response and mutual dialogue; to individualism, which ignores the gift and task of unity because it centers more on personal, private rights, rather than on the good of the community.

How do we Grow?

But the question then is – if we accept our understanding of the unity of the Church in faith as it has been described so far, than how do we move forward? How do we grow?

Cardinal Bernardin's elaboration also provides a fine answer to this question in a section of the Pastoral Constitution on the Church in the Modern World of the Second Vatican Council. Here the Cardinal shows us how the Council Fathers noted, drawing on the Seventeenth Chapter of John – i.e., on the above mentioned prayer of Jesus – that the unity of the Church moves in accordance with a pattern set by the Trinity.

Continental and American theologians have helped the community of believers recover an ecclesiological sense rooted in Trinitarian theology, as well as in Christology and theological understanding of the Holy Spirit. Coupled with these theological developments is a renewed appreciation of the Trinitarian theology of the Eastern Church. This begins in a fashion unlike that of the Western Church: it proclaims the plurality of persons and moves toward the unity of the Godhead. These theological movements and historical reappraisals help us greatly in our understanding of how the unity of the Church is to grow.

In this regard, the Cardinal asserts that, according to the theological tradition, the inner life of the Trinity consists of mutual knowledge and reciprocal love. This is exactly what we mean when we speak of the "inner life" of God. Mutual knowledge and reciprocal love, then, are also the inner life of the Church. Furthermore, his conclusions are that they are the way in which unity grows within the Church.

We clearly see, then, how in the end the Church's unity is a luminous hope that we will ourselves find in God, who is in all. No shadow of present division or alienation can dim such hope. Its promise already has sunk deep roots. We must hold on to it, with every fiber of our being, insists Bernardin.

This exhortation concludes some of the best pages of Cardinal Bernardin's exposition of the fundamental questions faced by contemporary theologians. Such questions, if addressed with genine ecumenical efforts, constitute the best lead to move towards the third millennium of Christianity in a fruitful ecumenical context.

6

A Consistent
Ethic of Life

*Leading a consistent ethical life is one of the principal con-
cepts in Cardinal Bernardin's thought. He gives two reasons
for personal commitment to such a life – it helps us overcome
obstacles that we encounter daily and it provides an enlarged
value of our moral vision.*

*Nuclear war, abortion, capital punishment, and euthanasia are
impending threats to life. A consistent ethical life manifests
the positive potential of the Catholic moral and social tradition. It calls for positive legal action to prevent the killing of
the unborn and to promote human dignity through programs
for nutrition, health care and housing. Each one of us is called
to give his contribution. In its four dimensions, a consistent
ethical life works to defend the integrity of moral principles
which prohibit attacks on unborn life, direct attacks on civilians in war actions, and intentional killing of patients in nursing homes. Cardinal Bernardin asserts that in an "ethical life"
we must examine each case individually and apply moral principles accordingly. Catholics must express their commitment
to moral principles in their everyday life, and politicians must
make political choices with moral principles in mind. This is
true for all public issues, from abortion to "arms racing," from
social programs to foreign policies.*

*Cardinal Bernardin concludes that the Church legitimately ful-
fills a public role by articulating a framework for political
choices, by relating such a framework to specific issues, and by*

calling for a systematic moral analysis in all areas of public poli-cies.

Aconsistent ethic of life – a concept for which Cardinal Bernardin has been the principal spokesperson – is one of the dominant themes of the addresses and writings of the Archbishop of Chicago. It underlies the specific issues that he has been ad-dressing with more consistency, dedication, and depth in the course of his numerous reflections.

He specifies why a consistent ethic of life is needed and also what is actually being advocated when we call for this ethic. In his view, there are two reasons why Catholics need to embrace a consistent ethic of life. The first of these is provided by the magnitude of the threats to life we constantly face today. The latter is given by the value of our moral vision.

The Cardinal sees nuclear war as one of the major threats to human life, and this has a haunting presence; he also views abortion as taking life daily and on a horrendous scale. Then there is capital punishment, which is making executions almost weekly events in the most advanced technologi-cal society in history – i.e., the United States; and there is euthanasia, an issue which is not only publicly discussed but even advocated by some nowadays. Confronted with these threats, "it is only through a conscious choice and through a deliberate policy that humanity can be saved," as Pope John Paul II rightly observed.

The Protection of Life and the Promotion of Human Dignity

The reason why Cardinal Bernardin has stressed the idea of a consistent ethic of life is twofold: he is persuaded that these diverse problems are interrelated, and he is convinced that the Catholic moral vision has the scope, the strength, and the subtlety to address this wide range of issues in an effective fashion. The case for a consistent ethic of life – one which stands for the protection of the right to life and the promotion of those rights which enhance life from conception to natural death – manifests the positive potential of the Catholic moral and social tradition.

This is both a complex and a demanding tradition. It joins the humanity of the unborn infant and the humanity of the hungry; it calls for positive legal action to prevent the killing of the unborn or the aged and positive societal action to provide shelter for the homeless and education for the illiterate. The Cardinal points out that the potential for a moral and social vision can only be fully and properly appreciated when the "systemic" vision of Catholic ethics is seen as the background for the "specific" positions taken by the Church on a range of issues.

A consistent ethic of life, the Cardinal goes on to observe, does not equate the problem of taking innocent life (for instance, by abortion or the killing of noncombatants in war) with the question of promoting human dignity (for example, through humane programs for nutrition, health care, and housing). Nevertheless, he emphasizes, a consistent ethic identifies both the protection of life and its promotion as moral questions. It argues for a continuum of life which must be sustained in the face of diverse and distinct threats.

What is important to understand is that a consistent ethic does not say that everyone in the Church must do all things. The Cardinal specifies that, instead, a consistent ethic requires that, as individuals and groups pursue a specific issue, whether that is opposing abortion or capital punishment, the way Catholics oppose one threat should be related to giving support for a systemic vision of life. Actually, it is not possible nor necessary for every person to engage in each and all issues. On the contrary, it is both possible and necessary for the Church as a whole to cultivate a conscious and explicit connection among the several issues.

It is important to note how Cardinal Bernardin underlines that no one is called upon to do everything, while each one of us is called to do something. Our full appreciation of this point will lead us to understand that Catholics can strive, at least, not to stand against each other when the protection and promotion of life are at stake.

Four Dimensions of a Consistent Ethic

A consistent ethic of life should in the final analysis honor the multiple issues it is called upon to address. The Cardinal is convinced that it is necessary to distinguish several levels of this question, and he sets himself the task of exploring four distinct dimensions of a consistent ethic.

The first dimension he identifies regards the level of general moral principles. Here it is possible to identify a single principle with diverse applications. In his first address on this theme, when he spoke at Fordham University on December 6, 1983, the Cardinal used the prohibition against direct attacks on innocent lives as an example. This principle is both central to the Catholic moral vision and systematically related to a range of specific moral issues. In fact, it prohibits attacks on unborn life in the womb, direct attacks on civilians in warfare, and the direct killing of patients in nursing homes. Each of these topics, insists the Cardinal, has a consistency in society concerned with the morality of abortion, war, and care for the aged and the dying. A consistent ethic of life encourages the specific concerns of each constituency, but it also calls them to see the interrelatedness of their efforts. The need to defend the integrity of the moral principle in the full range of its application is a responsibility of each distinct constituency, concludes the Cardinal in his address.

A second level of a consistent ethic stresses the distinction among cases, rather than their similarities. As Cardinal Bernardin points out, we need different moral principles to apply to diverse cases. The classical distinction between ordinary and extraordinary means has applicability in the care of the dying, but no relevance in the case of warfare. Actually, not all moral principles have relevance across the whole range of life issues. Nonetheless, he finds compelling the argument that there is a need to relate the cases while keeping them distinctly divided into different categories. As an example, he cites the fact that abortion is taking life in ever growing numbers in our society and those concerned about it will find their case enhanced by taking note of the rapidly expanding use of capital punishment. In a similar way, those who are particularly concerned about the growing numbers of executions should recognize the elementary truth that a society which can be indifferent to the innocent life of an unborn child will not be easily stirred to concern for a convicted criminal. He firmly believes that a comprehensive vision of life must expand the moral imagination of a society, and not partition it into airtight categories.

A third level of a consistent ethic involves how Catholics relate their commitment to moral principles to their public witness of life. Of course, no one can do everything as it has been pointed out above; in fact, there are limits to both competency and energy. Both point to the wisdom of setting priorities and defining distinct functions. However, as Cardinal Bernardin emphasizes, the Church must be credible across a wide range of issues; the very scope of the Catholic moral vision requires a commitment to a multiplicity of questions. In this way, the teaching of the Church will sustain a variety of individual commitments.

A fourth level and one where dialogue is sorely needed, as the Cardinal notes, is the level of the relationship between moral principles and concrete political choices. The moral questions of abortion, the arms race, the fate of social programs for the poor, and the role of human rights in foreign policy are all public issues with a moral dimension. The arena in which they are ultimately decided is the political process. A consistent ethic of life seeks to present a coherent linkage among a diverse set of issues. In adopting such an ethic, as Cardinal Bernardin concludes, the Church legitimately fulfills a public role by articulating a framework for political choices, by relating such a framework to specific issues, and by calling for a systemic moral analysis in all areas of public policy.

The Role of the Church in the Public Arena

The Church is primarily a teacher in the political order; it possesses a carefully cultivated tradition of moral analysis within the fields of personal and public issues. It makes this tradition available in a special manner through the community of the Church, but it also offers something to all who find meaning and guidance in its moral teaching. This is the reason why the U.S. Bishops' Conference has published "A Statement on Political Responsibility" during each of the presidential and congressional election years. The purpose of such publications, explains the Cardinal, is surely not to tell citizens how to vote, but simply to help them shape the public debate and form a personal conscience such that every citizen will become capable of voting thoughtfully and responsibly.

The moral teaching of the Church, according to Joseph Bernardin, has both pastoral and public significance. Pastorally, a consistent ethic of life is a contribution to the witness of the Church's defense of the human person. Publicly, a consistent ethic fills a void in the public policy debate of our times.

From the pastoral point of view, he maintains that a Church standing forth on the entire range of life issues, which the logic of the Catholic moral vision bids us to confront, will be a Church in the style of the values asserted by Vatican II's *Gaudium et Spes* and also in the style of Pope John Paul II's consistent witness of life. Actually, the Cardinal observes, the capacity of faith to shed light on the concrete questions of personal and public life today is a positive way in which the values of the Gospel are applied to current realities.

The public value of a consistent ethic of life is connected directly to its pastoral role. It informs both the conscience and the concrete ethical choices of Catholics as they confront issues of public policy. The unique public possibility for a consistent ethic is provided precisely by the unstructured character of the public debate over the important questions of life. Each of the issues the Cardinal's insightful analysis has taken into account – abortion, war, hunger, human rights, euthanasia, capital punishment – is treated as a separate, self-contained topic in today's public life. Each is distinct; thus, an approach to each one fails to illustrate how our choices in one area can affect our decisions in another. There must then be, the Cardinal insists, a public attitude of respect for all of life in order for public actions to be respectful of life in each specific case.

This powerful exhortation concludes by reminding us that this is precisely where our consistent ethic must really be demonstrated. The Cardinal firmly believes that a clear witness to a consistent ethic of life will provide us with the moral basis to grasp opportunities to serve both the sacredness of every human life and the God of Life who is the origin and the support of our common humanity.

7

The Economy and the Poor

Joseph Bernardin asserts that the bishop has a full right and a compelling duty to come to terms with important topics such as the economy. It is the bishops' duty – a duty which arises from their roles as teachers of moral truth – to address economic questions. However, the real questions concern the people. Are poor people protected against suffering rooted in economic disadvantage? Every society has a moral obligation to take the necessary steps to ensure that none of its members suffer from hunger, homelessness, and unemployment, or is denied what is necessary for a dignified life. Poverty in the world is so massive that we do not know yet how to deal with it. In political debates the question of the poor still exercises very little leverage.

The concept of "economic justice for all" is deeply rooted in the Scriptures. We must make space for the faces of the poor not only in our personal consciences but also in public agendas; the Church must speak for the poor and view the world from their perspective.

In conclusion, Cardinal Bernardin states that a consistent ethical life is a contribution that the Church can and should make in any nation's public debates. These consistent ethics, as defined by Cardinal Bernardin, must include a substantial commitment to the poor, because to stand for the needs of the poor means to stand for life.

T aking as his starting point the 1984 pastoral letter on the economy, "Catholic Social Teaching and the U.S. Economy", and answering those who assert that the bishops simply have no right, competence, or authority to speak out on economic questions, Cardinal Bernardin affirms in no uncertain terms that the bishops not only have a full right, but also a compelling duty to come to terms with this important topic.

Catholic social teaching and the economy are intertwined issues. It is the bishops' duty – a duty which arises precisely from the bishops' role as teachers of moral truth – to address economic questions. The Cardinal repeatedly emphasizes that, in their capacity as moral teachers, the bishops do have an obligation and must build an adequate competence to speak about the fundamental issues pertaining to the various economic systems in which they operate; naturally, they must speak from the perspective of Catholic moral teaching. The main question they are called upon to address is: how do economic theories, programs, and practices affect the lives of people?

People and Not Gross National Product as a Moral Test

Talking specifically about the U.S. economy, Cardinal Bernardin adds that this is not immune to criticism and that it is not beyond improvement. The crucial moral test is not the gross national product (GNP), inflation rates, or other similar measures: it is people. The real questions to be addressed are questions concerning people. The Cardinal insists that we must ask how wide the benefits generated by this powerful economy are and to what extent so much abundance is shared. Moreover, how successful are we in lifting individuals and groups out of poverty in all countries? And also, how vulnerable are such individuals and groups because of their age, health, or other reasons? How protected are they against suffering as a result of economic disadvantage? It is questions like these – observes Cardinal Bernardin – that point to the moral context within which any economic system can and should be evaluated.

In the first draft of the above-mentioned pastoral letter, the bishops affirm: "The dignity of the human person, realized in community with others, is the criterion against which all aspects of economic life must be measured. [Every] society has a moral obligation to take the necessary steps to ensure that no one among its members is hungry, homeless, unemployed or otherwise denied what is necessary to live with dignity." In sum, the bishops have both the right and the duty to express themselves on economic matters, and this is so because the theme of human dignity is central to Catholic social thought.

The Feminization of Poverty

In his analysis of this question, the Cardinal addresses also the question of how many poor there are in the United States. In an address at Georgetown University in 1984, he said that, according to the then current statistics, more than 35 million people in his country lived below the poverty line; between 2 and 3 million were homeless; the hidden poor, those living just above the poverty line, numbered another 20 to 30 million. In addition to these startling figures, estimates placed the number of people without any medical insurance at 35 million. The Cardinal also pointed out that the poor represent every race and religion in the nation; they are both men and women, and also very often children. Moreover, the number of poor women is increasing all the time.

As a matter of fact, Joseph Bernardin notes the disturbing phenomenon of the so-called feminization of poverty. A closer look at poverty among women reveals that it is intimately related to two sets of factors: on the one hand, job and wage discrimination; on the other, the responsibility for the care and support of children. Discrimination against women in the labor market leaves women concentrated in the lowest-paying jobs, with many more problems in finding full-time, year-round jobs. In this regard, the Cardinal remarks that even when women manage to overcome these difficulties, they still earn substantially less than men.

The situation is much worse for women raising their children alone. These women are often financially responsible for most or for all of their children's support. The increased rates of divorce and out-of-wedlock births have left more women than ever solely responsible for the support of an increasing number of children. A single parent – widowed, divorced, or unmarried – finds it in any case very difficult to keep her family above the poverty line. When this parent faces additional obstacles, such as costs for day care (which can easily amount to one-fourth of the average salary of a woman), in addition to sexual discrimination in employment, concludes the Cardinal, the cards are overwhelmingly stacked against the woman.

A Daily Confrontation with the Faces of Poverty

Continuing in his analysis of poverty and stressing the dramatic spreading of this social ill, Cardinal Bernardin asserts that the faces of poverty are all around us and that the only way to hide the poor from our sight is to confine ourselves to our rooms or our homes. After walking through the poverty of the city during the day, he adds, we are confronted with the faces of poverty on a wider scale in the nightly news. Actually, the fact of poverty is the dominant social reality for over 100 countries in the whole world.

Naturally, he focuses on his own reality – poverty in the United States. The fact of world poverty, he observes, is so overwhelming that it might paralyze us. Poverty in the world is so massive that we do not yet know how to deal with it.

More Space for the Faces of the Poor in the Public Agenda

Poverty is present in the United States, he argues, but the poor have not been central to public planning in recent years. Again, poverty is present, but in the policy debates of the nation, the poor have exercised too little leverage. Therefore, he concludes, we need to make space for the faces of the poor not only in our personal consciences, but also in the public agenda. In fact, reality tells us that poverty is not marginal in the United States.

The role of the Church in this regard must be shaped by the perspective provided by the Scriptures, as they are read within the Catholic tradition. The lesson the Church is trying to draw from the biblical perspective is contained symbolically in the phrase which is quoted in the bishops' pastoral letter, "Economic Justice for All": the Church must have a "preferential option for the poor." This concept is rooted in the Scriptures, and it shows the special place the poor have within the care of God. It has been developed with extreme originality by the Church in Latin America, for instance, and it illustrates how the Church learns anew from the Scriptures in every succeeding stage of its history.

However, underlines the Cardinal, the power of this phrase lies in the fact that it summarizes a number of different biblical themes. In fact, he explains, it calls the Church to speak for the poor, to see the world from their perspective, and to empty itself so that it may experience the power of God in the midst of poverty and powerlessness.

Nevertheless, the Cardinal also believes that it is necessary to inquire what the phrase "preferential option for the poor" might really mean for the ministry of the Church in the United States. His answer to this important question offers him the opportunity of illuminating us with another of his fine exegetic analyses of the Scriptures.

Two Dimensions of the Church's Work: Social Service and Advocate for the Poor

Cardinal Bernardin situates the answer in a wider perspective. He says that the Church as a social institution has given two different responses to the tragic question of poverty. The first has been to organize itself in order to carry out effectively all possible works of mercy. The fulfillment of the command to feed the hungry, clothe the naked, and care for the sick has found direct and immediate expression in the Church since the apostolic age. Although the methods of performing such work have been varied over the centuries, all can be now classified as direct, social service provided by the Church to the advantage of the poor.

The second and complementary witness to the option for the poor is given by the Church's role as an advocate and actor in the public life of society. The roots of this dimension of social ministry are found in the prophets who teach us to ask questions about how we organize our life as a society. The purpose of this social teaching is to measure the social and economic life of our country by the standards of social justice and charity.

Cardinal Bernardin's emphasis on these two dimensions of the Church's work – its ministry of direct social service and its role as an advocate for the poor in society – is very strong; in his opinion, these remain the principal channels through which the Church can respond to the tragedy of poverty in our lives.

The Cardinal's teaching, however, is never generic nor theoretical, and his analysis is closely related to the reality of the United States. With regard to this country, he states that, in a large, complex, bureaucratic, and secular society like the United States, the Church's social service role is more needed than ever. In fact, the Church must bring two dimensions to the national system of social care.

On the one hand, it must deliver some social services through a system of distribution based on a decentralized local model. As the Cardinal carefully explains, for a number of social services today, only the taxing power of the State can raise sufficient funds to meet human needs. But the State is often not the best agency to administer services to the people in need. Indeed, the Church can often deliver those services in a more humane and compassionate way than the State can provide.

On the other hand, the Church's agencies of direct social service should be not only a source of compassion but also of creativity. In fact, the public bureaucracy is not famous for its creative innovation, observes the Cardinal ironically. Its size and complexity often prevent it from acting in anything but routine patterns. In every field, from housing to health care and hospice care for the dying, there is room from new creative methods of public-private cooperation and intervention, so that more of the hungry can be fed, increased numbers of the homeless sheltered, and the sick healed. Here – stresses the Cardinal – is where the Church should creatively intervene.

Cardinal Bernardin's reflection addresses a second challenge to the Church in the United States: how to fulfill the role of advocate in the public debate. This is precisely the role which the U.S. Bishops' Conference sought to fulfill in its pastoral letter concerning the issue of poverty. The failure of the bishops to speak on issues such as poverty would be a dereliction of civic responsibility and religious duty. The role of the bishops, as the Cardinal underlines, is not to design or legislate programs; rather, it is to help shape the questions society asks and to help set the right terms for a fruitful debate on public policy.

A Commitment Part of a Consistent Ethic

Cardinal Bernardin defends the opinion that the fiscal deficit debate, in recent years, has provided an excellent example on how Christians should confront the administration of the government. He states that the question of how the country faces the deficit is clearly part of what the Church should do as a moral advocate in the social system.

In many of his addresses, Cardinal Bernardin has pointed out that a consistent ethic of life is a specific contribution which the Church can and should make in any nation's public debate. Central to a consistent ethic of life is the imperative that the Church stands for the protection and promotion of life from conception to natural death. The Cardinal has always insisted that a substantial commitment to the poor is part of a consistent ethic, since to stand for life is equal to standing for the needs of the poor.

In the end, he asserts, every social institution is known by what it stands for. He thinks that all Catholics in the United States should collaborate in the Church's mission in order for it to be known as a community which has committed itself to the protection and promotion of life – i.e., a community that has helped its own society to fulfill as adequately as possible these two complementary tasks.

Global Market and Human Costs

In his last speech at Georgetown University, on September 9, 1996, Cardinal Bernardin called for all Christians to bare their public religious witness in social and economic affairs. He indicated the example of the pastoral letter on the U.S. economy, Economic Justice for All, as a clear explanation of his words. Since its publication ten years ago – the Cardinal pointed out – the U.S. economy has continued to experience deep and far-reaching change generated by broad global patterns of economic interdependence, making is impossible to isolate the U.S economy for analysis apart from the global economy. Sustained economic growth, competitiveness of American workers and indus-try, and unemployment statistics are "macro" indicators of critical importance, but they do not address crucial moral questions that must be part of our assessment of U.S. economic life. The dynamic of the global market – one that does not address the human costs of global competition – must be complemented by a broader framework of social policy that attends to the needs of those who lose in the economic lottery. Catholic social and economic teaching is deeply concerned for the welfare of society as a whole and for the dignity and human rights of each person.

The healthcare debate of the early 1990s and the welfare debate of this past year – two of our major socioeconomic policy debates of the 1990s – should make us think deeply about our societal contract, or conception of moral obligation among the citizens of this nation. Cardinal Bernardin acknowledged that healthcare policy must address the exponential increase in healthcare costs, the need to restructure parts of our delivery system, and the need to strike a balance between competing objectives of quality of care and the kinds of care provided in the healthcare system. In his view, however, both of the extended policy debates on these issues failed to meet basic standards of responsible policy. We have "changed" health care and welfare. But from the perspective of those for whom we bear moral responsibility – women, children, the poor – change does not equal reform. It looks more like abandonment. In order to be fair and just, social policy must meet both the standards of effectiveness and justice.

The Subsidiarity Principle

The state has to find its appropriate role in our common life as a society. The concept of "subsidiarity," a principle of Catholic social theory, explicitly requires that responses to social needs not start with the State. But the State has specific moral duties toward those afflicted by illness, hardship, unemployment, and the lack of adequate nutrition and housing. Thus, a conception of what the State's moral role is in society cannot be omitted. However, we cannot discuss the moral obligations of the State without making first a substantive analysis of the obligations we have to each other as members of civil society. A sense of social responsibility must be showed by all. This can be done in many ways, as beautifully pointed out by Pope John Paul II. Cardinal Bernardin makes a distinction between solidarity and subsidiarity. Solidarity precedes subsidiarity. The first defines our moral relationship; the second regulates how we will fulfill the duty of solidarity.

Social solidarity helps to define the moral responsibility of the State and its citizenry and points toward the neuralgic issue of U.S. politics: taxation, a secular issue rooted in moral obligations. A fair tax policy, one which obliges each of us to play a role in sustaining the human dignity of all in our society, is thus seen as a requirement of distributive justice. The same distributive justice through which our obligations towards the poor are met.

Subsidiarity, solidarity, and socialization – three key ideas to Catholic social teaching – need to be held in tandem since the first establishes the basis of common obligation, the second argues that private voluntary institutions are needed to fulfill our obligations, and the third maintains that increased societal interdependence requires an activist State to meet the needs that private institutions cannot meet alone.

8

Civil Rights

Catholic teaching must be the basis of any Catholic commitment to civil rights. The right to life is the first and utmost right, and, consequently, respect for freedom and personal responsibility play an important role in society. In fact, when the freedom and the dignity of a person are violated in any way, the entire human family is devalued.

Its imperative that Christians respect civil rights, demostrated through their actions to establish a lasting national and international peace. Cardinal Bernardin underlines that peace engendered by arms races proves to be a illusion. Security at the expense of another country's insecurity is unacceptable. Moreover, security is not a reality for the world if people still suffer from hunger, children die every minute, exorbitant military expenditures are continually planned, and racism, segregation, poverty, hopelessness and despair are still so prevalent. In light of this, Joseph Bernardin invites all Christians to act upon their convictions as people of faith. Abortion, he asserts, must not be included among civic rights, but rather the right to life must be considered as the first and foremost among fundamental human rights.

Among other civil right violations, apartheid has not yet been eliminated in South Africa. In countless nations violent civic wars have diminished human dignity, providing examples of social injustice. Immigration has been charged with creating problems; however, immigrating people move from one country to another in search of a better life and most times find themselves, once again, in poverty. When nations, in a desperate attempt to solve immigration problems, try to build a pro-

tective wall around their borders to keep other people out, they
forget we are all members of a single human family in which
every individual's rights must be respected.

Respect for human dignity involves respect for freedom and personal responsibility; thus, it involves the respect for civil rights. In turn, Catholic teaching asserts that every person is created in the image of God. Upon these two fundamental considerations is grounded Cardinal Bernardin's thinking on civil rights. In fact, he observes that Catholic teaching must be considered the basis for any Catholic commitment to civil rights.

The Cardinal emphasizes the extent to which any form of unjust discrimination ultimately results in an attack on the image of God present in our midst, every person being created in His image. The right to life is the first and utmost right, though the Cardinal emphasizes that respect for freedom and personal responsibility play an important role in society as well.

In fact, he goes on to develop his argument by showing that there cannot be any recognition of sin in the absence of responsibility. The reverse is also equally true: to deny the reality of sin is in effect to deny the fact of freedom. There is a very important dimension to all this. As Cardinal Bernardin states, borrowing from the British sociologist Christy Davis, crime rates have risen in Great Britain precisely as cultural factors have combined to weaken and diminish the sense of personal responsibility. Thus, there is no adequate reason to deny or to dismiss it, because defending the fact of human freedom is essential both within the sphere of individual behavior and on the level of society itself.

Respect for Civil Rights Is Required by Freedom and Peace

To this analysis, Cardinal Bernardin adds the remark that, when the freedom and the dignity of any person are violated in any way, the entire human family is devalued. We are social creatures by nature, and we are essentially linked within an interdependent community.

Joseph Bernardin goes on to observe that today many people claim to hold the values of freedom and justice, yet, when it comes to translating such values into concrete action or practical public policy, they pause, hesitate, or perhaps even back away from the commitment to action which this belief implies. On the contrary, it is precisely the duty of every Christian – insists the Cardinal – to act on their beliefs and help create a just society. In such a society everyone is expected to live in a way that allows the enjoyment of equal opportunities and at the same time full participation in the economy and in the decisionmaking processes that affect their lives.

Besides, Cardinal Bernardin argues that the respect of civil rights is also required in order to establish a stable national and international peace. In fact, as Dr. Martin Luther King Jr. observed in the 1960s, a stable peace within nations and among nations cannot exist apart from the claims of justice; moreover, such claims must be acknowledged by individuals and groups alike. An imposed peace is a transitory illusion; an unjust peace is purchased for some at the price of the lives of others. From these observations, Bernardin's argument concludes by stating that the peace engendered by the arms race proves to be a transitory illusion, too.

The Cardinal embraces Martin Luther King Jr.'s thought to show how those who claim that the substantial and continually increasing amounts of money spent on the arms race are justified as contributions to national security are wrong, because the relationship of peace to justice forces us to examine what we mean by security. He also emphasizes that a security at the expense of another country's insecurity is not acceptable.

Hungry, Homeless, and Hopeless

As Cardinal Bernardin emphasizes, we cannot be secure in a world in which, according to reputable studies, more than 450 million people go hungry and more than 30 children die every minute for want of food and vaccinations, while the global military expenditures are more than U.S. $1.3 million per minute. Therefore, the fact that we all must face is that we are clearly in a situation in which every dollar spent for military measures is in competition with the increased resources so much required to satisfy human and social needs.

Considering the situation of the United States, and in particular analyzing the severe cuts in social programs, accompanied by a consistent rise in military spending – a decision taken by the U.S. Administration and Congress not too many years ago – the Cardinal asks what is the view of security that the American government wants to promote. What definition of security can possibly move the United States to believe that hungry, homeless, and hopeless people in the world's wealthiest democracy are a basis for a stable domestic peace?

As he specifies, however, his argument is not meant to imply that there should be no military component to a true definition of security. He acknowledges the fact that a nation has an obligation to defend itself against unjust aggressors and a certain military capability is needed for this purpose in today's world. However, his position is that peace must be joined with a reasonable concept of security for this to be truly secure, both on a national and on an international scale.

Peace Needs Justice

Peace and security are thus seen as things which should grow from justice. Justice in turn, should grow out of the respect for civil rights – first among these the right to live.

As Cardinal Bernardin observes, Dr. Martin Luther King well understood this point and felt a moral duty to disrupt the unjust domestic peace of the United States in a nonviolent way. He forced the country to face the real reasons why the peace in the strongest nation on earth was actually precarious and unstable: one dimension of that peace was rooted in the denial of full human and civil rights to a whole sector of the nation. He forced America to face squarely the moral, political, and constitutional crisis caused by, on the one hand, basing the political system on the principles of human dignity and equality while, on the other, basing the practice of the law on a systematic denial of those great principles.

Racism: An Obstacle to Peace

The civil rights movement exposed a reality which many had so far refused to acknowledge: the sin of racism and segregation, poverty and hunger, hopelessness and despair. Unfortunately, Cardinal Bernardin says, even though it is evident that there must be no gap between the principles we profess and the way we live as a society, the ugly features of racism and discrimination remain alive in the hearts and attitudes of many people. Racism in the United States is a fact, not a mere perception or opinion. Racism is an obstacle on the way to national security and a stable peace.

This is the reason why Cardinal Bernardin invites all Christians, as people of faith and believers in the risen Lord, to act upon their convictions. They must challenge the inconsistencies between professed beliefs and accepted actions. They must undertake the task to overcome the obstacle of racism and discrimination, in order to create a just society based on the respect of civil rights.

The Right to Abortion Is No Civil Right

The Catholic bishops of the United States are irrevocably and unequivocally in favor of civil rights, but Cardinal Bernardin emphasizes that they are just as firmly opposed to the notion that abortion can be properly viewed as a "civil right." And the U.S. Catholic Conference asserts that, precisely because they are testifying in support of civil rights, the Catholic bishops want to reaffirm their opposition to including in any way the right to abortion as a civil right. In fact, the right to life is the fundamental civil right, and it applies to the unborn as well as to any other human being.

Unfortunately, since the U.S. Supreme Court decisions of 1973 legalized abortion, a strange and disturbing thing has been happening: there has been a pronounced tendency for some people to maintain that abortion and abortion-related services constitute a "civil right," and to assert that these activities are entitled to the corresponding constitutional protection and legal enforcement. The bishops simply do not accept this, and they want the Congress to affirm clearly which is the real civil right – the right to life, not abortion.

Violation of the Immigrants' Civil Rights

Cardinal Bernardin observes that there are still many nations where civil rights are manifestly violated, among them, for example, South Africa – where the heresy of apartheid, which impedes and dishonors human dignity, has not yet been eliminated – and some countries in Central and South America – where civil wars have diminished the value of human life, where violence occurs daily, and where, besides these constant threats, most people live in utter poverty, itself the result of social injustice.

These political and social problems are the cause of the large number of immigrants and refugees who seek peace and justice in other countries. There are many immigrants in the United States, and their numbers increase daily. But there are also people in the United States, already citizens but who themselves are the descendants of immigrants, who want to build a "protective wall" to keep the new immigrants out, thus refusing to grant to these people the fundamental right to a peaceful and secure life.

As Cardinal Bernardin suggests, however, the end of the inscription on the Statue of Liberty may offer a useful perspective from which to confront this dramatic question properly. It reads: "Send these, the homeless, the tempest-tossed, to me: I will lift my lamp beside the golden door." Joseph Bernardin thus asserts that the citizens of the United States must face the fact that it is not feasible, nor would it be in accordance with the values of the nation, to build a protective wall around the borders of the country to keep other people out. On the contrary, both justice and generosity must be extended in allowing immigrants and refugees to become members of their society. And they must do so in ways that do not jeopardize the legitimate rights of those who are already citizens.

At the same time, he concludes, Americans cannot afford to ignore the serious problems that cause people to immigrate to their safe shores and elsewhere. When parents see that their children do not have enough to eat, or are exposed to the daily danger and violence of war, can anyone blame them for wanting to move to a land such as the United States, which is known throughout the world as a safe refuge and a land of opportunity? In a complex world, immigrants remind us of a simple fact: we are all sisters and brothers, members of one human family, and the rights of all people must be respected, since any violation harms the entire human family.

9

Religious Women and Men

Joseph Bernardin acknowledges the importance of religious congregations and the fundamental role played by women in the local and universal Church.

A dramatic decrease in new vocations, together with the perception of the lack of authority in religious life, are both causes of pain for religious women congregations. Women, he notes, feel hostility from the Holy See, local bishops, parish priests, and lay people; as a result they experience feelings of discord, isolation, fragmentation, and polarization is pervading them. Nonetheless, because of their great faith and commitment, women are signs of fidelity and life in the Church.

The Archbishop of Chicago, likewise, talks about men who, together with religious women, have worked diligently to shape their lives and their ministry according to the vision and mandate of Vatican II. In so doing, they have performed a service both for themselves and for the entire Church, providing helpful insight and direction for other Catholics. Cardinal Bernardin also touches on the existing tensions in the Catholic world that, he notes, do not have to be destructive or debilitating.

He expresses that working working hand in hand with auxiliary bishops, diocesan priests, permanent deacons, lay ministers, and religious women and men is a joyful aspect of his ministry, and hopes that his commitment will encourage them to work more closely together.

Cardinal Bernardin concludes by underlining the importance of our own personal relationship with God, noting that relig-

ious men and women must allow themselves to become instruments of our Lord.

Cardinal Bernardin expresses his deep understanding for the problems of religious life and, at the same time, his appreciation and gratitude for the work done by religious women and men. He also acknowledges the importance of the existence of religious congregations for the life of the universal, as well as the local, Church.

On the occasion of a meeting of all the religious women of the Archdiocese of Chicago on April 9, 1984, he wisely summarized his remarks on this subject under three headings since it became obvious to him that religious women are: women of sorrow, women of faith, and women of hope.

Women of Sorrow

They are women of sorrow because they suffer from the lack of appreciation and understanding, whether on the part of their own sisters, or of priests and bishops, or of the lay people whom they serve. The broader Church does not appreciate their gifts as persons, as women, as religious.

For many among them, however, the pain is the result of the effort to effect renewal. For some, Cardinal Bernardin explains, renewal came too slowly after the Second Vatican Council; for others, too quickly. Some feel as though all the values of religious life have been lost. For others, the cause of pain is just the opposite. These religious women are convinced that their renewal efforts have indeed resulted in a deeper understanding of religious life and a more radical commitment to it; yet they still feel that they sometimes face misunderstanding, disagreement, or even hostility on the part of the Holy See, the local bishops, the parish priests, or the people.

Another cause of pain has been the polarization within communities and between congregations. There have been struggles over questions of habit, lifestyle, style of leadership, living situations, and ministries. As Cardinal Bernardin recognizes and applauds, these struggles have subsided to some extent, but the healing process is not yet complete.

Another serious concern, and a major cause of pain for the religious congregations of women, is a dramatic decline in new vocations which, obviously, raises questions about the future of the same congregations.

Another troubling question, of which the Cardinal proves to be well aware, is that of authority. Some religious women, as Joseph Bernardin observes, are pained by what they perceive as the lack of authority in religious life. For them, the vow of obedience has lost its significance, and this has affected the meaning of their choice of life. On the contrary, there are other religious women who want even more independence.

Cardinal Bernardin underlines that there is always much pain in what he hears about or from religious women, and this pain is caused by a sense of disharmony, isolation, fragmentation, and polarization; for this reason, he feels almost compelled to consider them as women of sorrow.

Women of Faith

Beyond the pain and anxiety, however, it is very evident that they are women of great faith who thirst for intimacy with the Lord. Their years of service; their struggles to form community, to live their vows, to renew their congregations; the breadth and richness of their diversity; the intensity of their desire to dialogue and to collaborate with the rest of the Church in continuing Jesus' mission – all these gifts, Cardinal Bernardin emphasizes, can only flow from the deep faith which gives tremendous witness to the risen Lord. He also adds that he sees them – with all their gifts, skills, and charisms – as a precious gift to the Church. He sees them as signs and witnesses of fidelity in a Church and in a society where faithfulness is not always valued and where recognition and appreciation are not always given.

Women of Hope

Because of their great faith, Cardinal Bernardin also sees religious women as women of hope. In faith they know it is the Spirit who renews the Church, religious life, and the whole face of the earth. In faith they have accepted their pain and suffering as part of the paschal mystery which is integral to Christian lives. In faith they know that the fundamental call of the Gospel, the call to renewal, must involve both dying and raising. Even though all the problems have not yet been resolved and the future is not crystal clear, the religious women have begun to experience resurrection. This is why, Cardinal Bernardin concludes, they are women of life and not of death. This is why, despite the trying and sometimes painful experiences of the last decades, they are women of enthusiasm and hope.

Examining the issue of the renewal of the Church called for by Vatican II, Cardinal Bernardin insightfully observes that it is easier for members of religious congregations to move ahead on renewal because, while they represent a rich diversity of gifts and charisms, there is a unity of purpose which binds them together. Moreover, they are able to stand back and to take the steps needed to discern, to affirm or correct, and finally to renew. The result is, as Joseph Bernardin underlines, that the progress of renewal in religious congregations has frequently gone forward at a faster pace than in the rest of the Church. This has had both positive and negative results. As he explains, the problematic side is that because religious women and men have proceeded with renewal more quickly, there is great likelihood that their efforts will be misunderstood. Furthermore, as with any vanguard, they have made some mistakes because they are working without precedents; consequently, there have been few opportunities to learn from the mistakes of others.

A Service for the Entire Church

Cardinal Bernardin, however, does not forget to stress that there is, of course, a positive side. In fact, their strong commitment to the Church and to religious life has not permitted them to sit by idly and let things happen on their own. Instead, both religious women and men have worked diligently to shape their lives and their ministry according to the Second Vatican Council's vision and mandate. This is evident in the new constitutions they have developed for their congregations in the post-conciliar years. And in doing this, as Cardinal Bernardin warmly acknowledges, they have performed a service not only for themselves but for the entire Church. In fact, they have given other Catholics many needed and helpful insights and directions.

However, he continues, the renewal has not yet been completed, either in the religious congregations or in the overall Church. There are many issues which still need attention, and there is no doubt that, in facing them, the Catholic world will encounter a certain amount of tension. Tension, however, need not be destructive or debilitating. The tension of which he speaks is rooted in the reality of religious life as a gift in the Church. It is a dynamic, growth-inducing tension that has been evident in the Church since the earliest days. Cardinal Bernardin explains the nature of this tension by speaking of the "institutional" and the "charismatic" side of the Church's life.

The institutional side is that of the ongoing care for a limited and fixed area and population, the everyday ministries and, as in his own case, the pastoral administration of a local church. The charismatic side is that of the opening of ways of seeing new possibilities for living the life of the Church, new possibilities for the life of discipleship, new possibilities for the radical nature of the Gospel to affect and indeed shape today's society, as Pope John Paul II said in his address to the U.S. bishops on September 19, 1983. Demonstrating once again a deep understanding of the manifold aspects of the life of the Church, Cardinal Bernardin insists that both institutional and charismatic dimensions belong to the Church and they should not be in opposition. They should create a tension, and through this tension the Church can grow and become a more effective servant and witness of the Gospel in the world.

Working Closely with Religious Women and Men

Cardinal Bernardin further developed his reflections on this important subject when he addressed the religious women and men of his Archdiocese in 1984. He openly admitted that, when he thinks about religious life in the Church, and when he reflects on the men and women with whom he has collaborated and from whom he has drawn inspiring witness, he has one deep feeling. It is gratitude, a deep sense of gratitude for God's gift of religious life to the Church. He also joyfully asserted that he wants to work more closely with these women and men as together they serve God's people. He wants to work more closely with all of them, and, in the process, he hopes that this will also encourage them to work together more closely with one another. He very much wants them to be full partners and active collaborators in the life and the ministry of the archdiocese. They will have to help him take whatever next steps are necessary to ensure that this becomes a reality.

Cardinal Bernardin offers religious men and women the challenge of joining with others in developing a more collaborative model of ministry, but one that does not weaken the many contributions they are already making in their own apostolates. This collaboration must include not only the archbishop and the auxiliary bishops, Joseph Bernardin concludes, but also the diocesan priests, permanent deacons, lay ministers, and, of course, both religious women and men. And he adds that, if they say YES to such collaboration, it will mean that they will have to invest some personal resources into such a process. It will demand their time, energy, and talents. But it will also mean a lot of dialogue, and he asserts that he is firmly committed to the process of dialogue as a way of solving problems and asks them, all of the religious women and men to whom his address is directed, to respond with such a commitment.

Understanding and Working Together

Cardinal Bernardin has stated on numerous occasions that he hopes that the above-mentioned gifts and tension will work in the direction of building up the Body of Christ, the Church. This hope hinges on three conditions. First, every religious woman and man must be convinced of the great urgency of the need for healing and redemption in the world today. This sense of urgency must continuously lift them up and beyond merely intramural concerns. Second, they need to attend deliberately to the process of creating a climate of openness within themselves to the movement of God's Spirit today. Third, they need to make continuous efforts to return to the core of their faith and renew their sense of mission and service.

Cardinal Bernardin finally asserts that, if they move responsibly in these directions, he is confident that they will become a community of many gifts. At the same time, they will be a community of effective witness and service in the world.

In the last analysis, however, the most important thing is every religious' relationship with the Lord. Religious women and men must place themselves totally in His hands and allow themselves to become His instruments; they must be very holy people. As a man of faith, Cardinal Bernardin freely admits that no program, no strategy, no structure will be fully successful unless they are, and they are perceived to be, men and women of deep faith, and unless there is a transparency in them which allows people to see Jesus working in and through them.

To understand fully Cardinal Bernardin's attitude towards religious women and men it is useful to bear in mind his eloquent presentation to them, when he says that beneath his titles he is a very human person – their brother, Joseph – who, like them, is weak and sinful, in need of affirmation and support, and at times full of doubts and anxieties, very sensitive, easily hurt and frustrated. But he asks them to accept his person as one who has a great respect and affection for them, as one who stands in solidarity with them, who is proud of them, and who, for the sake of the Lord, is ready and willing to lay down his life for them.

10

Racism

Cardinal Bernardin examines the prejudice and racism that are still alive and strong in our world. Racism manifests itself in problems such as inadequate housing, unemployment, of job forced choice, poor education, and distance between people of different ethnic and racial backgrounds. In worst cases, it can take the form of open hostility and violence. There will be no end to acute racial crises if we do not defy chronic problems of racism in all parts of the world. Racism can also manifest itself economically, making one's economic status as determining as the color of one's skin.

People feel a sense of helplessness – Cardinal Bernardin continues – when they lack control over their own destiny. Each one of us is hostage of racism and needs to free ourselves from it. Catholics must not forget that they, too, have experienced discrimination and rejection which, the Archbishop of Chicago asserts, must not be repeated. Racism must be seen as an attack on Christianity at its roots, and as an insidious sin.

Different colors of skins or different races cannot exist for Christians since all human beings are one in Christ. In our own fight against racial problems, Cardinal Bernardin calls us to examine the example provided by Martin Luther King, who prophetically illuminated the moral issues of his own time. Dr. King knew that the problem of racism required profound changes not only in people's thought but also in political attitudes. Dr. King began an important process that the present generation must continue.

The problem of racism in the United States has been confronted and analyzed in its effects on contemporary society by Cardinal Bernardin from three different and important points of view: as citizens, as Catholics, and as the Church. His understanding of this important and complex problem has been illuminated by this approach.

Considering the issue of racism as it is felt from the point of view of citizens, the Archbishop of Chicago observes that racial tension in contemporary society, and most especially in Chicago, cannot be a surprise, even to the most naive resident. He underlines the fact that prejudice and racism is, in fact, still alive and well. In the metropolitan area of Chicago, the Cardinal adds, racial tension appears in two main forms.

Chronic Racism and Racial Tension

First, there is a low-key, chronic form of racism that manifests itself in the usual ways: inadequate housing, jobs, and education, as well as a certain distance between people of different ethnic and racial backgrounds. This form of racism has been described as the "quiet riots" which grip society today. Second, there are moments of acute racial tension, when words and actions become openly hostile and even violent.

We often assume that the silent wounds of chronic racism are incurable conditions of contemporary life. So, we usually live with the so-called quiet riots. However, even the perennially optimistic person will recognize that such silent racism is a problem waiting to turn into a deafening crisis. To put it bluntly, there will be no end to acute racial crises if we do not attend to the chronic problems of racism in Chicago, or in any part of the world where they manifest themselves.

Whether it involves white against black or black against white, Cardinal Bernardin affirms in no uncertain terms that racism is a sin. The sin of racist behavior must be identified, named, and then eliminated from our lives, personally and collectively. The last task, undoubtedly, will be the most challenging, because changing destructive patterns of behavior takes patience and commitment. Authentic reconciliation will certainly take time. This healing process, Cardinal Bernardin concludes, will demand discipline, forbearance, and compassion.

Racism Affects All of Us

Racism, he has stressed over and over again, is not a sin of a single ethnic or racial group. It affects all Americans – black, white, brown, yellow, or any other color. It is their problem, whether their ancestors came from Europe, Asia, Africa, or Latin America. This is why they must remain sensitive to the concerns of all citizens. They also have an obligation to reject explicitly and resist intemperate, irrational, or inflammatory accusations, no matter what their source may be.

Cardinal Bernardin observes that racism has a particular shape and face in Chicago. It involves housing and jobs. It takes the form of economic questions which can be as determining as the color of one's skin. It is the sense of helplessness, he continues, which persons feel when they lack control over their own destiny. It is the frustration of knowing that we are all potential victims of exploitation when racism prevails. Racism permits us to create enemies and then to assign them the blame for all that is wrong and for every one of our fears and anxieties. Ultimately, each of us is held hostage by racism. This is why we need to struggle to free ourselves from racism.

It is, however, necessary to approach this issue not only as citizens but also as Catholics. As immigrants and newcomers to the United States and to the city of Chicago, in fact, Catholics themselves have, at times, experienced discrimination and rejection. Cardinal Bernardin asserts firmly that they must not allow this to be repeated. As followers of the risen Lord, they are called to eliminate any and all false distinctions which would separate us from one another or imply that some are superior to others. There is no room in the Catholic community for the false premise that, because we differ in color or heritage, we may forget or ignore what binds us together in our common humanity. To say it simply, we are all sons and daughters of the same God, and, therefore, brothers and sisters.

Racism Attacks Christianity at Its Roots

The main goal of Cardinal Bernardin is to speak out against the racism that divides, insults, and seeks to dominate. He emphasizes that we must oppose the racism that seeks to hold down, to keep out, to hurt, to exclude, to infuriate, to inflame – whatever its source may be, and whether it is done by word, action, or conspiracy, and regardless of whether it is perpetrated by white, black, brown, or yellow.

Joseph Bernardin considers the problem of racism as a challenge to every Christian. He also underlines that racism will be a social problem as long as it is a personal problem, and he adds that every lasting social change obviously and undoubtedly requires a profound change of heart. For Christians, this means grasping the truth of the frequently repeated statement that racism is a sin and a heresy, too. The idea of racism, as he explains exhaustively, is in fundamental contradiction to some of the basic doctrines of Christianity. Basically, it is a denial of the essential quality of all human beings, which is based on their relationship to God as their Creator and to Jesus Christ as their redeemer. One who refuses to accept the fundamental unity of the human race in its origin and destiny rejects, knowingly or unknowingly, the truth that God created us all and that Christ died for us all.

From this important perspective, racism must be seen as an attack on Christianity at its roots. In a special way, racism repudiates the saving mission of Christ, and Cardinal Bernardin acknowledges that it is one of the scandals of history that Christians should so often have lapsed into the racist frame of mind. St. Paul wrote that in Christ there is neither Jew nor Greek, for "all are one in Christ Jesus" (Gal. 3: 28). If he were writing in our world today, Joseph Bernardin adds, he would undoubtedly say that for Christians there is no longer black, white, or brown – all are one in Christ. To the extent that it denies and rejects this doctrine, racism reflects a pre-Christian mentality which no sincere follower of Christ can deliberately make his own.

The Church Must Be Firm

Analysing racism as a dramatic and urgent issue of our time, Cardinal Bernardin underlines his own convictions and speaks of the Church's necessity to take a definite position on the matter. He asserts that since his arrival in the archdiocese, he has tried always to speak out as strongly as he can – in homilies, in addresses, in his columns in *The Chicago Catholic*, and especially in his actions – against the sin of racism. For instance, he visited Marillac House and saw firsthand the pain, the despair, and the desolation of people living in public housing projects. This visit – he said – highlighted a reality that has become very apparent to him in the years that he has been visiting the parishes and institutions of the archdiocese: the citizens of Chicago live not in one city, but two! There is the shining downtown and the beautiful residential areas, both within the city and in the suburbs. Then there is the other city: the city marked by poverty, high unemployment, and decaying housing – and it is this city that breeds despair. If the Church is to minister effectively and if it is to witness the Gospel in a credible way, observes the Archbishop of Chicago, it must first understand the reality and complexity of these two entities and how they relate to one another.

He believes that charity begins "at home." The Archdiocese of Chicago is predominantly white, and he is aware that this fact can, at times, cause its members to be insensitive to others. They must, therefore, examine and challenge any and all racist attitudes, language, and actions, explicit or implicit, which they find in the Church itself. He also believes and suggests that the priests must be honest with their people. In their preaching and teaching about racism and other justice issues they help their people most when they simply and humbly share with them their own painful stories of how they, too, wrestle with the challenge of the Gospel in their own hearts.

The Example of Dr. Martin Luther King

Racism is an insidious sin. It is a human reality not confined to any single racial, social, or economic group. This allows Cardinal Bernardin to observe astutely, and with a wry sense of humor, that dealing with racism is like peeling an onion. One works hard to remove one layer only to discover that he must start all over on yet another layer – all the while feeling like weeping.

In order to fight racial problems and injustice and, at the same time, to witness to the Gospel and to be real peacemakers, Cardinal Bernardin believes that Christians should look at the example of Martin Luther King, Jr. Dr. King was first and foremost a man of the Gospel and the Church. He fused the Old Testament cry for justice with the New Testament witness of nonviolence to create a social revolution that reshaped the substance of the public life in the United States.

Dr. King was not only an outstanding pastor and eloquent preacher; he was also a prophet, since a prophet's purpose is not primarily to describe the future but to illuminate the moral issues of his own time. Prophetic messages are pre-eminently focused on the issue of justice – the community's correct relationship with God as that is measured by its members' relationships with one another. Dr. King assessed the degree of justice in American society in the 1960s and found it wanting.

He knew the dilemma of the treatment of Black Americans would be resolved only by a series of political-moral decisions reaching all the way from the innermost personal relationships up to the highest levels of public institutions. The issue of race was so deeply embedded in U.S. life that it required profound changes in the way Americans thought and in the way they acted, in the way they voted, and in the way they allocated resources. Cardinal Bernardin observes that the decisions required were essentially moral, and the prophetic vision of Martin Luther King forced every one to face squarely the moral, political, and constitutional crises that existed for them, as individuals and as a nation, by basing their political system on the principles of human dignity and equality, while basing their everyday practice on a systematic denial of those principles.

The leader of the antiracism movement disturbed the domestic peace of the United States in a nonviolent and positive way. One dimension of that peace was rooted in the denial of full human and civil rights to a whole sector of the nation. It was an unjust peace, and Dr. King created a constitutional crisis because only by exposing the constitutional question could the crisis of conscience in the nation be addressed. As Cardinal Bernardin concludes, Martin Luther King began an important process, and it is up to the present generation to continue it.

11

Family and Marriage

Cardinal Bernardin also analyzes the widespread topic of pregnancy at very young age in the United States. When teenage girls are not offered a proper education, a job, and a realistic prospect for self-improvement, they can make wrong choices.

Moreover, providing contraceptive services in school-based clinics merely escapes the problem, and encourages young people to engage in sexual behavior by giving it a veneer of social acceptability. Furthermore, along with a permissive attitude toward premature sexual activity, we send young people the message that casual sex is a socially acceptable norm.

A real solution – the Archbishop of Chicago says – is a strong education that helps teenagers develop into sexually mature adults. Despite difficult challenges facing families of today, they must play an active role in the education of teenagers and provide positive examples through their behavior. Christian families are very important to our society and it is necessary that young couples thoroughly understand the Sacrament of marriage.

Joseph Bernardin underlines the importance of an extensive and correct marriage preparation, noting that unhealthy formative circumstances may eventually lead to separation and divorce. Marriage preparation must be realistic about faithfully maintaining the marriage covenant in a changing world. In doing so, the family will grow as a positive and healthy example for modern society and for young people in particular.

Cardinal Bernardin confirms that the family has a central importance in our society as nurturer of new life and transmitter of values. He notes though that the survival of the modern

family is in danger based on the high rate of divorce (one mar-
riage out of two ends in a divorce). Not only economic but
moral issues, he concludes, play an important role in family
problems, which encompass values, attitudes, and mistaken
use of personal freedom.

The existence of the problem of teenage pregnancy has provided Cardinal Bernardin with a favorable opportunity to analyze the importance of the family, which he emphasizes is central to the health and well-being of all societies as the bearer of values and principles. The Cardinal maintains that the solution to teenage pregnancy is not to be found in the provision of contraceptive counseling and the dispensing, prescribing, or selling of contraceptives to teenagers. On the contrary, by doing this under the guise of helping young people at risk, society is well on its way towards doing them even further injury.

In his lucid analysis, the Archbishop of Chicago observes that nobody doubts that teenage pregnancy is a real problem in the United States. For some years now a million or more teenage girls become pregnant every year, and several thousand of these pregnancies annually end in abortion. What Joseph Bernardin suggests is to stop and reflect on what the real causes of teenage pregnancy are.

The Health in a Hopeful Youth

He finds extremely interesting a document of the National Academy of Science, which analyzes why some teenagers engage in premature sexual activity. The answer that applies to a very substantial group of teenagers boils down to one of "self-perception." In other words, those who are hopeful and optimistic about their future tend to avoid such sexual activity; those who lack this outlook are most likely to engage in this type of activity, with all the problems that it entails. In the words of William Raspberry:

> Youngsters who believe, on whatever evidence, that they have a bright fu-
> ture ahead of them – who have a positive and clear idea of who they are
> – find it easier to make positive decisions, easier to resist peer pressure,
> easier to make sacrifices necessary for academic excellence, and easier to
> say no to drugs, sex and other future-threatening temptations.

By contrast, the Cardinal argues, the approach embodied in school-based clinics, which facilitate the dispensing or selling of contraceptives, is that it is easier for society to thrust contraception on vulnerable young people than to offer them reasons – education, jobs, and realistic prospects for self-improvement – for looking to the future with hope. Proponents of contraception will object that the aim of these efforts is precisely to preserve young people's positive options by helping them avoid premature pregnancies. But no less pertinent is the argument that urging contraception on teenagers simply encourages them to engage in sexual behavior before marriage by giving it a veneer of social acceptability.

Joseph Bernardin is aware that, if a Catholic bishop says things like this, he risks being accused of trying to impose the Church's teaching about birth control and premarital sex on the population at large. But here he is only asking whether society cannot – and ought not – do better by young people than urge on them a doubtful solution which does not respond to their real problems and needs.

Actually, providing contraceptive services through school-based clinics is not an answer but an evasion, and the Cardinal's position is that pursuing this pseudosolution delays the day when the problem will be addressed realistically and, very likely, we make lasting remedies more difficult to find and apply. Consequently, and consistently, he urges governmental policy-makers to reexamine their headlong plunge into school-based contraceptive services. Neither as a short-term solution nor as a long-term policy will this meet the complex needs of teens and their families.

Why Contraceptives Are Not the Right Solution

Cardinal Bernardin not only opposes the solution of the increased avail-ability of contraceptives on moral grounds but also because it simply does not work. He affirms, in fact, that for some years contraceptives have been available practically for the asking, and it is precisely during this time that the incidence of teenage pregnancy has risen dramatically. What is even worse, and here he goes back to the moral grounds against this solution, is that along with a permissive attitude toward premature sexual activity, we have been indoctrinating young people in a contraceptive mentality whose fundamental principle is that casual sex is the socially acceptable norm. Obviously, he agrees that more education of teenagers is needed, but he believes it should be education in such things as family, values, a healthy and integrated acceptance of sexuality, stability in marital relationships, a sense of obligation toward other persons, and a willingness to accept the consequences of one's actions. In other words, expanded and improved education for teenagers should seek to help them grow up as sexually mature adults. Cardinal Bernardin concludes that he is certain that this is the solution – the only morally correct and practically workable one in sight.

The Active Role of the Family

The solution suggested by Cardinal Bernardin requires a more active and positive role of the family in the education of teenagers, but he is well aware that many families are struggling with multiple problems today. In fact, there are important changes affecting the family, and, obviously, whenever there is change, there are also difficulties. These are particularly evident in three main areas: economics, interpersonal relationships, and spirituality.

In the past 100 years, the United States has moved from an agricultural through an industrial to an information/service-oriented economy and lifestyle. In the past, millions of families took care of themselves and one another while the number of public institutions to assist them were comparatively few. This is not the case today. Many of the services once handled primarily within families, such as education and health care, are now provided largely by outside sources, most particularly the various branches and levels of government. There is less parental control of the influences affecting children, leading many parents to feel, at least some of the time, quite helpless.

A second area where changes are occurring at a rapid rate is in the relationship between women and men. They are learning to be friends, and to share ideas, feelings, the responsibilities of being parents, and household tasks. It is an ongoing process that has many positive aspects, but the transition is difficult and sometimes very confusing.

A third area of change is in the way the Catholic Church views marriage. Prior to the Second Vatican Council, the purpose of marriage was described as, first, the procreation of children and, second, the well-being of the spouses. The Council defined marriage as an intimate partnership of life and love, recognizing the well-being of the spouses as being as important as the creation of new life.

Promoting a Family Perspective

The Church should promote a family perspective because it works closely with the family in fulfilling many basic family responsibilities, such as education, religious and value formation, socialization, religious practice, health care, and social services. As Cardinal Bernardin emphasizes, the family is central to the health and well-being of all societies, including the Church. He suggests thus that the solution to the problems of teenage sexuality and pregnancy may be also found in the family, which must be seen and treated as the most important model of behavior and keeper of values in society.

Since families, and especially healthy, Christian families, are so important to our society, Cardinal Bernardin affirms that it is necessary that young couples understand well the sacrament of marriage in all its aspects. He also firmly believes that young people first learn about marriage and family life from their own parents and what they experience at home. Later, many other persons and events certainly help shape their ideas, attitudes, beliefs, fears, questions, dreams, and hopes for their own marriage.

A Correct Marriage Preparation

Many children are fortunate to be raised in families where there is respect for one another among family members, effective communication, and the healthy resolution of conflicts. But others, unfortunately, have different experiences which may include considerable hurt and pain. If the latter do not face and resolve these unhealthy formative circumstances in a positive way that contributes to their personal growth, their own subsequent marriage may become problematic. It may also lead to separation and divorce. This is the reason why Joseph Bernardin strongly urges marriage preparation for all young couples.

The goal of marriage preparation is to help couples develop the kind of relationship that will grow and deepen through all the stages of their marriage, each of which has its own challenges and rewards. Marriage preparation must be realistic about faithfully living a marriage covenant in a changing world. That world often tries to undermine or deny the basic values of a Christian marriage: fidelity, unselfishness, permanence, mutuality, and openness to having children. This implies that engaged couples should realize that the Christian beliefs and ideals about marriage are in some ways countercultural. This, in turn, means that for their marriage to survive and grow in this environment, they will have to do at least three things. First, they must place their own relationship as husband and wife before all others. Second, they must safeguard their marriage by developing the kind of unity that protects the marriage from all outside and inside pressures. Third, they should realize that they have an important mission: to celebrate their love, to be open to new life as a sign from God, and to turn outward to others in witness and service. Cardinal Bernardin strongly believes that in this way the family will grow as a positive, educative, and healthy example for modern society in general, and for young people in particular.

Centrality of the Family

Over the years, Cardinal Bernardin emphasizes, few institutions have received as much attention from the Church as the family has. The fundamental reason, valid in all times and places, concerns the family's central importance for the well-being of individuals, society, and the Church itself. No other social institution can possibly surpass the influence of the family as nurturer of new life and transmitter of values.

As the Cardinal astutely observes, however, linked to this fact is a disturbing, contemporary reality. In fact, in the United States and in many other countries, the family is in trouble. Today, as always, there are many solid, healthy families, but, generally speaking, these are really hard times for marriage and family life. As Cardinal Bernardin explains, new marriages in the United States now have a 50-50 chance of ending in divorce.

Abortion and illegitimacy rates are both soaring. Cohabitation without marriage is widespread. The Cardinal maintains that these developments are probably both symptoms and causes, and underlines that these developments clearly point to a genuine and dangerous crisis for family life and the moral values that it represents and transmits.

The Importance of Moral Roots

Obviously, problems require solutions; solutions require understanding of what causes the problems. As Cardinal Bernardin asserts, for a long time it has been the conventional wisdom that family problems are only economic problems. He agrees that many family ills are economic and require economic solutions – training, jobs, and enlightened welfare programs for those incapable of working – but he strongly disagrees and cannot accept that all family problems can be reduced to economics or can be solved by economic measures alone. In fact, many family ills have moral roots – that is, they concern values, attitudes, and the way individuals use their personal freedom. He stresses the need to recognize that the cultural upheavals in thinking about personal morality which have taken place in recent decades have – to say the least – not been entirely beneficial, either for individuals or society. Yet, the Church's efforts to assist with the maintenance and development of family life are fiercely opposed from many directions, with the excuse that the Church, in doing so, violates the principle of Church-State separation, since it tries to deal with the problems of marital and family life according to religious values. As Joseph Bernardin emphasizes, this form of opposition proves only to be shortsighted and destructive, particularly when one considers the conspicuous failure of secular remedies.

12

Issues and Challenges of the Church in Modern Society

Cardinal Bernardin acknowledges that the Church has to deal with great ethnic and racial diversities, especially in the United States, making solidarity and collaboration difficult. The Archbishop of Chicago believes that genuine solutions to social, economic, and political problems require the collaboration of all citizens, who must work together for the common good. He says that ethnic and social diversities are also a great opportunity for the Church. In fact, they greatly contribute to enrich the community.

It is out of doubt that we live in a period of history in which technology and its capacity to threaten and diminish human life are at hand. This is especially true for genetic engineering, abortion, capital punishment, modern warfare, euthanasia, prostitution, pornography, sexism, and racism. The importance of the family in modern society must be restated. Today the family is very fragile, and the priests may be more aware of that fact than anyone else in their knowledge of the private and inner lives of people they serve.

The condition of women within the Church is another critical issue. Women feel that they are not undervalued and their potential is unrealized. The Church acknowledges that women

*deserve to take their rightful place in equality with men but, un-
fortunately, the Catholic tradition does not yet permit the admission of women to priesthood.*

*The Church, too, is facing its own internal ecclesiastical pains.
It is necessary to heal the divisions and tensions which exist
within the Church, and face the problem of vocational decrease
in both lay and religious people. Priests, Cardinal Bernardin
says, must be intrinsically united with the Lord, strengthened
through the breaking of the bread and pouring of the wine during the celebration of the Holy Eucharist.*

The Church has to face many problematic issues and challenges
in modern society, acknowledges Cardinal Bernardin in his
capacity as a leader of one of the largest archdioceses in the world,
a role which gives him the opportunity of coming to terms with
a variety of issues every day. It is his constant concern, but on the occasion
of a meeting with the Jesuits of the Chicago Province he analyzed these
topics more exhaustively.

First, he lists a number of the issues the Church faces. He explains that
some of these issues are societal in nature. Others are also societal, but
they have a more direct impact on the life and ministry of the Church. Still
others are rooted in the internal life, teaching, or discipline of the Church.

Ethnic and Racial Diversity

The first issue is American ethnic and racial diversity. The Church in the
United States must deal with a diversity of population not found in many
other countries. Unfortunately, this diversity all too easily translates into
ethnic and social divisions which make solidarity and collaboration difficult, if not altogether impossible. Cardinal Bernardin believes that genuine
solutions to social, economic, and political problems require that all
citizens work together for the common good. Mutual understanding,
collaboration, and acceptance among the many ethnic groups that make
up the population of the country must be such that they are not pitted
against each other for attention and resources. He adds that a special
challenge is outreach to Hispanic Catholics, so many of whom are alienated
from the Church or are in danger of being alienated.

Nevertheless, Cardinal Bernardin emphasizes how this ethnic and racial
diversity is also a great opportunity for the Church. In fact, it greatly
contributes to its richness as a community. He says that today the
Christ-in-others often speaks Spanish with a Central or South American
accent, or French with a Haitian inflection, or English with a Vietnamese

or Polish inflection, and this gives us a better understanding of the universal Church with its many diverse peoples and cultures.

A Threat to Life

A second issue is the manifold threat to – and diminishment of – human life. Cardinal Bernardin observes that, even though there have always been threats to it, we live now in a period of history when we have produced, sometimes with the best of intentions, a technology and a capacity to threaten and diminish human life on a scale which previous generations could not even imagine. He refers especially to genetics, abortion, capital punishment, modern warfare, and euthanasia, but also to longstanding problems like prostitution, pornography, sexism, and racism. All of these developments threaten or diminish human life, but each is a distinct problem, enormously complex, and deserving of individual treatment. No single answer and no simple response will solve them.

The Fragility of Family Life

Another issue the Church has to face nowadays concerns family life and sexuality. Family life is very fragile. As Joseph Bernardin observes, priests, and especially those who enter into the lives of people in parishes and educational institutions as well as in hospitals and retreat centers, may be more aware of that fact than anyone else in the entire country. They know the pain and despair of children with alcoholic parents. They also know the agony of parents who watch helplessly as their children are drawn more and more deeply into the dead-end tunnel of drug addiction. Priests know the pain of husbands and wives who are unable to communicate. They know, too, the pain of separation, divorce, and remarriage, which are complex problems often without simple solutions.

The Condition of Women

Another critical issue is that of women within society and within the Church. Today there is a growing consciousness that women have been diminished, their potential unrealized, their dreams cut short by cultural biases and expectations; the Church, too, has come to acknowledge that women deserve to take their full, rightful place alongside men. One of the greatest challenges the Church will face during the rest of this century is that of promoting the dignity of women and facilitating the use of their talents and charisms in the service of the Church itself and within the bounds of the Catholic faith.

What makes this issue more difficult and complicated is the Catholic tradition which does not permit the admission of women to the priesthood. Church teaching does not see this as a justice issue but one related to the way Christ structured the Church. The real problem is that this has become a neuralgic issue which frequently erodes the credibility of Catholic efforts to promote the equality of women in other ways, and it engages the priests in an adversarial rather than a collaborative relationship with many women.

Ecclesiastical Pain

Cardinal Bernardin believes that the Church – and he stresses how this must be said frankly, without hesitation – faces its own internal ecclesiastical pains. Sometimes these difficulties derive from living in a particular time and culture. Sometimes they are rooted in a lag between the momentum of the Second Vatican Council and the religious community's lumbering way of moving towards renewal. He adds that now it is necessary to begin to heal the divisions and tensions which exist within the Church. These divisions are caused in part by "conservative" and "liberal" interpretations of the teaching of Vatican II. Actually, it is not so much the different interpretations, as it is the inflexibility that makes it impossible for one side to talk reasonably with the other. But these divisions and tensions are also caused by an inability which some ministers have, including priests and religious women and men, to work together in harmony.

There are also problems within the priesthood and religious life – in particular, the effect the decline in numbers is having on priests and the religious orders and on their ministry. There are fewer active priests and religious women and men today, the median age is rising, as are the workload and peoples' expectations. Cardinal Bernardin says that the solution to this problem is to be found in the teaching of Vatican II, which directs that the laity assume more responsibility for the well-being of the Church.

Special Challenges to Chicago Church

Also, the Archdiocese of Chicago is facing particular issues. First, each parish, each institution seems often to forget that it is part of a whole and that it does not stand alone. It is essential to help the local Church become – spiritually and pastorally – a true community of faith in which all members feel they belong to the whole and share responsibility for the whole. A second need of the Church in Chicago is better allocation of resources – physical facilities, finances, and personnel. The demographic patterns have changed, and so it is necessary to consolidate and reallocate where needed.

After this list of issues, and continuing his reflection, Cardinal Bernardin analyzes the challenges, which are how to face the issues and needs. He focuses on four crucial challenges.

He says that the first challenge priests have to face is to suffer with their people. They love as Jesus loved when they suffer with their people, because that is what He did. Then, the issues they face all bespeak suffering. Like Jesus, they have to walk with their people in the valley of darkness. They need to walk the dark valley of moral dilemmas, the dark valley of physical and spiritual sickness, the dark valley of injustice and oppressive structures.

To understand and accept the redemptive, life-giving value of suffering in their own lives and in the lives of those they love, priests must first be intimately united with the Lord, especially through prayer.

How Weaknesses Can Be Turned into Strength

So, suffering must remain a part of priests' lives. Speaking of his own personal experience, Cardinal Bernardin says that he has learned that his weakness and vulnerability have become his strength, because he no longer pretends that it is he who "calls the shots," he who is in control – it is the Lord Jesus! It is then that he understands Jesus' suffering. It is then that he understands and accepts his own suffering and that of his people – a suffering which is redemptive, a suffering that has meaning, a suffering that gives life.

The second challenge priests face is celebration. Together with their people, they must stop the merry-go-round on which they find themselves. They all need a vacation from the many problems and issues which confront them. They need to learn how to celebrate. As priests, they are expected to do more than simply say the words and preside over the actions of the Eucharistic ritual. They are called to be effective signs of Christ present among the people with whom they celebrate.

In the Eucharist, Cardinal Bernardin explains, the Church learns what it means to be a self-giving servant. This essential dimension of the Eucharist has special meaning for priests and religious. For, if their outreach to others becomes disconnected from the Church's sacramental life, it will lose its unique, compelling character. Their ministry will soon lose its spark, its inner dynamism, its capability of continually renewing itself. He deepens this concept by adding that they must become the bread broken and the wine poured out for the life of the world, and concludes by saying that this is why the liturgy, particularly the Eucharist, must always be at the heart of their life and ministry.

Another great challenge is that of creativity. Actually, Cardinal Bernardin says, priests cannot merely repeat conventional wisdom or hand out cliches. On the contrary, they are called to the strenuous exercise of creativity so that the power of the Gospel can truly come alive and support people who live in a new, always changing world. They need also to find creative solutions to new and complex issues and questions, creative ways of meeting new and complex needs, new and creative ways of using available, but limited, resources. This is the challenge of creativity.

The final challenge analyzed by Cardinal Bernardin is that of continuing the ministry of healing reconciliation in all the circumstances in which they find themselves. All the issues he mentioned have, as their common root, the sort of brokenness into which we are born. We desperately need, he says, the healing touch of the Lord Jesus. To the extent that priests have felt in themselves the reconciliation of their own inner conflicts and wounds – not necessarily their perfect resolution – they will succeed in mediating the healing and reconciliation which Jesus wants his people to experience. So many of the issues He raised bespeak brokenness and a bleeding of the spirit, which is why there is such a tremendous need in the Church and in the world for healing reconciliation.

The issues are many. They are complex. They give rise to specific needs. The challenges also seem to be many and, at times, out of reach. But Cardinal Bernardin is convinced that what the people want of priests is really far simpler. They want priests to be present to them – in faith, hope, and love – present to them in such a way that they know that God cares and will safely deliver them home. To be present – this is the task of the Church.

The ultimate challenge, Joseph Bernardin notes, lies within one's self, and it is the challenge to be intimate with the Lord. He is aware that growing spiritually – investing the time it takes to be truly intimate with Jesus – is very difficult, while it is very easy to become discouraged and to give up. But the effort is necessary, because the greatest need facing the Church – at all levels – is that of spiritual renewal, and the need – the hunger and thirst, as he describes them – for spirituality must be met. And to meet it fully implies that priests have grown so much spiritually that they can share their experiences, they can feed others.

13

Immigration

Immigration is a very real and a very difficult problem currently facing our society. Religious communities have large concentrations of undocumented people, many of whom are Spanish-speaking Catholics escaping poor economic conditions, and the Church is called to play a special role in order to help them.

Their presence is a large pastoral challenge for the Catholic community. Cardinal Bernardin is conscious that no simple route to immigration reform seems available. Nevertheless, he believes it is a challenge which needs to be met nationally and internationally. Countries need to apply justice and generosity in their immigration policies.

Furthermore, he points out that immigrants are often marginalized by society and therefore, find themselves among the unemployed, the hungry, and the homeless. As a community – Cardinal Bernardin insists we have a duty to respond to their needs, regardless of race, nationality, or legal status.

Cardinal Bernardin recognizes the present reality of immigration patterns as a very important and vital question which needs to be addressed. He stresses the fact that immigration reform is a continuing issue in the United States and around the world.

An Urgent Issue for Congress

The fact that this question remains unresolved underlines the intractability of the problem and the diversity of views about how to cope with it. The failure up to now to find satisfactory solutions reflects not ill will or indifference but the complexity of the issue itself. Discussions about immigration reform have a tendency to become heated and even rather acrimonious.

Cardinal Bernardin admits that there are good reasons for the strong feelings, but sees no reasons to doubt the sincerity of the groups and individuals who are trying to grapple with the question.

That there is a problem – or rather a series of overlapping problems – nobody seriously doubts. Numbers alone demonstrate little, because nobody knows exactly how many undocumented aliens – i.e., people who have entered the country illegally – are in the United States at the present time. In other words, this is a very large problem that must be addressed by the undocumented aliens themselves and the communities with large concentrations of such persons. This is why, in turn, the Church is called to play a special role.

The Special Role of the Church

The Catholic Church is especially concerned about this question because most undocumented aliens are Spanish-speaking persons who identify with the Church. If their presence in the United States is a large economic and social challenge for the government and the civic community, it is an even larger pastoral challenge for the Catholic community. This argument is illustrated very clearly by the Cardinal.

At the heart of the matter two questions stand out: What to do about the undocumented aliens already in the United States? How is the flow of prospective newcomers to be reduced, or at least controlled?

The Cardinal states that the notion of simply rounding them up and shipping them home must be rejected out of hand, because such an approach would be not only impossible, but grossly inhumane. Many of these people already have deep personal and family roots in the United States. It is therefore unthinkable to work out a solution that simply excludes them from the United States.

Resolving the Reasons for Illegal Immigration is Essential

The more difficult question to date, however, is identified by the Cardinal in addressing the root causes of continued immigration. In this regard, he acknowledges that there is no consensus on what can or should be done.

The fact that people enter the United States as the consequence of economic deprivation should invite us to undertake some reflections. The first, commonsense solution would seem to lie in improving economic conditions in their countries of origin, which is of course a long-term challenge of enormous magnitude. On the other hand, with regard to a short-term solution, Cardinal Bernardin seems to recognize that reform proposals focused on a system of sanctions against U.S. employers who knowingly hire undocumented aliens has not resolved the problem. Moreover, this system sometimes penalizes those who have a legitimate right to seek employment. But over the long term the Cardinal is also painfully aware of the fact that no simple route to immigration reform seems available. Nevertheless, he believes that it is a challenge which needs to be met nationally and internationally.

It is clear that the country needs to reexamine its immigration policy, Cardinal Bernardin underlines, and we must face up to this task with justice and generosity. He is especially concerned because this group of people find themselves excluded from the community, while socially and economically they are among the most vulnerable. In addition, they often face the tragic prospect of being separated from their families and deported.

Cardinal Bernardin remembers the time when a new and reformed immigration law was being discussed; he recollects his hopes and that of the many immigrants of Chicago, because it seemed to represent a welcome opportunity for many of them to regularize their status in the U.S. and to become recognized participants in their new home.

He remembers the disappointment when, in 1986, certain provisions of the finally enacted law seemed contrary to the positive and desired solution of this problem. For example, the cutoff date of required residency for "amnesty" was set at January 1982, which automatically excluded many of the undocumented people who came to this nation since that date.

The Helpful Role of the Archdiocese of Chicago in the 1986 Amnesty

Cardinal Bernardin stresses the fact that despite the law's shortcomings, the archdiocese, through its parishes and Catholic Charities, made a significant effort to help people avail themselves of the opportunity to participate in the legalization process. To encourage the maximum participation, his staff and volunteers worked very hard to improve these services. The Cardinal established a special lay advisory group, representing people from different ethnic and cultural backgrounds.

Unfortunately however, as the program came to an end, Cardinal Bernardin became aware that the hopes and dreams it once encouraged were far from fully realized: many people were excluded by the very law whose stated purpose was to help the undocumented. Moreover, those who wanted to apply were often intimidated by extensive paperwork and exclusionary regulations, some of which could separate them from their families. Finally, as the employers sanctions took effect, the flaws in this provision of the law began to be felt.

Cardinal Bernardin publicly expressed concern about these matters on several occasions in order to raise awareness about the thousands who were excluded from or did not participate in this legalization process in order to remain among the U.S. people. The Cardinal never ceased to remind the American people that the overwhelming majority of those aliens had lived in the country for some time and were already part of families, neighborhoods, and parishes in the United States.

Immigrants Are Members of Our Family

Bernardin insists that the larger community must respond to these people's needs, to prevent them from being pushed even further toward the margins of society. He observes with deep concern the effects of the law on the undocumented. They are very vulnerable. This law makes them more likely to be found among the unemployed, the hungry, and the homeless. Furthermore, they are very limited in their job opportunities because of employers' sanctions. Those who already have jobs are vulnerable to exploitation and discrimination; they often have no health insurance or other ordinary employee benefits, in addition to all the other problems that they have to face as illegal aliens.

As a Christian community, we are obliged to serve others without reference to their race, nationality, or legal status. He is confident that the parishes and other institutions will continue to provide social and pastoral services to these individuals and their families. The Catholic Church will continue to provide a voice for the voiceless – as he effectively puts it – to seek justice for these people by raising these issues for discussion and action. The Cardinal is well aware that the plight of the undocumented will not disappear of itself; neither will the economic conditions of Mexico nor the political turmoil in Central America – the impetus that prompted many undocumented persons to come to the United States in the first place – change overnight.

That is why, Cardinal Bernardin reminds us, it is the duty of everyone to help these unfortunate people; we must stand in solidarity with the undocumented, for they too are our brothers and sisters.

14

AIDS

A Challenge and Commitment for Everybody

The Church faces a significant pastoral issue in AIDS, a growing reality of our time. This human disease must be answered in a consistent manner, with the best medical and scientific information available.

As members of the Church and society we have the responsibility to share AIDS victims' pain in solidarity, providing them spiritual and pastoral care, as well as social support for their families and friends. Cardinal Bernardin asserts that the Church does not approve practices of "safe sex" or the use of condoms. Catholic programs must communicate the Church's vision of human sexuality and behavior as well as its doctrinal and moral tradition.

As a community of faith we are called to confront courageously and compassionately the suffering and death which AIDS has brought to the world. Cardinal Bernardin emphasizes that AIDS is not a disease restricted to homosexuals. Many people have been otherwise infected.

The entire civic and religious community must collaborate in its battle against AIDS. Catholics cannot permit the discrimination against AIDS victims and must face the scourge of AIDS

as a challenge that needs Christian solutions. Such a discrimina-
tion clearly violates basic human dignity and it is inconsistent
with a Christian ethic of life.

With the increase of AIDS cases in our society, we must call
upon civic, governmental, religious, and community leaders to
respond to the human and religious needs at hand. The Arch-
bishop of Chicago has supported the development of an Inter-
faith Pastoral Counseling Center for AIDS victims, while the
Archdiocese Department of Personnel Services has developed a
general employment policy for all those with life-threatening ill-
nesses. The Department of Human Services also coordinates in-
itiatives in the AIDS ministry.

I n the life of society, as in the life of individuals, there are events of significance and moments of decision. Today, Cardinal Bernardin says, society is experiencing such an occasion: the ominous presence of the disease known as AIDS (Acquired Immunodeficiency Syndrome). AIDS is a reality that we all must face, and with this disease the Church confronts a significant pastoral issue.

Our Responsibilities in Caring for and Supporting AIDS Patients

Cardinal Bernardin recognizes that society is faced with serious moral decisions concerning the etiology of this deadly epidemic, its prevention, and the care of those stricken by it. How are we to relate to those who have been exposed to the virus and to those who have the disease? What are our responsibilities as members of the Church and society with regard to their care and support?

Cardinal Bernardin recalls that the Administrative Board of the U.S. Catholic Conference published an important statement entitled, "The Many Faces of AIDS: A Gospel Response." His feelings and thoughts about this terrible illness are reflected in the short summary that opens this document:

> As with all other diseases, AIDS is a human illness to which we must
> respond in a manner consistent with the best medical and scientific
> information available. As members of the Church and society, we have a
> responsibility to stand in solidarity with, and reach out with compassion
> and understanding to those exposed to or experiencing this disease. We
> must provide spiritual and pastoral care as well as medical and social
> support for their families and friends. Discrimination or violence
> directed against persons with AIDS is unjust and immoral.

Since the publication of this booklet, Cardinal Bernardin has committed himself to answering the numerous questions provoked by this statement. Many people interpret the document in different ways, and the interpretations of the media are often distorted. The Cardinal is always ready to clarify those points that prove to be useful for a correct and humane view of the problem.

For instance, he emphasizes that it is groundless to believe that the Administrative Board statement implies or suggests a change in the Church's teaching on sexual morality. The use of prophylactics as well as the practice of "safe sex" are not promoted, remarks the Cardinal.

Safe Sex Is Not a Catholic Solution

It should be clear, he insists, that Catholic educational programs must communicate directly the Church's vision of and teaching about human sexuality and behavior. Therefore – the Cardinal underscores – such programs cannot encourage a "safe sex" mentality. On the contrary, teachers must discuss – in accordance with the ability and maturity of their students and within the context of the Church's teaching – what these programs recommend, and assess their medical accuracy and moral failure.

Cardinal Bernardin lays an important stress upon faithfulness to the Catholic doctrinal and moral tradition in order to prevent unsatisfactory approaches. In addition, he does not forget to underline the emotional impact of contracting this fatal disease.

AIDS is a growing threat to our society, he reminds us, and our response to it cannot be fear, ignorance, or alienation. As followers of Jesus, he says, we have learned a different, better way, because He has taught us to show compassion for the sick and suffering, and to be ministers of reconciliation so that our wounds and alienation may be healed.

The Community of Faith Must Have Courage and Compassion

And this is the purpose of the pastoral response to AIDS, Cardinal Bernardin stresses: as a community of faith, we are called to confront courageously and compassionately the suffering and death which AIDS has brought to our world. To do this, we must put aside our fears, prejudices, and whatever other unhelpful sentiments we may at first feel. Cardinal Bernardin has extensively articulated his position on the disease. He disagrees with the opinion that AIDS is divine punishment for homosexual activity.

First, medically speaking, AIDS is not a disease restricted to homosexuals; it appears that originally it might have been spread through heterosexual sexual encounters. In the United States many people have been exposed to AIDS or have contracted it through the use of drugs, tainted blood transfusions, and heterosexual sexual activity.

AIDS – A Human, Not a Homosexual Disease

That is why the Cardinal calls AIDS a human disease, not a specifically homosexual one. God can't be considered as vengeful: He is loving and compassionate, and for Him every human being is of inestimable worth, and every life is sacred and worthy of respect.

The Gospel itself reveals that, while Jesus did not hesitate to proclaim a radical ethic of life grounded in the promise of God's kingdom, he never ceased reaching out to the lowly and the outcasts of this time – even if they did not live up to the full demands of his teaching. Jesus offered forgiveness and healing to all who sought it; Cardinal Bernardin exhorts us to keep this in mind when facing the complex problems caused by AIDS. That is why we who are followers of Jesus see the AIDS crisis as both a challenge to relate in a truly Christian way to persons who are in dire need, and as our responsibility to work with others in our society to respond to that need.

Cardinal Bernardin's analysis illustrates the facts of the matter: the illness is present in every community; the percentage of women with AIDS is also increasing. These are the facts that – according to the Cardinal – the whole civic and religious community must face as a challenge for a Christian solution to the problem.

It is understandable that this disease, which spreads so quickly and is invariably fatal, occasions misunderstanding, fear, prejudice, and discrimination. Cardinal Bernardin stresses the fact that this is not a new phenomenon: the same happened to tubercular patients who were completely isolated, and similarly many people still speak with moral righteousness and indignation about the "sin" of alcoholism.

Cardinal Bernardin underscores that now is the time that we must recognize the importance of relating in an enlightened and just way to those suffering from AIDS itself or from AIDS-Related Complex (ARC), as well as to those who have been exposed to the AIDS virus. We must, he emphasizes, make sure that our attitudes and actions are based on facts and not on fiction.

At the present time, there is no medical justification for discrimination against these people; in fact, such discrimination is a violation of their basic human dignity and inconsistent with the Christian ethic. To the extent that they can, persons with AIDS should be encouraged to continue to lead productive lives in their community and place of work.

Cardinal Bernardin encourages the government as well as health providers and human service agencies to collaborate, and for the former to provide adequate funding and care for AIDS patients. Moreover, people with AIDS have a right to decent housing, and landlords are not justified in denying them this right merely because of their illness.

Community Collaboration Is Urgently Called For

The whole community must collaborate, and Cardinal Bernardin reminds us of a number of specific actions in order to fight this terrible illness. He also affirms and commends the concern that so many professionals and volunteers have shown toward AIDS patients. The increasing seriousness of the problem, however, requires that more should be done. Cardinal Bernardin therefore joins his voice with the many others who have called upon civic, governmental, religious, and community leaders to intensify their efforts to respond to the many human and religious needs caused by AIDS.

Cardinal Bernardin underlines the need to expand and encourage acute and long-care facilities, to develop sufficient patient advocacy procedures to ensure the respectful and compassionate care of persons with AIDS. He also focuses attention upon the importance of educational programs, utilizing the media in order to help reduce prejudice and discrimination toward people with AIDS and to assist the families and friends of these patients.

The Proposal to Establish an Interfaith Pastoral Counseling Center

The Church must collaborate in this effort, and Cardinal Bernardin stresses this role and the responsibilities that it entails: the Church must work with public, private, and other religious and community groups to achieve these vital objectives. Cardinal Bernardin supported the development of an Interfaith Pastoral Counseling Center to assist people, and also a program to develop a group of priests, religious, and lay leaders to provide accurate information about the medical, psychosocial, and pastoral issues related to AIDS. He focuses on the importance of making accurate information about AIDS available to schools and religious education programs in order to help young people to understand the illness and how to fight it.

Another critical concern is the employment of persons who have contracted the AIDS virus or AIDS itself. Cardinal Bernardin underlines the fact that the

Church has a responsibility to provide a good example in such situations. The archdiocesan Department of Personnel Services has developed a general employment policy for all those with life-threatening illnesses, and this must be scrupulously applied to all those that suffer from AIDS.

In order to ensure that the many dimensions of the AIDS crisis are effectively addressed, Cardinal Bernardin appointed a pastoral care coordinator for AIDS ministry. Working within the archdiocesan Department of Human Services, this person oversees and coordinates initiatives in the AIDS ministry. Cardinal Bernardin also called upon the parishes of the archdiocese to open their hearts to those who are touched in any way by AIDS and to minister to them with love and compassion. It is only in this way that we will develop a deeper conversion and healing process.

We should not make judgments, but rather encourage people to live in a way that will enhance life and not threaten or destroy it, the Cardinal emphasizes. It is essential, Cardinal Bernardin reminds us, to remember the call to use God's gift of sexuality morally and responsibly.

He calls upon Christian responsibility to provide for the necessities of our suffering brothers and sisters in a context of spiritual support and prayer, because they need the special help of God. To overcome ignorance and prejudice and to achieve reconciliation, a unity of unconditional love must be created. As the Cardinal underscores so movingly, we are not alone and together we can face up to the challenge of AIDS and fulfill our responsibilities.

15

Priests and Bishops

The Community of faith of which all priests are members has became a counter-cultural reality and today is not only constantly questioned but also often ridiculed. The priesthood is called to develop spirituality and come to grips with their own selves, so that they don't negatively affect their ministry. Their life and ministry, he continues, are indeed intimately related and cannot be separated.

Priests must also deepen their faith on a practical level, in order to live more trustful lives. Cardinal Bernardin emphasizes that priests must avoid the temptation to forget God and put their trust only in themselves, and likewise they must remember that they are important as individuals loved by God and entrusted by the Church with a special ministry.

Of course, they, too, need support and affirmation from one another. Annual retreats and spiritual direction on a continuing basis are both essential for priests' spiritual growth. However, we cannot talk about priests' spirituality without taking into account their sexuality too. As members of the priesthood, they must observe celibacy, but, as human beings, they are not exempted from experiencing all the phases of human growth. They profess a central commitment to the Lord and, therefore are invited and trusted to share many of the deepest moments of others' lives.

Priests have a fundamental role as teachers. Christ has delegated them the responsibility of passing on His message, and their primary duty is to proclaim the Gospel of God to all.

Priests must follow the example of Jesus as a shepherd, and as loving, caring and forgiving men, they must help people handle frustration. In conclusion, Cardinal Bernardin speaks about the role of the Archbishop who is called to perform a role of leadership. They must be men of prayer, faith, mercy, and compassion who proclaim Jesus' Gospel as their primary duty and exercise Episcopal authority with prudence. Bishops must know how to exercise the prudence of a good shepherd, judging times and persons, potentials and limitations, frailties and talents. In conclusion, the Archbishop of Chicago believes in a "participating" style of leadership from the bishops.

P riests confront difficulties and challenges that directly affect their morale and the efficiency of their ministry. Aware of this situation, Cardinal Bernardin observes how they are daily buffeted by a culture that is becoming increasingly more detached from the Judeo-Christian values which have shaped our societies and institutions for so many generations.

The Community of Faith Is a Countercultural Reality

Every day he becomes more and more aware that the community of faith to which all priests belong has become a countercultural reality. The Cardinal is of the opinion that the community of Christians has become a minority and that it cannot assume that values which traditionally have given meaning and credibility to the priests' ministry and their lifestyle are still operative; indeed, he remarks, they are not only questioned constantly but also sometimes ridiculed.

In this context, Joseph Bernardin asserts the necessity of developing a deeper and more mature spirituality for the priesthood. He also emphasizes the need for bringing into clear focus the identity of priests: Who are they today? What are their roles and responsibilities in contemporary society? Furthermore, he notes that once they have fully comprehended who they are, they must ask how they can respond to their personal needs as celibate men ministering in a society that is becoming increasingly secularized.

By addressing these numerous and important questions, the Cardinal emphasizes that, unless priests come to grips with their own selves – i.e. unless they are capable of developing as healthy human beings – they will negatively affect their ministry. In fact, there is really no split, no dichotomy between life and ministry; the Cardinal points out that the two are indeed so intimately related that the well-being of the one has an extensive impact on the well-being of the other.

Trust, Self-Image, Support, Affirmation, Prayer, and Spiritual Life

But the Cardinal has never been prepared to dismiss a complex issue with a simplistic argument. He understands that he cannot provide answers for all the troublesome questions that priests might have. Nevertheless, certain specific points must be taken into account and deserve to be highlighted. The points that he is most concerned about are trust, self-image, the desire for support and affirmation, and the need to intensify prayer and spiritual life.

As for trust, Cardinal Bernardin says that there is a great necessity for priests to deepen their faith on a practical level – i.e., in order to live more trustful lives. Unfortunately, they too have been affected by the changes in the times in which they live. The Cardinal notes how in our age the mystery that constitutes the core of the Church and its priesthood has been obscured to the point that the transcendent no longer gives any meaning or purpose to much of what they are called to be and do. Of course, this weakens faith and diminishes trust in the Lord; priests may no longer be willing to let go because they are no longer convinced that the Lord will never abandon them.

Encouragement from Trust in the Lord

Cardinal Bernardin shows his understanding for this lack of trust, but his reaction is quite strong – how foolish to think along these lines, he observes. He then goes on to exhort the priests: You must trust in the Lord! You must leave room for Jesus' power and strength! Moreover, you must be open to the movement of His Spirit and avoid the temptation to put your trust only in yourselves, forgetting the Lord.

However, he acknowledges, if priests put their trust in the Lord, they are not necessarily expected to cultivate a poor self-image; they are by no means supposed to demean themselves constantly. On the contrary, since they are created – as every human being is – in God's image, they must acknowledge the good that is in them, even when they place themselves totally in His hands. As the Cardinal maintains, their self-image is strictly related to their sense of self-worth, their ability to witness and recruit those who will follow them. In the face of a shaky image, they must recall that they are truly important – not on the level of personal grandiosity, but as individuals loved by God and entrusted by the Church with a special ministry. In their personal uniqueness and in their sacramental ministry, priests offer something of irreplaceable value to the world. If they don't believe this, then why do they bother with the struggles of priesthood? Why shouldn't they return to service among lay people? The Cardinal's questions are obviously a provocative exhortation to his priests.

He continues this discourse by underlining how each one of them needs support and affirmation, whether they admit it or not. Moreover, he believes that priests need a better system for supporting one another and finding the strength for self-affirmation.

In this regard the Cardinal observes that the difficulty lies in the fact that too often priests tend to think that giving affirmation is someone else's responsibility. This is wrong, because if they all look to someone else, no one will ever think to be in charge of giving affirmation. Cardinal Bernardin argues that the solution to this dilemma is that each of them must be willing to support and affirm the others. One problem may simply be that they are too bashful and, hence, feel too awkard to do it. Sometimes they may even be afraid that their sincerity might be questioned. Whatever the obstacles, says the Cardinal, they need to talk about it more; they need to learn how to give affirmation and support in a relaxed and credible way.

However, one must recognize that this reluctance to affirm and support people is not a problem which is confined to priesthood. For example, many marriages go sour and ultimately break up because of a lack of communication and affirmation.

The final point highlighted by Cardinal Bernardin is an indispensable part of the ministry of priesthood: How should priests encourage the development of their prayer life? How can they intensify their spiritual growth in a culture that places so much emphasis on the "quick fix," the tangible, and the attraction of material things? The answers offered by the Cardinal are simple and reassuring.

Spiritual Growth

First, a good annual retreat is essential for spiritual growth. Some priests may say that they do not need to withdraw from their ministry to recoup their focus and spiritual energy. But that is simply not true; they are fooling themselves. Even Jesus retreated from His public ministry to restore His spiritual strength. Why shouldn't the priests need it? They must challenge each other to take the time to make a spiritually productive retreat at least once a year, the Cardinal firmly believes.

Second, spiritual direction on a continuing basis is also essential to spiritual growth. Priests need the insights and the objectivity of someone other than themselves. However, the difficulty is that often priests are not inclined to give spiritual direction to one another, even when they have no difficulty giving it to lay people. What is needed, argues the Cardinal, is a greater willingness to give one another the time to listen with care and compassion, to reflect with honesty and trust, and to encourage one another's best instincts.

The Problem of the Priests' Sexuality

Finally, Cardinal Bernardin asserts that it is not possible to talk about priests' spirituality without also taking into account their sexuality. We must never forget that priests are actually men: they experience all the phases of human growth and personal integration common to other men; they are men who profess a central commitment to the Lord and who, for that very reason, are invited and trusted to share many of the deeper moments of others' lives. They are celibate; but what is important to keep in mind is that they are celibate and relational at the same time. Both are dynamic realities which priests grapple with and grow into day by day. They cannot turn away from this challenge – whether they find it problematic, joyful, or "messy," states the Cardinal.

He reassures them of the fact that theirs is certainly not the first generation of priests who have discovered sexuality. Nonetheless, they must address this question in the context of today's world with all its pressures and countervalues. And they must do so from a spiritual perspective, not only from a psychological viewpoint.

However, the point of departure for any reflection on priesthood is Jesus. This is a fundamental aspect of the Cardinal's reflections on this issue. The Roman Pontifical points out that those who are ordained priests are teachers, shepherds, and leaders of the worshipping community for the very same reason that Christ Himself is Teacher, Shepherd, and Priest.

Priests Are Teachers

Priests are teachers because, according to the Second Vatican Council, they have as their primary duty the proclamation of the Gospel of God to all. They must not place obstacles in the way of its saving power, and they must act faithfully toward the teaching authority of the Church, to which Christ has delegated the responsibility of handing down the message in all its richness and without any error. Moreover, people look at the priest as one who can make the teaching of the Church come alive for them in the home, at work, in the factory, the office, the courtroom, or the research laboratory.

These are demanding expectations, admits the Cardinal. They call for continued reading, consultation, and reflection on the part of the priest. Yet, this challenging task is also extremely rewarding.

There is also an important ecclesial dimension to the teaching role of priesthood. Teachers of religion are to be faithful collaborators of the bishop. They must present the Church's teaching, and they must present it as the Church's teaching, emphasizes the Cardinal.

Priests Are Shepherds

Priests are shepherds because, like Jesus Himself, they are called to have great concern and affection for the flock entrusted to them, to be shepherds eager to do all they can to help their people, even to the point of giving their own lives. In his ministry, Cardinal Bernardin is trying to imitate the example of the Good Shepherd. He is willing to give his life for the flock entrusted to him.

But more than anything else, the Cardinal asserts, people look to priests for their presence as loving, caring, forgiving men. They want their help in their efforts to handle pain and frustration. People want someone whose presence will remind them that, no matter what or how great their difficulties might be, God really loves them and cares for them. They want assurance that God will never abandon them.

Eventually, as ordained ministers, priests share in Christ's sanctifying power through the celebration of the sacraments, which are real encounters with the Lord. To be good leaders of worship, priests must be gentle, hospitable, and humble. They must never lord it over people, never give an impression of moral superiority or increase the burden of guilt which others may already bear.

To be effective leaders of the worshipping community, priests must also understand the importance of celebration in the life of their people. They must lead it and inspire it, gathering their people in prayer to celebrate the ordinary and the extraordinary moments of life. But, as Cardinal Bernardin adds, as priests, they are expected to do more than simply say the words and preside over the actions of the ritual. They are called to be effective signs of Christ who is present to the people with whom they celebrate.

Cardinal Bernardin concludes his reflections on priests by saying that the world and the church have changed dramatically in the past years. What has not changed is the need for holy priests. He also observes that people can forgive a priest many failings, if they perceive him as a man of prayer, a man who strives to know and love the Lord. Nonetheless, Jesus promised joy and peace to those who seek Him, but He also promised the cross – the symbol of suffering and rejection. Priests who have committed themselves to the work of Jesus and attempt to model their lives on Him must also expect the cross. There is really no valid way to avoid it.

The Role of Bishops

Finally, Cardinal Bernardin reflects on the role of bishops. He says that in the Church as a whole and in the Church of each locality, the bishops are called to take a leadership role, because this is the way Christ ordered the Church. However, after the Second Vatican Council, bishops are called to a more collegial style of leadership – consultative as well as directive – and they are called upon to attend to the many voices that participate in the ongoing life of the Church.

The role of the bishop in the local Church is often misunderstood by many people. On this subject, Cardinal Bernardin agrees with Bishop Kenneth Untener, who asserted that many Catholics see bishops as mere "branch managers," with the significant authority and leadership in Rome. That is why some bypass the local bishop or even the episcopal conference in sending letters to the Pro-Nuncio or directly to the Holy See. This practice often belies a faulty ecclesiology. In fact, whereas the lines of authority are clear and each bishop is directly subject to the Holy Father, the danger remains that this mentality can reduce both the efficiency and the legitimate authority of the local bishop.

The Cardinal affirms that a bishop's primary role is to proclaim the Lord Jesus and His Gospel. He must thus be a man of faith, understanding love, mercy, and compassion. For this to be a consistent way of life and ministry, it means that a bishop must be a man of prayer. Reflection on Scripture, discourse with the Lord, and discernment through the Spirit have to be deeply rooted in one's daily life.

Second, Cardinal Bernardin explains, a bishop exercises leadership in the local Christian community. His ministry is akin to that of a shepherd, caring for others, nourishing them, guiding them, defending them when their rights or lives are threatened or diminished. Moreover, episcopal authority is God-given and irreplaceable, but it must be exercised with the prudence which would be expected of a good shepherd who knows how to judge times and persons, potentials and limitations, frailty and talents.

There is another important dimension of episcopal leadership. The bishop, together with his priests, has the serious responsibility of helping all the members of the community discover, develop, and use their God-given talents and charisms for the well-being of the Church and society. Thus, a successful shepherd is one who not only uses his own gifts, but also knows how to help others use theirs.

Third, Joseph Bernardin notes, there is a prophetic dimension to the episcopacy which has come more to the forefront in recent years. Like all prophets, bishops who exercise such an office can expect opposition and even rejection. This makes the task very challenging, though the ministry is supported by God's gifts of courage and prudence, perseverance and fidelity.

In his lucid analysis of the role of bishops, Cardinal Bernardin says that another problem that they face is their personal limitations as they attempt to address the moral dimension of any issue. At times they lack the courage to set forth their convictions clearly and without hesitation. Sometimes they simply do not know what to do. A key solution, he suggests, is to engage in frequent dialogue with others – with experts in various fields, with respected colleagues, with trusted advisors, and with the public at large.

To the question, "How should a bishop exercise leadership in the local church?" Cardinal Bernardin answers that he believes in a style of leadership which is "participative." Leadership is truly effective, he believes, only when it succeeds in involving many other people. Such leadership does not hesitate to make decisions, explore new ground, or take stands which may sometimes be unpopular. But it does not want to stand alone. It seeks guidance; it needs support. Consequently, before it acts, it consults. It challenges people to use their own talents, energy, and creativity in analyzing a situation, and to come up with solutions. It also tries, at all times, to be charitable and respectful. It tries to deal with people as they are rather than as they should be. This kind of leadership takes time; it requires persistence and patience.

As Cardinal Bernardin concludes, exercising episcopal leadership is a most worthwhile service to perform in the Church. When a bishop gets a glimpse of the Kingdom of God in the midst of his people, when he sees ministers caring for the poor, the sick, and the marginalized, he knows that it is good to be alive and a part of the Church's mission in the world.

16

Synod, Episcopal Conferences, and Collegiality

Starting from the deliberations of the Second Vatican Council on the Church Ministry and its performance in collegiality, Cardinal Bernardin carries on a study about its manifold aspects. The diversities of the Catholic Church are put forward as a source of richness; its unity must be firmly established and maintained. The balance between diversity and unity is given by collegiality. If the duties of the Church are performed through the exercise of collegiality, unity and diversities are maintained and harmonized. If there is an element that can be defined as constant and overwhelming in Bernardin's work, that element is collegiality. He did a great job for the church in the United States. He linked it deeply with Roman authorities and taught the latter not to fear it as a superpower. His work helped the Conference of American Bishops become a real instrument of effective weight in the American social and Catholic life. He did all this by constantly promoting the exercise of collegiality and its application in every decision and in every matter. If the U.S. Church is what it is today, this is also thanks to Bernardin's dedication to and promotion of collegiality.

Pope John Paul II has said that the Second Vatican Council was "the fundamental event in the life of the modern Church" and declared that it is constantly necessary to return to the Council's deliberations as a source for our meditations.

The Second Vatican Council and Collegiality

The Council brought into clear focus the fact that the Catholic Church is a world church whose richness is in its diversity. In the midst of this diversity, but not apart from it, it is necessary to remember that the unity of the Church must be maintained and promoted, emphasizes Cardinal Bernardin. As he goes on to explain, it is through the exercise of collegiality that the balance between diversity and unity is maintained at all levels of the Church. Collegiality, in the strict sense of the term, refers to the relationship between the Holy Father and the world episcopate. Each bishop, by virtue of his consecration and not through delegation, receives the office of sanctifying, teaching, and governing.

Synods are a direct expression of the teaching on collegiality. They are therefore a consultative means of collaboration between the Holy Father and all the bishops in the world. The Synods also exemplify the tension of renewal and reform within the Church. Many have argued that the institution of the synod could be used more effectively by being given more than a consultative status, and might thereby play a larger role in directing Church policy.

Cardinal Bernardin is convinced of the importance and validity of synods. In order to illustrate his opinion, he asks first: What organization – secular or religious – does not periodically evaluate its own operation, in order to check whether it is realizing its visions, or could improve the goals and objectives which are needed to implement such a vision? It is clear in the Cardinal's mind that the Church has no better way to make this review than to call a session of the Synod of Bishops, the consultative and representative structure set up by Vatican II. Synods present the Church with a unique opportunity for reflecting on the progress made in implementing the renewal proposed by the Council.

It is important to know that the Synod is a consultative and not a legislative body. Therefore, it makes no decisions. Rather, its conclusions are contained in "propositions" or "affirmations," which are turned over to the Holy Father. Because the propositions are intended for the Pope, they are not published, although a summary is usually made available to the press. These propositions, together with all the interventions made by individual bishops and the reports of small group discussions, usually provide the basis for the Apostolic Letter that follows. The Synod of Bishops gathers every three years to examine an issue determined by the Pope after consultation with the world's bishops.

In the light of the original vision set by Vatican II, and in light of the U.S. experience since the Council, Cardinal Bernardin believes that it is worth commenting on three major issues related to the topic of the Synod. More precisely, these issues are collegiality and its future, the social ministry of the episcopal conference, and the role of theology and theologians.

The Future of Collegiality

The first issue is the future of collegiality as a principle and as a style of leadership within the Church. One crucial dimension of this topic is the status and function of episcopal conferences as an expression of collegiality. The Cardinal asserts that since Vatican II, the episcopal conferences have served to enhance the pastoral role of each bishop, precisely because they provide a framework and a forum for sharing ideas, setting a pastoral direction, and projecting policy positions on the major issues of the day. While it is necessary to understand the legitimate concerns of some people that a conference structure might inhibit creative, individual initiatives, much more would be lost if the capability to project a unified voice on both pastoral and policy questions were diminished. Both the theology and the practice of the post-conciliar period point toward an enhanced role of episcopal conferences, precisely as a means of implementing the collegial principle in the Church. Such collegiality or shared authority is not a power struggle: it is a proven means of effective service to the Church and to society.

The Episcopal Conference and Social Ministry

The second issue addressed by Cardinal Bernardin concerns that aspect of ministry which emphasizes the indispensable role of the episcopal conference in social ministry. It has been the direct involvement of the Cardinal as chairman of both the ad hoc Committee which drafted the bishops' pastoral letter on war and peace and the Committee for Pro-Life Activities that has convinced him of the immediate and necessary connection between an active, engaged, social ministry, and the work of evangelization in the Church. Especially in a society like the United States, the social witness of the Church is an integral element in its pastoral credibility. In fact, in the face of the threats to life – asserts the Cardinal – silence or passivity on the part of the Church and its leadership comes very close to pastoral scandal. On this issue the Cardinal expresses his most passionate and deeply-felt thoughts.

The Role of Theology

The third question he addresses is that of the role of theology and theologians in the life of the Church. The starting point for the Cardinal's reflection is, once again, the experience of Vatican II. He says that Catholic faith, in the end, is the work of the Holy Spirit. This fundamental truth should not lead us into believing that human collaboration is not determining, too. Actually, the beneficial impact of Vatican II has been in great measure the result of the theological work which preceded it.

This fact is shown by the Cardinal as pointing up the indispensable role of theological research and writing. Research requires an atmosphere of freedom because freedom is a natural habitat where the exchange of ideas keeps what Bernardin calls, in his widening of the concept, the "growing edge" of the Catholic tradition alive and productive of creative insights. At this growing edge mistakes are sometimes made, but it is also here that truth is found.

Theologians and other scholars, continues the Cardinal, are the primary agents of the growing edge. Nonetheless, bishops have a distinct but complementary function. In fact, they must have a concern for the public order of the Church's life, for pastoral guidance, and for the quality of Catholic teaching and preaching in the community of faith. They must ensure that work at the growing edge of the tradition ultimately enriches the center and will never erode its substance.

The relationship between bishops and theologians has always been deemed as somewhat problematic, the Cardinal acknowledges. But he exhorts both groups to find a proper balance. Today, those areas which need most attention by both theologians and bishops are ecclesiology and moral theology. In fact, these fields are experiencing the most conflicts, observes Bernardin.

The Life of Faith in an Age of Knowledge Explosion

As he subsequently underlines, we live in an age of a "knowledge explosion" and in a culture which prizes an educated citizenry. The life of faith needs to be presented as an enhancement of all that we know – not in isolation from the frontiers of human knowledge and creativity. Theological research is a requirement of evangelization in our culture and demands the cooperation of bishops and theologians.

A further point to be made is that the joining of reason and faith is a permanent element of the Church's ministry in the world. To this Cardinal Bernardin adds that another perennial responsibility is that the Church, as a community and as an institution, must be a sign of hope in the world in its worship, witness, and words. And precisely here we are to find the great test for the Synod, observes the Cardinal. The test consists of carrying forward its deliberations and shaping its conclusions in a way that gives hope to members of the Church in their daily lives, and to the wider society as it confronts everyday decisions and dilemmas.

Cardinal Bernardin describes his taking part in all the world synods of bishops (except the Extraordinary Synod of 1985) as a great privilege. Most of all he is grateful for having participated in the 1986 Synod whose theme was "The Vocation and Mission of the Laity in the Church and in the World." He is very interested in summoning lay people to their mission in the Church and in the world, and has made this one of his main tasks. However, his argument develops a fine distinction in reasoning that is worth pointing out here. The Cardinal asserts that the very phrasing of the theme as "in the Church and in the world" points to a distinction that needs to be not only noted but also probed.

As he observes, the Second Vatican Council viewed the role of lay people in distinct categories: on the one hand, the place of lay people and the functions they are called to perform within the Christian community; on the other hand, the apostolic engagement of lay people in the secular order arising from their vocation and state of life. However, Cardinal Bernardin does not hesitate to underline, progress "in the Church" has been much greater than progress "in the world."

The Role of the Laity

To support his statement, he takes the United States as an example which clearly demonstrates that lay people today play a much more active role in ecclesial life than they did in the days before the Council. Lay people are clearly visible and vocal in the Church today, he observes.

But then he moves on to analyze what is happening "in the world." Here, he notes, it is another story. In fact, there are indeed many admirable Catholic lay people who are hard at work bringing Christian values into the public arena, but this is not universally true. Joseph Bernardin asserts that this is not a question only for marginal or indifferent Catholics. On the contrary, the issue involves those who unquestionably practice their religion and live good lives, but who do not seem to realize to what extent their vocation summons them to do their part in transforming the world, in accordance with the vision and the values of the Gospel.

The Cardinal insists that their task is to relate the Gospel to the issues of the day in a multitude of settings – on the job, at school, within the family, and in the neighborhood. But the expansion of lay participation "in the Church" since the Second Vatican Council has not been paralleled by a comparable new thrust of a committed lay apostolate "in the world." In no uncertain terms, today all of us need to come to grips with the fact that the authentic Christian vocation calls lay people to engage in the apostolate in the world. The mission of Catholic lay people today, whether "in the Church" or "in the world," ultimately depends upon the quality of their spiritual lives. In fact, Cardinal Bernardin notes, ministries, apostolates, and programs are very important but, without a healthy, lay spirituality, there may be a great deal of activity but very little in the way of solid accomplishment.

An interior life is thus crucial, he concludes, and fostering lay spirituality will be essential in the expanded lay role of the future.

17

Chicago

The Challenge of a Big Metropolis

Cardinal Bernardin discusses the social inadequacies that exist in a big metropolis like Chicago, highlighting collaboration and negotiation as real solution to these problems. People living in Chicago, or any metropolitan area, want to eliminate crime, violence, immigration, hunger. Fighting racism, the Cardinal says, is the first step to improve life conditions in a city.

Nowadays, Hispanic people represent a large part of the American population. Racial and ethnic obstacles, however, often prevent them from obtaining a standard of living comparable to that of other Americans. The Church's mission is to work towards the dignity and the equality of all people and respond to the particular needs of Black and Hispanic communities. First and foremost, the Church must help eliminate the racial obstacles that marginalize these ethnic groups in society. Cardinal Bernardin dreams of the creation of a "Chicagoland" where people work together to renovate the structures of modern urban life, thereby destroying the roots of poverty, crime and racism.

Society needs a new generation of young leaders who have the capacity to think of a better future with the help of the Church. Young people have the right to seek help in every step

*of their life, from childhood to adulthood. They need safe
schools, secure home lives, and safe places like the Church
where they can meet other young people. To implement all of
this, the Church requires good organization and a pastoral plan,
along with a Catholic response to the need for Hispanic integration that respects both the culture and the language of this ethnic group.*

I n a metropolis like Chicago, most social problems are connected with
criminality, ethnic discrimination, and ignorance – all of which are
fundamental problems which effect a large proportion of the people
who live in big cities. The solution to these problems advocated and
practiced by Cardinal Bernardin is basically that of promoting a serious,
deep collaboration among Chicagoans themselves.

Cardinal Bernardin observes that special interest groups threaten everywhere to defeat the democratic traditions of the United States. Those who
champion narrow interests make claims for "their own," rejecting, as part
of their strategy, even the possibility of compromise and sacrifice for the
common good. True progress always depends on persons who can support
their own legitimate interests while maintaining sympathy and making
room – in a family, a school, a business, or a city – for the rights and
concerns of others. America – and Chicago is indeed one of its greatest
cities – suffers from groups who refuse negotiation and cooperation, and
who insist that their claims must be recognized and their demands must
be immediately addressed without regard for others.

People want friendship, love, and opportunity; they want a good world
for their children. This is one of the Cardinal's firmest convictions. These
are gifts which we can have only if we make sacrifices to ensure that
everyone, regardless of race, color, or creed enjoys them. This is the time
to contemplate how much a common hope makes all people alike as
members of the same family, rather than to focus on what may dangerously
divide people from one another.

Racism: Enemy Number One of a Good Community

The first step to building a better, more united community of people in
Chicago – or elsewhere – is to fight racism, an evil which Cardinal
Bernardin does not hesitate to define as a sin. His role as the Archbishop
of Chicago is that of a reconciler. His task is to help create the kind of
atmosphere in all parts of the Archdiocese where people will be willing to
come together, communicate with one another, and thereby create a new
and united community.

Hispanic Population: A Major Concern

What is of special interest to Cardinal Bernardin is the increase of the Hispanic population in the United States generally, and in Chicago particularly. He is very concerned about the difficulties faced by these brothers and sisters of ours. The Hispanic population in metropolitan Chicago is very diverse, with representatives from nineteen Latin American republics, Puerto Rico, and Spain. Although they differ in racial origins, color, history, achievements, expressions of faith, and degree of disadvantage, they share many elements of culture such as a common language (spoken with different accents) and a deep-seated commitment to the extended family. By and large, Hispanics face the same racial or ethnic obstacles that are faced by the Black community. For example, lack of adequate education is an important factor in keeping both Blacks and Hispanics poor.

Cardinal Bernardin considers it to be an important step to include representatives of the Hispanic community in Catholic organizations, and he encourages all those involved with the Church to continue searching for ways to include this segment of the population within the purview of the Church's mission. In this sense, Catholic commitments are basically threefold:

1. Continue to work for the dignity, equality, and sanctity of all persons.

2. Continue to be sensitive to the particular needs of the Black and Hispanic communities and providing corresponding pastoral services.

3. Continue to provide education and other social services to as many people in the Black and Hispanic communities as the limited resources of the Catholic Church will allow.

Cardinal Bernardin's task is to help create the kind of atmosphere in all parts of the Archdiocese that will encourage people to come together, communicate with one another, and thereby create a new, united community. He is persuaded that social and ethnic diversity can, indeed, work to the advantage of all, though sometimes, unfortunately, it can also lead to conflict. When such diversity becomes the focus of fear or indolence – when it is manipulated to maintain group power, prerogatives, or material advantages – the ensuing hostility and conflict impact negatively on the quality of life and greatly impede the resolution of community problems.

It is to the advantage of all people that we learn to live in harmony. This means that we must tear down the fences which separate people from one another. The high fences around different communities have only increased the suspicion, the fear, and the distrust which threaten to isolate people from one another, thereby destroying the harmony of the community. These fences have become obsolete and destructive because they make it impossible for people to behave like brothers and sisters towards one another. They also make it impossible for people to confront the problems which can only be resolved through joint efforts.

Turning Chicago into a Chicagoland

One of the main factors that hinders and destroys sound relationships among people is racism. According to Cardinal Bernardin, it alienates people from their better selves and allows their weaknesses to control their thoughts and behavior. In short, it causes a tremendous waste of gifts, energy, and resources. It is an insidious sin, but it is not confined to any single racial, social, or economic group. Moreover, it is often associated with other convictions, fears, or emotions. It can be found among Blacks as well as Whites. It is coupled with a legitimate desire to have a larger house, live in a more pleasant neighborhood, enjoy the fruits of hard work. And what is really sad about this matter is that young people – Black and White and Hispanic – are often the flash point for racial violence. But frequently, they are merely acting out the attitudes and prejudices which they learn from their elders.

Cardinal Bernardin hopes that metropolitan Chicago can be turned into a "Chicagoland." He dreams of a coalition of dedicated people in the metropolitan area working together to renovate those structures of modern urban life which are at the root of poverty, crime, and racism. He hopes that young people can be enthusiastic about themselves and the possibilities of life rather than taking refuge in drugs, sex, and violence.

New Leaders

The task of adult society is to prepare the next generation of leaders: people who have the capacity to continue developing a broad vision which can embrace the ethnic and cultural diversity of the metropolis, people who have the courage to work collaboratively and creatively in solving the problems facing the people of Chicagoland, people who have the compassion and concern to help all their brothers and sisters, especially those who are most vulnerable.

Thus, Cardinal Bernardin's concerns are the young people of Chicago, especially those of the neighborhoods like Humbold Park, Logan Square, the West Town community, and indeed of the entire city. They represent the future, and they have a right to learn that they belong to God, not to a gang leader; they must understand that they belong to a family and friends, and to a Church that cares for them. They must be prepared to assume their full and rightful role as citizens of this great city and nation.

The environment in which many young people in Chicago live is often very dangerous. Their classmates may belong to rival gangs. Their brothers and sisters may be in jeopardy unless they cooperate with ruthless gang leaders. New members are often recruited through intimidation and promises of false security. Sometimes mere children are set up to do some of the most dangerous deeds for the professionals who hide behind them.

Many young people do not really want to belong to a gang – if they are given a free choice or a better alternative. Adolescence has always been a time to wrestle with conforming to the ideas and manners of peers. But to be forced to conform under penalty of violence or death erodes individual dignity and tends to rob the individual of a very important God-given resource – the ability to decide for oneself.

Schools often are not the places of safety that parents want for their children. This is not due to negligence on the part of dedicated administrators or teachers, but rather to the pervasive presence of gangs. Cardinal Bernardin commends the efforts and sacrifices made by many teachers and administrators representing both the public and the Catholic school systems. However, because of the number of weapons brought to school, these places of potential opportunity have become, instead, powder kegs of potential violence and destruction. In this connection, Cardinal Bernardin challenges the federal government to take these harsh realities into account.

According to Cardinal Bernardin, violence and the fear of violence can also lead individuals and families to retreat into the safety of their own homes – in a kind of isolation from others. However, in doing so, they simply become more vulnerable because, in not reaching out to others, they can expect no help themselves.

A Real Home for the Young

Young people need real homes to return to after school. They need some place where they are not only safe but also where they are loved. They need someone to talk to – with whom to share their dreams and their fears, their hopes and their despair. They need parents who show concern about who their friends are, what they do outside the home, where they go and why. They need parents who care enough to learn whether they are really going to school, and whether they are gang members. They need parents who care and are willing to take the tremendous effort it requires to help them deal with the problems that they are facing. Thus, Cardinal Bernardin is thoroughly persuaded that parents – mothers, fathers, single parents – are those who hold the key.

The Mobile Teams Program

A special archdiocesan initiative was created in 1985 to help the community fight against criminal youth gangs; this program was known as Mobile Teams. Cardinal Bernardin explained that these bilingual, interracial teams were designed to have an immediate impact. The Mobile Teams focused on education and information. For example, they assisted parents in identifying and responding to gang presence and pressure on their children. They offered similar assistance to churches, schools, and youth workers. They also dealt directly with young people, informing them about the implications of gang participation and about alternatives. In all of this, they cooperated with the police, social service agencies, other churches, school authorities, and recreational programs in each area.

Cooperation and Integration vs. Assimilation

According to Cardinal Bernardin, all citizens are responsible for the well-being of the society in which they live. The nation is based on laws which protect human rights, order, and harmony in society and are derived from respect and commitment to justice and fairness. Respect for and observance of the law is, therefore, a responsibility of each citizen.

The Church plays a very important role in this relationship. There are certain tasks which the Church, by its very nature, must perform: worship, education, and service. In order to do all this the Church needs good organization and a pastoral plan. And given the diversity within the Archdiocese of Chicago, it would be difficult for Cardinal Bernardin to develop an overall plan which would apply everywhere. Moreover, he notes that a multiplication of churches, often within a short distance of one another, has been the Catholic Church's response in the past to the diverse ethnic needs of immigrants.

Cardinal Bernardin underlines that, while his pastoral plan has many important dimensions, its most significant contribution is its call for Hispanic Catholics to be integrated, not assimilated, into the Church in the United States. This implies, for example, that they are to be served in their own language when possible, and that their cultural values and religious traditions are to be respected. It is also a sign of the Church's fundamental unity, because the plan is not intended to separate or isolate

Hispanics, but to acknowledge their heritage and talents so that they take their rightful place, alongside everyone else, in announcing the Kingdom of God to which everyone is invited.

While Cardinal Bernardin wants the people to participate in the planning process, he also has some expectations of them, as he knows they have of him. He expects mutual respect and trust, and he is committed to sitting down with people – through his representatives or even personally – to look at the facts realistically, to examine the options, and to analyze the alternatives. Cardinal Bernardin also expects people to respect the fact that he is ultimately responsible for all the resources of the Archdiocese and that decisions that are made in one area impact the well-being in other areas as well. He states that in the end, "we may disagree about a particular decision that has to be made, but we can disagree as Christians and as friends."

In this regard, there are certain kinds of behavior that are not appropriate in the Christian community. According to Cardinal Bernardin, one of these would be making decisions entirely on his own, without taking into serious consideration the lives or desires of the people affected by the decisions. Another would be for the people to use power plays in vain attempts to influence his ultimate decisions: spreading false rumors, saying outlandish or exaggerated things to the media, or invoking the claim of racism when none is present. Such tools of division and alienation are contrary to the gospel and foreign to the community of faith founded by Jesus.

18

Education

Delinquency is a plague which can be fought only with education, in particular religious education. The government should help the Church in this difficult task, one that has become increasingly difficult since religion has been removed from public schools. Joseph Bernardin notes that Church and society are traditionally recognized as having distinct, important roles in a child's education. Therefore a good and conscientious cooperation among parents and educators is necessary. Catholic schools, the Cardinal asserts, better prepare children both for life and for successive educational steps. For this reason the number of lay teachers and administrators in Catholic schools has recently increased, giving rise to further challenges and perplexities.

Another serious concern regards the media. Advertisement that publicizes the use of contraceptives or shows violent scenes should not be aired because it violates parents' rights and responsibilities to provide clear guidance to children. Another aspect is increased financial support in the private sector by the government so that low-income parents have the option of choosing Catholic education for their children. Elitism, Cardinal Bernardin concludes, does not belong to the Catholic heritage.

Delinquency, poverty, and generally poor conditions of life plague much of the population of Chicago. It seems to be an almost irreversible situation, and even from the most optimistic perspective there always seem to be new dimensions to these problems. Unfortunately, they seem to keep growing and causing severe suffering both to their immediate victims and to the members of the entire society.

According to Cardinal Bernardin, one of the most important and effective weapons against youth gangs and delinquency is education, and more specifically, religious education. He is persuaded that the government should help the Church in its educational work. On this topic, he refers to James Reichley's study, *Religion in American Public Life*. One of this author's central conclusions is that a democratic government "depends for its health on values that over the not-so-long run must come from religion." This is necessarily so because through religion – and only through religion – human rights are rooted in the moral worth with which the loving Creator has endowed each human life, and social authority is legitimized by making it answerable to a transcendant moral law.

According to Cardinal Bernardin, the Reichley study rejects the thesis that the removal of religion from public settings is an expression of government neutrality towards religion and secularism. On the contrary, he indicates that the "banishment of religion does not represent neutrality between religion and secularism; conduct of public institutions without any acknowledgement of religion is secularism."

Cardinal Bernardin observes that schooling occupies a great deal of time in the lives of children. Moreover, it exerts a critical influence on their entire growth process. Thus, excluding religion from the school experience of the young cheats them and their parents of something that they have a right and an obligation to seek – a well-rounded education that makes provision for spiritual growth as well as intellectual, emotional, and physical development.

To expect children to pray spontaneously – affirms Cardinal Bernardin – is to ask something very nearly impossible. Thus in legal terms, the problems should be focused on a constitutional measure: to allow children not only to pray voluntarily but to receive religious instruction provided by their own church or denomination in their school.

Institutional Role of the Parents

A very important side of the educational matter is the role played by parents' rights. Cardinal Bernardin underlines that the Catholic Church has long taught that parents are the primary educators of their children. The Second Vatican Council, in its Declaration on Christian Education, puts it this way:

> Since parents have conferred life on their children, they have the most solemn obligation to educate their offspring. Hence, parents must be ac-
> knowledged as the first and foremost educators of their children. In con-

ceiving and giving birth to a child, the parents take on the obligation to provide both for the physical well-being and the psychic well-being and development of the child.

However, Cardinal Bernardin is persuaded that this does not imply that parents have exclusive educational rights and responsibilities with regard to their children. The Church and society are also traditionally recognized as having distinct, important roles. Today, too, a realistic view must also acknowledge that popular culture, especially through the media, has an enormous "educational" impact on children, for good or ill.

Furthermore, Cardinal Bernardin states that, if parents are seriously unable or unwilling to provide for the education of their children, some other educational agent – in fulfillment of its obligations and also out of respect for the children's rights to be educated – must step in and fill the gap. Cardinal Bernardin is categorical in asserting that the parental right does not mean "carte blanche" for neglect or abuse.

In our complex world, the parental right to educate is necessarily exercised in large part by providing for schooling of children. Even so, parents' rights do not stop at the school door. Without intervening in the legitimate decisions which professional educators have a right to make, parents should be closely involved in decisions affecting the formal education of their children.

According to Cardinal Bernardin, parents and educators will be able to resolve specific problems to the extent that they approach the issues in an atmosphere of mutual respect and with a commitment to authentic dialogue. Both sides must be willing to listen with open minds and hearts. In the end, the children will benefit from such an approach, based on a correct understanding of parents' rights in education.

Parental Rights Usurped by the Media

Cardinal Bernardin states that parents' rights and duties concerning their children's education are usurped and hindered by the media. For example, according to recent reports, contraceptive advertisements have begun to appear on some cable television systems and local TV and radio stations. Cardinal Bernardin thinks that there are many good reasons why such contraceptive advertising should not be aired. One of his most serious concerns is that advertising violates parents' rights and responsibilities in providing guidance to their children. This is not a matter where instruction of young people can rightly be turned over to the purveyors of a commercial product whose built-in motive is to promote circumstances favorable to its use.

Another aspect of the problem of the media's role in education concerns the portrayal of violence. A study by the U.S. Surgeon General in 1972 and a followup study by the National Institute of Health in 1982 concluded that there is a significant link between children's exposure to televised violence and antisocial behavior. Yet violence remains a staple of TV entertainment programming. Cardinal Bernardin obviously has no specific solution for this problem but a wise general suggestion: the media need more formal and extensive procedures than they have now for consulting the public and responding to the public interest.

The Richness in Values of the Catholic School

Cardinal Bernardin's reflections on education have naturally focused extensively on the proud tradition and important role of Catholic schools. Their purpose even in the past was much broader than simply "protecting" the faith of children in a sometimes religiously hostile environment – as important as that was. Catholic schools have been a source of vigorous Catholic life in the United States. Catholic educators have always maintained that a Catholic school does much more than merely teach a religion class each day. Rather, the whole atmosphere of the school is animated by the Christian spirit; all who participate in it – students, teachers, and parents – experience a community of faith. It goes without saying that Catholic schools must be able to provide an education that conforms to the highest professional standards. They must also be prepared to nourish a vital faith in young people and help them to bear witness to that faith today.

Cardinal Bernardin observes that from a study concerning different educational systems, it was agreed by almost all of the participants that Catholic schools are indeed good schools. Even those parents who choose to send their children to public schools acknowledged that students in Catholic schools are better students and better behaved, that the schools have higher academic standards, and that their graduates are better prepared for college. Another impressive finding is the fact that parents are still choosing a Catholic elementary school because of its connection with the Church. It is good to know that families with children in Catholic elementary schools feel closer to the Church and tend to involve themselves more in Church activities. According to the same study, parents and children who do not attend Catholic schools do not feel as close to the Church and are not as involved in its life as are the parents and children in Catholic schools.

The study also revealed another factor in parental decisions to send their children to Catholic schools: the sense that they "prepare children better for life" by instilling religion, values, and respect for themselves and others. The findings of the study demonstrate that the Catholic elementary school continues to play an important role in the development and formation of the faith life of individual persons and, indirectly, of parishes and the archdiocese as a whole. Thus, according to the Cardinal, it is clearly proper to speak of the ministry of Catholic elementary education.

Cardinal Bernardin is persuaded that Catholic schools are different from public schools. In its educational ministry the Church promotes both academic achievement and value or religious formation. In other words, Catholic schools are concerned with the minds of high school students, and provide excellent instruction in the sciences as well as the faith and values that will provide nourishment and guidance for their lives. A Catholic education helps students develop a disposition for service. It aims to spark within the students a passion for justice, and helps to evoke a genuine commitment to creating and building community.

Involvement of Lay Teachers

Cardinal Bernardin recognizes that there are many vehicles for carrying out this mission, but none is as essential as the individual teachers – and, of course, the principals. Recently, there has been increasing involvement of lay women and men as teachers and administrators, and a concurrent decreasing number of religious people in these roles. Cardinal Bernardin applauds and supports the integration of laity into teaching and administrative positions. At the same time, this opportunity gives rise to further challenges and perplexities: What impact do lay teachers in Catholic high schools have on their students in regard to religious formation? Where do these teachers stand on issues of Catholic faith and values? In 1985, a report on full-time teachers noted that, although the non-Catholic teachers who participated in the survey are not hostile to the religious identity of Catholic schools in which they teach, neither are they enthusiastic supporters of Catholic teaching in a number of areas. The challenge before such schools is how to balance respect for the conscience and competence of its non-Catholic teachers – many of whom are unquestionably people of faith and good will – with institutional commitments to a specifically Catholic religious formation for their students.

Over the last twenty years, public schools have increased their share of total enrollment while private schools' share has declined. However, according to the findings of the study discussed above, nearly half of all public-school parents would send their children to private schools if they were tuition-free. Cardinal Bernardin's perspective on this matter is quite clear. He does not argue against public education or against government aid to the public sector. The United States needs strong public schools. The better the public schools, the better for everyone. But he also favors introducing a new element of equity into the picture by increasing aid to the private sector. In particular he favors maximizing the opportunities for parents to exercise a real choice in the schooling of their children. That is the central argument for tuition tax credits. Before 1986 the idea of education vouchers was adopted on the level of higher education, where "Pell grants" helped nearly 2 million financially needy students attend the public or private college of their choice.

Helping Needy Students

In 1986, U.S. Secretary of Education Bennet's proposal extended this system to the elementary and secondary levels and tied it in directly with the provision of remedial services for needy students. This program gives low-income parents a real choice in the schooling of their children, increases parental involvement, and provides some healthy competition for the public schools. The intention is to make it easier for parents – especially low-income parents – to exercise a modicum of choice in the education of their children. Cardinal Bernardin is convinced that, whatever new form of financing is developed, it must ensure that the truly poor and the economically disadvantaged – as well as the middle class – are not excluded from access to Catholic education. He emphasizes that elitism has not been a Catholic heritage, and it cannot become so in the future.

A Moral Vision

A very interesting aspect of education is it mutual interrelationship with business. In fact, businesses are dependent on the educational community for scientific research and future employees and managers. The educational institutions are dependent on the business community for funds and the interdisciplinary dialogue which will help ensure both the quality and the relevance of educational endeavors. Throughout U.S. history, education was considered more important than the best industrial system or the strongest military force, because neither industry nor defence can long endure without education.

Cardinal Bernardin remarks that – quite sadly – we use our genius for less than noble purposes. For example, our ability to develop and control atomic energy and lasers has had a tremendous impact on many fields of human endeavor, from medicine to the development of weaponry. In order to achieve a new international order and peace, the key moral question is how to relate politics, economics, and ethics so as to shape our material interdependence in the direction of moral interdependence, and to bring the technology of the arms race to its appropriate subordinate role. To accomplish this, we need a moral vision. The absence of any sense of a necessary relationship with an ethical world larger than oneself results in individuals taking less and less a role in public life and feeling little, if any, responsibility for anyone but themselves. Individualism and isolationism go hand-in-hand.

Illiteracy

Another widespread plague in the United States that can only be cured with education is illiteracy. A few years ago, the federal Department of Labor estimated that adult illiteracy cost the nation $225 billion annually in lost industrial productivity, unrealized tax revenues, welfare assistance, prison costs, and criminal activity. The U.S. Catholic bishops expressed their deep concern about this situation in a pastoral letter on the economy. They write: "Illiteracy condemns many people to joblessness or chronically low wages. Moreover, it excludes them in many ways from sharing in the political and spiritual life of the community." Cardinal Bernardin underlines that there is shock and shame in the realization that in 1986, among the 159 members of the United Nations, the United States ranked 49th in literacy! Think of the implications: individuals who cannot function at all in our information society, Christians who cannot read scriptures, wage earners who cannot find employment in an economy with a declining need for unskilled labor, parents who cannot write letters to their children who live away from home. Cardinal Bernardin is persuaded that, since the problem of illiteracy is both personal and social, the solution must involve both individuals and communities.

Some important measures have been taken on a local level. In Illinois, for example, a Literacy Council accepts volunteer tutors and would-be students. Tutors are trained, and the students are assigned. Tutor-student teams are encouraged to meet for about two hours weekly over several months so that real progress can be made.

A Lifelong Effort

To sum up Cardinal Bernardin's views on education, it is helpful to think of his idea that education can be seen as a seamless garment, in two senses. First, in the sense that our commitment to Christian education cannot exclude anyone, regardless of who the person is or where he or she goes to school. Education must also be seen as a seamless garment in the sense that it is a lifelong effort. As a Church we can never be content to focus only on one period in a person's life. Our educational ministry begins early and continues to the end, from early infancy through adulthood.

19

Sexuality

Between Human Fulfillment and Abuse

The Church's position on sexuality is an important topic in human relationships. Cardinal Bernardin clarifies this position, stressing the importance of people understanding the Church's message and its traditional teaching. The Cardinal emphasizes that sexuality is a great gift of God that is central to our identity as persons and must not be abused. As Christians, we must strengthen the virtue of chastity by putting our sexual instinct at the service of love and development of the person God created. Human sexuality becomes very important when discussing the spirituality of marital intimacy. Profound spiritual intimacy and sexuality in a married couple are deeply related. An inability to be intimate can cause people to become lonely and embittered. In Christian asceticism, i.e., the diligent practice of love, an important common project and a mutual goal for both men and women is to be achieved personally and in the realm of the family. Women have to protect their human dignity and life when they are subject to random violence. Men must be aware of these realities since they are part of the problem; they must work to develop appropriate solutions among themselves.

The idea that the Church should not talk about sex and sexuality, or else that it should say something other than it does, offers the possibility of misunderstanding and hostility concerning what the Church really has to say. Underlining this point, Cardinal Bernardin clarifies that the position of the Church and its message about this matter is essential to human happiness and authentic fulfillment. Sex and sexuality are too important for the Church not to talk about them, and his wish is to show the relevance and importance of its traditional teaching.

Since the Church takes a comprehensive view of human life, it cannot omit sexuality as one of the central elements in human relationships. Cardinal Bernardin recognizes that much of the desire "to drop the subject" arises from a body/soul dualism. The common attitude is that the immaterial part of a human being is what really counts, and it is this dualistic denigration of the body that stresses the false ideas and practices in regard to sexuality. Human beings are unique body/soul composites, and the bodies are as truly human as the souls. Jesus Christ Himself was not a disembodied soul: he was a human being with a body.

Morality, then, is concerned with human beings as they are, and it is therefore necessarily concerned with the integrity of the body and bodily behavior. "Glorify God in your body" (I Cor. 6:15,20), St. Paul recounts; thus, bodily behavior has a moral character. The positive theology of sexuality, as Cardinal Bernardin points out, provides a necessary basis for appreciating what the Church teaches about sex. He even emphasizes that sexuality is a great gift of God, central to our identity as persons, and must not as such be abused. That is why understanding and observance of the Church's teaching are vital to the correct use of this precious gift.

Chastity and Healthy Sexual Attitude

As Cardinal Bernardin observes, as Christians, we must rehabilitate, when necessary, the virtue of chastity in order to have a healthy attitude and behavior towards sexuality. The virtue of chastity is something positive. The Holy See's Congregation for Catholic Education published the "Educational Guidance in Human Love" as the outline for sex education. Here, the virtue of chastity is described as the capacity for guiding the sexual instinct to the service of love and to the development of the person. Chastity, being the fruit of the grace of God, serves to harmonize the different components of a person. Each person can follow the vocation to which God has called, while overcoming the frailty of human nature.

Like any other virtue, chastity must be acquired not as something repressive and neurotic, but on the contrary as something which is necessary for human fulfillment. There are serious internal obstacles to reach it, and first of all we must take into account the reality of original sin and its consequences. Original sin results in a tendency toward defective relationships both with God and with our fellow human beings. To avoid the inner disintegration of the elements of our personhood, chastity contributes to the integration of our inner selves in a way which is consonant with God's plan and vision for society. Sexuality under the influence of chastity is then healing and good.

As Pope John Paul II points out, authentic Christian sex education is in fact "education in chastity." Acquiring chastity is, then, an educational task, and to reach it people must experience conversion. They must experience faith in their lives because God's love, mercy, understanding, and compassion must be real to them. Only then will they be willing to commit themselves to Him and accept the demands He makes of them. One of the most important ecclesial tasks is to motivate people to dispose themselves to be open to the grace of conversion, so that they can be called to a totally new way of life involving new personal and social responsibilities.

This new way of life runs counter to many of the values of contemporary culture, but as a result of God's grace and the strength it confers, it should be accepted willingly and joyfully. As far as sexuality is concerned, chastity and conversion are the inseparable keys to this state of mind and style of life.

Marital Intimacy

Cardinal Bernardin emphasizes the subject of human sexuality when discussing the spirituality of marital intimacy, as a certain psychological and physical nearness of one's being with another. The nearness is profoundly spiritual, and, since we need intimacy, it also has an important physical dimension. Human intimacy is a pale but real reflection of the divine intimacy of the Trinity, and it is part of the lives of everyone.

The inability to be intimate causes people to become lonely and embittered. Married people may separate and even divorce – all because they have never learned to be intimate. Intimacy and sexuality are integrally related, but intimacy involves the willingness to become vulnerable by being honest about oneself with others and to let others become a part of and an influence on one's own life.

A four-phase cycle – of falling in love, settling into a routine, descending into a crisis, and beginning again – repeats itself often in a marriage. But if a marriage stops at a crisis stage, the cycle seems both unnatural and unhealthy. An initially unconscious evil in married life is an increasing indifference of spouses toward each other which arises from their need for autonomy and freedom. This state of affairs becomes conscious sin when spouses withhold communication; this sin then becomes hatred, until at last there is an explosion in which torrents of vicious recrimination are let loose. But we as Christians – says the Cardinal – can purify ourselves through the love of our Lord and call forth mutual forgiveness; in this way, our relationships can be born anew.

The Mutual Goal of Family Life and Behavior

Cardinal Bernardin recognizes that out of sin and sorrow, forgiveness and resurrection will save spouses. They generate powerful creative forces in order to be born again as "new" persons with a new and deeper love. Pope John Paul II underlines the asceticism based on the "nuptial meaning of the body," which takes into account the difficult virtues and skills required to realize this meaning fully. In the Old and New Testaments, and especially in the Easter story, there exist enormously rich resources for developing an asceticism of the "nuptial meaning of the body."

Christian asceticism is, then, the diligent practice of love. The notion of detachment in the Christian tradition is then practiced not so that we might arrive at a state of impassibility or neutrality, but so that the right "attachments" might take root. Understanding and observance of the Church's teaching are indispensible to the correct use of this gift, and its correct use is essential to our fulfillment in this world and in the next.

Cardinal Bernardin stresses the importance of both women and men for realizing this common project, and for reaching the mutual goal of family life and behavior. However, many Catholic women endure female tasks and responsibilities which seem to belong only to them. Moreover, many parents and teachers in matters of sexual responsibility set and enforce only for girls the standards necessary to confront the consequences of pregnancy. We seem to forget that fatherhood plays a vital role in children's lives.

Crime and Violence

In the effort to defend human dignity and life, the full spectrum of crime and violence must be addressed. Women are aware from experience that they are subject to random violence. Cardinal Bernardin is cognizant of the level of victimization experienced by women, of the anxiety they must feel, and the precautions they routinely take. Just look at the statistics. In a nation where experts estimate that only one-in-four forcible rapes is reported, there were 84,233 reported forcible rapes in 1984. These are not simple numbers; these are women with faces and families. As Cardinal

Bernardin clarifies, all men are not the enemy, but they must know these realities and, since they are part of the problem, they must struggle to develop appropriate solutions among themselves.

As for women, they must articulate the enormity of the pain they suffer in order to unmask the problem. Society itself should help women through appropriate programs and recognize that the so-called "women's concerns" are fundamentally human concerns. The community cannot violate, belittle, or ignore women without harming the whole fabric of human life.

20

Death Penalty in Our Time

Capital punishment is one of the most complex and intensive questions to debate. We must always remember that human life is sacred and has a social value. We have the duty to protect it. The death penalty must be examined in the light of a consistent ethic. The growing awareness of human dignity must be acknowledged as a dominant factor in our culture. Consequently, a consistent ethical life must be based on the need to ensure the sacredness of human life, the ultimate source of human dignity. The Church cannot accept the viewpoints of some political leaders on capital punishment. These leaders point out that such punishment might satisfy certain vindictive desires of the victim, and can be justified as punishment for reasons of deterrence, retribution, reform or protection of society. On the contrary, the Church affirms that the death penalty can never be justified as such, and cannot be the humane and Christian approach to punishment. The best example, the Cardinal points out, comes from Jesus Himself, who offered forgiveness for His own unfair death. He calls us to view the judgment of these matters as shifting to a "higher court" that possesses wrath and tenderness, law and grace. In light of this, we must seriously question the appropriateness of capital punishment and the right of society to impose lifetime imprisonment.

A consistent ethical life requires that society struggle to eradicate poverty, racism, and other forces that nurture and encourage violence. Capital punishment is an example of meeting violence with violence, with the aim of revenge. It is a shame, the Cardinal feels, that a great percentage of the population favors capital punishment despite studies that have shown its

negative impact on crime prevention. Violence cannot be an-
swered with other violence. An effective means to protect and
enhance human life must be found.

The question of capital punishment has always stimulated broad and intensive debate, not only in the United States but also in many other societies. Recently, a number of specific facts has increased the interest and also actualized the problem in the United States, where the death penalty is applied in some states and not in others. These facts have drawn the attention of the whole world and triggered petitions and other such mass initiatives. A typical example is that of Paula Cooper, a young minor sentenced to death for having killed her teacher.

When we speak of the death penalty, we must bear in mind the two basic truths of Catholic social teaching with regard to the human person: human life is both sacred and social. Because human life is sacred, we have the duty to protect and foster it at all stages of development, from conception to natural death, and in all its circumstances. Acknowledging that human life is also social means that society must protect and foster it. And since life is sacred, it follows that the taking of even one life is an awesome event.

Cardinal Bernardin addresses this issue by situating it in the context of a consistent ethic of life and then examining the death penalty in the light of this ethic.

The Context: A Consistent Ethic of Life

It must first be remembered that, historically, traditional Catholic teaching has allowed the taking of human life in particular situations by way of exception. For example, it has permitted it in the cases of self-defense and capital punishment. In recent decades, however, the presumptions against taking human life have been strengthened, and the exceptions to them made ever more restrictive. Fundamental to this shift in emphasis is a more acute perception of the multiple ways in which life is threatened today. Obviously, such questions as war, aggression, and capital punishment have been with us for centuries; they are not new. But what *is* new is the context in which these ancient questions arise and the way in which the changed circumstances shape the content of our ethic of life.

In this regard within the Catholic Church, the Second Vatican Council has acknowledged that "a sense of the dignity of the human person has been impressing itself more and more deeply on the consciousness of contemporary man" (Declaration on Religious Freedom, 1). The official recognition of this growing awareness of human dignity has been a dominant factor within Western culture in our times. In the United States, the struggle to appreciate human worth more fully has materialized in the civil rights movement, as well as in the public debate about U.S. foreign policy toward totalitarian regimes of both the right and left. Such deepening awareness has been precipitated in part by a growing recognition of the frailty of human life today. Faced with the threat of nuclear war and escalating technological developments, the human family encounters a qualitatively new range of moral problems. It is a fact that life is threatened on a scale previously unimaginable.

For these reasons the U.S. Catholic bishops, among others, have been visible and vocal in the public debate this past decade or two, asserting belief in the sacredness of human life and the responsibilities we have, personally and as a society, to protect and preserve the sanctity of life. Nonetheless, the simple assertion of such an ethical principle must impact all areas of human life. A consistent ethic of life is based on the need to ensure that the sacredness of human life – which is the ultimate source of human dignity – will be defended and fostered from conception to natural death, from the genetic laboratory to the cancer ward, from the ghetto to the prison.

Capital Punishment in Light of This Ethic

Since the time of St. Augustine, great thinkers in the Roman Catholic tradition – St. Thomas Aquinas, for example – have struggled with such ethical questions as the right of the State to execute criminals. Through the centuries, the Church has acknowledged that the State does have the right to take the life of someone guilty of an extremely serious crime. However, because such punishment involves the deliberate infliction of evil on another, it always needs justification. Usually, the indication of some good that would derive from the punishment – a good of such consequence that it justifies the taking of life – has been accepted as a valid reason.

The current discussion about capital punishment has brought up the question whether the State should exercise the right to inflict capital punishment altogether. The new perspective is dictated by doubts about whether in present circumstances there are sufficient reasons to justify the infliction of the evil of death on another human person. This question has been addressed by the U.S. Catholic bishops and others – the United States Catholic Conference in 1980, the Massachusetts Catholic Conference Board of Governors in 1982, Florida church leaders in 1985, and several other groups of bishops since then. Although there are differences of presentation, basically the reasoning of these positions follows two lines of thought.

First, they review four traditional arguments justifying capital punishment: retribution, deterrence, reform, and protection of the State. Based on their review, the religious leaders have argued that these reasons no longer apply in our age. They grant that the need of retribution does indeed justify punishment, for the practice of punishment both presupposes a previous transgression against the law and involves the involuntary deprivation of certain goods. But they maintain that this good does not require nor does it justify the taking of the life of the criminal, even in cases of murder." It is morally unsatisfactory and socially destructive for criminals to go unpunished, but the limits of punishment must be determined by moral objectives which go beyond the mere infliction of injury on the guilty," they state. Their argument defends the principle that "it is as barbarous and inhumane for a criminal who had tortured or maimed a victim to be tortured or maimed in return." In fact, they point out that such punishment might satisfy certain vindicative desires that we or the victim might feel, but the satisfaction of such desires is not and cannot be an objective of a humane and Christian approach to punishment. Therefore, many religious leaders conclude that, under our present circumstances, the death penalty as punishment for reasons of deterrence, retribution, reform, or protection of society cannot be justified.

Basing their judgement along similar lines of reasoning, they push their reflections even further. In fact they argue that there are "gospel insights which bespeak the inappropriateness of capital punishment." The best example of this comes from Jesus, offering forgiveness at the time of his own unfair death (Lk 23:24). Florida church leaders point out another challenging gospel theme especially visible in Jesus' ministry to outcasts, in his acceptance of sinners – that of "God's boundless love for every person, regardless of human merit or worthiness." Consistent with this theme and flowing from it is the biblical imperative of reconciliation – wherever there is division between persons, Christ calls them to forgiveness and reconciliation.

While these themes are specifically grounded in Christian teachings, they are not unique to it. People of good will recognize that these values ennoble human experience and make it more complete. Commitment to these values changes one's perspective on the strengths and weaknesses of the human family.

It is this change in perspective that the ecumenical leaders of Florida had in mind when they stated that Jesus shifted the locus of judgement in this matter to a higher court: a court where there is absolute knowledge of the evidence, good deeds and evil, faith and works of faith, things private and things public – a court in which there is both wrath and tenderness, both law and grace.

It is when we stand in this perspective of a "higher court" – that of God's judgment seat – and a more noble view of the human person that we seriously question the appropriateness of capital punishment. We ask ourselves: Is the human family made more complete – is human personhood made more loving – in a society which demands life for life, eye for eye, tooth for tooth? The State does have the responsibility to protect its citizens. It deserves and merits the full support of all in the exercise of that responsibility. Although we do not have an adequate understanding of the causes of violent crime, society "has the right and the duty to prevent such behavior including, in some cases, the right to impose terms of lifetime imprisonment" (Florida ecumenical leaders).

In agreement with these positions Cardinal Bernardin is thus not suggesting that society should be a prisoner of violence or violent crime. On the contrary, the consistent ethic of life requires that society struggle to eradicate poverty, racism, and other systemic forces which nurture and encourage violence. Similarly, the perpetrators of violence should be punished and given the opportunity to experience a change of heart and mind. Yet, having said this, he also emphasizes that capital punishment is not an appropriate response to the problem of crime. To take any human life, even that of someone who is not innocent, is awesome and tragic. In our culture today, it does seem that there are not sufficient reasons to justify the State continuing to exercise its right in this matter; there are other, better ways of protecting the interests of society.

The Gallup organization conducted a number of successive polls about capital punishment: in 1966, 42% of those polled favored capital punishment; in 1981, 66% favored it; in 1985, the proportion was 72%, and in 1988, the percentage that favored the death penalty increased once again. It is to these data that Cardinal Bernardin directs his reflection when he asks, "Why [has such a high percentage of the population] turned to favoring capital punishment in the last 27 years?" This question is even more urgent because that same poll reported that a high rate of the respondents said "they would still support capital punishment even if studies showed conclusively it does not deter crime!" This is striking, because people often use deterrence as a main argument to justify capital punishment. Then, if it is not to deter crime, why do people support capital punishment? Thirty percent of those who favored it indicated their reason was revenge. A simple but astounding answer. One might argue that the cycle of violence has become so intense in society that it is understandable and appropriate for people to support capital punishment. What alternative is there in a violent society, some ask, other than to meet violence with violence?

Yet any citizen in a democracy whose founding dream was that of human dignity and belief in God, must reject this alternative. Violence is not the answer – it is not the way to break the cycle of violence. Pope John Paul II, speaking to Peruvians who were living in the midst of a rebel stronghold, told them: "The pitiless logic of violence leads to nothing. No good is obtained by helping to increase violence."

Capital punishment, according to Cardinal Bernardin, is an example of meeting violence with violence, its sole reason often being revenge. He wonders what it says about the quality of our life when people celebrate the death of another human being. What does it say about the human spirit when some suggest a return to public executions, which only about twenty years ago would have been considered barbaric? His position encourages an attitude or atmosphere in society that will sustain a consistent defense and promotion of life, which nowadays is desperately needed. Where human life is considered "cheap" and easily "wasted," eventually nothing is held as sacred and all lives are in jeopardy. The purpose of proposing a consistent ethic of life is to argue that success on any of the issues threatening life requires a concern for the broader attitude in society about respect for life. Attitude is the place to root a consistent ethic of life. Change of attitude, in turn, can lead to change of policies and practices in society. Cardinal Bernardin invites us to find ways to break the cycle of violence which threatens to strangle a nation, to find an effective means of protecting and enhancing human life.

21

The Laity, the Church, and Society

The role of the Catholic laity in both the Church and the changing society of today is crucial. Lecturers and cantors, lay ministers of the Eucharist, lay teachers in Catholic schools provide perfect examples of this. The mission of laity in the Church finds consistent parallels with its mission in the world, both directed toward the actualization of Christ's message. The Church's specific mission is a religious one – to put into action the Kingdom of God; the lay, in virtue of their special vocation, must contribute to the sanctification of the world by fulfilling their respective duties at home, in the workplace, and in the public forum. Members of the Catholic laity find salvation not only in their service to the church on Sunday, but also through their daily lives. The importance of an interior life is crucial and so, says the Cardinal, the fostering of lay spirituality will be essential in the future roles of the Catholic laity. Everyone has a distinct role within the Church. For example, the Church should participate in politics via lay people, who in turn must be encouraged by bishops in undertaking this vocation. The U.S. Church has confronted many issues, such as war and peace, economy, abortion, capital punishment, human rights. New members of the church continue to see a growing open-mindedness in the Church's examination of these fundamental issues.

The dictionary definition of the term "lay" touches upon a number of meanings. Recently, the religious use of the term has gained significance. The international Synod of Bishops of 1987 explored the theme, "The Vocation and Mission of the Laity in the Church and in the World Twenty Years after the Second Vatican Council."

The role of Catholic laity – together with bishops, the clergy, and religious men and women – is essential today, independent of the lack of vocations to priesthood and religious life. Lay people, because of their baptism, have a fundamental role inside and outside the Church.

More than 25 years ago, the Second Vatican Council, in the light of the Church's mission in the world, delineated the respective roles of the laity, the priests, and the bishops. The 1987 Synod explored in greater detail the vocation and mission of Catholic lay people in the Church and in the changing society.

"In the United States, for example, the evidence is overwhelming that lay people today play a much more active role in the Church life than they did in the days before the council," Cardinal Bernardin points out. Lay people are clearly more visible and vocal in the Church than they were before. Lay lectors and cantors, lay extraordinary ministers of the Eucharist, lay teachers in Catholic schools, are examples of this.

A tremendous encouragement to the action of laity came from the apostolic exhortation, *Christi fideles laici*. Pope John Paul II signed this document on January 30, 1989. It constitutes a clear acknowledgement of the full dignity of lay activity for a new evangelization of a world which is increasingly being secularized.

The Church in the World and the Kingdom

Since the Council, during the Mass, it is not unusual to see lay people assisting the priest, and we see more and more lay people engaged in the teaching of religion.

These are only a few signs of the ever more active and vast role played by the Catholic laity in society to witness – together with the clergy – the evangelical message.

Cardinal Bernardin observes that this phenomenon is only partly due to the vocation crisis of our times. He says, "The basis for this participation and collaboration is not expediency and practical need (for example, because of fewer clergy or religious), but baptism which makes us all co-disciples of the Lord Jesus. As disciples, endowed with different gifts and called to various tasks and roles, we are coresponsible for the Church's well-being." The mission of the laity in the Church is therefore consistent with their mission in the world – both being directed toward the actualization of Christ's message.

The Church's specific mission to the world is not in the political, economic, or social order; its proper mission is a religious one. Nevertheless, this religious mission seeks to structure earthly realities in light of the vision of the Kingdom. The entire Church, through its efforts in society, sanctifies itself and makes present the Kingdom of God, underlines Cardinal Bernardin. Moreover, the

Church carries on Jesus' mission of proclaiming the Good News and building up the Kingdom, and all members of the Church share responsibility for its mission in virtue of their Baptism and Confirmation. While all are co-disciples of Jesus, there are different roles, which should not be allowed to disturb the unity and harmony of Jesus' community of disciples. As the Second Vatican Council pointed out clearly: Although by Christ's will some are established as teachers, dispensers of the mysteries, and pastors, for the others there remains, nevertheless, a true equality among all with regard to the dignity and the activity which is common to all the faithful in the building of the Body of Christ (*Lumen Gentium*, 32).

The laity – highlights *Lumen Gentium* – in virtue of their special vocation "seek the Kingdom of God by engaging in temporal affairs and directing them to God's will." In fact, they contribute to the sanctification of the world by fulfilling their respective duties in the home, the workplace, and the public forum. They are "to animate the world with the spirit of Christianity" and "to be witnesses to Christ in all circumstances and at the very heart of the community of mankind" (*Gaudium et Spes*, 43). The laity, indeed, find their salvation in and through daily lives in the world. *Gaudium et Spes* also reminds us that "The laity have a primary, though not exclusive, role in the world." Moreover, bishops, along with their priests, are "to preach the message of Christ in such a way that the light of the Gospel will shine on all activities of the faithful." They are also to provide guidance, to the extent they can, and spiritual strength to their lay sisters and brothers so that the latter may "shoulder their responsibility under the guidance of Christian wisdom and with eager attention to the teaching authority of the Church." Thus, working together as co-disciples, all members – both ordained and nonordained – carry out the Church's mission in the world.

The Council's Pastoral Constitution on the Church in the Modern World (*Gaudium et Spes*) states: "One of the gravest errors of our time is the dichotomy between the faith which many profess and the practice of their daily life." Although the Council accurately analyzed this problem – the "split" between faith and life – no one, notes the Cardinal, would seriously maintain that it has been solved in the two and a half decades since Vatican II. In some way it may even have grown worse. His discussion of the problem of the separation of faith from life is enlightening. He addresses directly the question of what it means to be true Catholics by reminding us that "to be a Catholic Christian is to have a personal vocation, a calling to a unique share in carrying on the mission of the Church which is the mission of Christ. That insight is essential to overcoming religious indifference, counteracting religious formalism, closing the gap between faith and life, and reestablishing the integrity of

Catholic identity in all members of the Church" (March 18, 1988). The Cardinal continues:

> Religion – to be authentic – must necessarily burst the bonds of Sunday morning worship so as to influence the whole week. A living, vital faith cannot be confined to a church or a cathedral. It must enliven every aspect of our lives and our society (Homily, March 2, 1986).

The mission of the laity in and to the secular order was a central element of Vatican II teaching about lay people. Indeed, the Council emphasizes that this is where their special work lies. "Guided by the Church's teaching, but using their own sphere of work, their task is to relate the Gospel to the issues of the day in a multitude of settings – on the job, at school, within the family, in the neighborhood," the Cardinal points out. And then he continues, showing a deep awareness of the problems involved:

> For example, although the number of lay people actively involved in Church-related ministeries and tasks is far greater than in the past, it remains, in relation to the total number of laity, comparatively small. The situation bears watching, for it could lead to an elitism. . . . Likewise, the danger of 'clericalizing' lay people should not be dismissed lightly. This would mean conveying the impression, usually unintended, that the more nearly they come to resemble the clergy, the closer they approach to the ideal. But that confuses the lay vocation with the clerical, and benefits neither.

The importance of the laity has been underlined by John Paul II's decision to canonize and beatify a number of lay people. "This gesture," notes the Cardinal says of the laity that they are "ultimately all about holiness."

In addressing the fundamental question of the relationship between the mission of Catholic lay people – whether "in the Church" or "in the world" – and their spiritual life, the Cardinal answers in unquestionable terms:

> It ultimately depends upon the quality of their spiritual lives. Ministries, apostolates, and programs are very important, but, without a healthy lay spirituality, there may be a greater amount of activity but very little solid accomplishment. Unless they are rooted in the interior life, lay activities – as well as clerical and religious activities – run the risk of superficiality and even counterproductivity.

He insists that "an interior life is crucial, and fostering lay spirituality will be essential in the expanded lay role of the future." In part, that was what the Cardinal meant when, in his own intervention at the Synod on the laity, he asked: "How can we help them [lay people] use that experience to develop spiritualities, stuctures, and programs that will support them in their vocation?"

The Experience of the Church in the United States

Throughout the history of the Church in the United States, and especially in this century, the Catholic bishops have taught the Church's social doctrine. In earlier decades, for example, they addressed such diverse topics as abortion, labor relations, secularism, and racism. As a result, they were successful in promoting human rights, in persuading the working classes to remain within the Church, and in developing a significant core of lay leadership.

In the decades immediately after World War II, many Social Action programs were developed, under the supervision of the hierarchy, with dedicated and competent lay leadership. Numerous lay organizations were established which have given effective witness to Gospel values in the family and the public arena. These new ventures have played a significant role in carrying out the Church's mission within the multiethnic U.S. society.

Today, the Church in the United States is no longer primarily a community of immigrants, even though new members continue to arrive from throughout the world. Especially since the Second Vatican Council, lay persons have been taking their rightful place within the Church as ministers and members of parish and diocesan pastoral councils. More recently, the laity themselves have seen the need for and have requested great support for their vocation in and to the world.

During this decade, the U.S. bishops have developed a consistent ethic of life which addresses a broad spectrum of life issues from conception to natural death, bringing the light of the Gospel and Church teaching to bear on such issues as war and peace, the economy, abortion, and the concerns of women. This has also enabled them to engage both the community of the Church and the wider society in reflection, debate, and examination of the moral dimensions of public policy. As part of this effort, the bishops developed two pastoral letters, one on peace issues and the other on the economy, in close collaboration with laity who had special expertise in those areas.

But these and other statements by the bishops will remain mere words – according to Bernardin – unless the laity assimilate the teaching. One way of implementing it is through the political order. It is very interesting to see how the Cardinal discusses opportunities and difficulties of doing so. He thinks that "the bishops should not be political partisans, but they can specify, examine, and press in the public debate the moral dimensions of issues as diverse as medical technology, capital punishment, human rights, economic policy, and military strategy." The experience of the U.S. episcopal conference in addressing the issues of nuclear and economic policies has shown the need to give high priority to this teaching task. Its critics have said that the bishops are usurping the proper role of the laity in the secular and, particularly, the political order.

It is Cardinal Bernardin's conviction that this is a mistaken criticism. He continues:

> In truth, the distinct teaching role of bishops in addressing the political order complements the indispensable role of the laity as participants in the political process. For that teaching role to be fullfilled, the character of the moral teaching must meet three requirements. First, it must be morally credible; that is, it must have the theoretical capacity to illuminate the human values and dimensions of political questions. Second, it must be empirically competent in its assessment of problems. Third, as noted above, it must lead toward specific recommendations and conclusions which are realizable.

The Church's direct engagement in the political order should be through lay people. Endowed with these capacities, Catholic lay men and women who enter the political process, whether by election or appointment, should have the encouragement of the bishops in undertaking this vocation. They must be addressed and treated as professionals in their sphere of competence. "It is the task of Catholic politicians, in cooperation with others of good will and a wide range of political coalitions" – adds the Cardinal – "to grapple with how the moral teaching should be joined with the concrete choices of the political order and the requirements of building public support for needed policies."

In the United States since the Council, the bishops have attempted to change the understanding of the Church as entirely separate from the world to its being an active agent in society. Moreover, individual Christians are becoming more aware of their responsibility to act as leaven in the world. Lay ministry, in this context, is seen both as service to the ecclesial community and as service and support for the lay vocation in the home, the workplace, and the public forum. Lay lectors and cantors, lay extraordinary ministers of the Eucharist, a vastly expanded corps of lay teachers in Catholic schools and religious education programs, lay editors of Catholic publications, lay people on parish councils and school boards, lay people in a host of Church-related roles – these realities, rare or nonexistent 30 years ago, are taken for granted today.

Although considerable progress has been made in the development of lay ministries within the Church, the great challenge in the United States is to help lay people become more aware of their vocation and mission in the world. They are to act as leaven in society, bringing gospel values and Church teaching to bear upon societal issues, as they build up the Kingdom in their home and workplace – in all they do.

The above reflections by Cardinal Bernardin bear the limitations of a particular national experience. Nevertheless, they may be useful in raising questions which pertain, *mutatis mutandis*, to the teaching and practice of the Church's life elsewhere.

22

Morality, Peace, and Nuclear War

In the following pages Cardinal Bernardin expresses his views on fundamental issues such as morality, peace, and nuclear war. Peace was God's eternal promise to mankind; nevertheless, we continue to face a world where the poor suffer injustice and oppression in a world of chaos. Anyway God continues to recreate, to reconcile, and to bring wholeness and peace to humankind through His Son's death and resurrection. Peace does not materialize, however, without human efforts; the desire for peace can be found in the hearts of all people. It is a gift that both challenges and inspires us to transform our world for the better. However, peace cannot exist where innocent are oppressed, human dignity is ignored, and life, from conception to natural death, is not viewed as sacred.

If peace is our goal, we must develop a keen sense of compassion and generosity toward the poor and those who live on the margin of society. Another constant threat to peace is nuclear war. Today the linkage between politics and war has been broken, and nuclear war threatens to destroy the very political values which once justified a resort to force. Present-day nuclear weapons can destroy the whole planet, and as a consequence, our ongoing goal must be the elimination of nuclear weapons.

We live in a time of anxiety and fear and also one of hope. With regards to this, Cardinal Bernardin underlines the Church's "Pastoral Letter on War and Peace" in which concern is expressed about the direction of the arms race, the role of

human rights in the United States, foreign policy, the United
States' posture on issues of international economic justice, and
U.S. policies in Latin America and in the Middle East. The let-
ter devotes over 30 pages to the challenge of constructing peace
in an increasingly interdependent world and emphasizes both
the threat and new moral dilemmas introduced with nuclear
weapons and nuclear strategy.

Cardinal Bernardin maintains the importance of the linkage be-tween morality, peace, and the many threats we are facing in the nuclear age, which represent the fundamental issues of our time. It is this principle that inspired the worldwide-known U.S. Catholic Bishops' pastoral letter "The Challenge of Peace: God's Promise and Our Response," which was published in May 1983 after three years of intensive work by an ad hoc committee chaired by Cardinal Bernardin.

The following text highlights the leading thoughts of the Cardinal on issues of war and peace in the nuclear age within the biblical perspective of peace. The description of the process used to develop the pastoral letter shows the deep responsibility and the courage of U.S. bishops, and espe-cially of Cardinal Bernardin, in addressing the main questions confronting us in the today's society.

Biblical Perspective of Peace

The Scriptures cannot give us detailed answers to specific questions we face today, but they provide us with an inspired vision of the world and humanity, as well as with guidance. They describe our world and human-kind in two contrasting ways: on the one hand, they envision the cosmos and all people as good – the world of order; on the other, they depict a broken, fragmented world of violence and hostility. We are destined to live in peace, and yet we are also doomed to live in a world very much like our own where the poor suffer injustice and oppression – the world of chaos.

The tension we find in the Bible is the same in which we find ourselves as believers. We live in both worlds each day. The people whom God inspired to write portrayed Him as a mighty leader in battle, but at the same time they longed constantly for peace. Peace was God's eternal promise to them, God's gift which flowed from their fidelity to the covenant. They learned that their quest for peace – for *shalom* – would be successful to the extent that they lived in right relationship with their environment, with one another, and with God. However, they also came to realize – from painful firsthand experience – that it is not easy for weak human beings to carry out the law and live in right relationships. They handed on many descriptions of the tragedy that results from breaking the covenant – estrangement, fragmentation, alienation. They also acknowledged that, of themselves, human beings can do nothing. Left to its own resources, humanity cannot realize its destiny of living in peace and harmony.

The Scriptures give witness to a loving God who continues to recreate, to reconcile, to bring wholeness and peace to humankind. The ultimate bad news may be the Tower of Babel where human beings are so totally alienated from one another that communication is no longer possible. But this is more than offset by the good news of Pentecost where languages are unscrambled so that we can once again listen to and understand one another. This is the word of God. Throughout the Scriptures we learn from God's promises and interventions that reconciliation and peace are first and foremost to the work of God and that He can accomplish whatever he promises. The concept of eschatological peace was proclaimed by the prophets. Basing their prophecies on the traditions of Israel – including God's promises to His people – they looked forward in faith and hope to a day when God's kingdom would be inaugurated and all people would live in justice and peace.

That kingdom has been definitively established by Jesus who has made peace through the blood of His cross. He came among us as a compassionate Shepherd, bringing healing and wholeness into human lives and relationships. He turned no one away from His ministry, not even those who disagreed with Him, and He even shared table fellowship with outcasts. He brought people to deeper levels of faith and wholeness within themselves, opened up new possibilities for building community, and led people into new and deeper relationships with God. He is the Lamb of God, victorious over the evil forces of chaos. Jesus proclaimed the coming of God's kingdom, challenging people to repentance. Those who heard Him had to change the way they lived – to live in accordance with God's reign and to prepare for its growth and expansion.

It is these readings that inspire the bishops to remind us that it is in Christ's resurrection that we have the clearest sign that God does, indeed, reign. Through His death and resurrection, Jesus gives God's peace to a broken, fragmented world. The Scriptures also make it clear that peace does not come about without human efforts. St. Paul tells us that "God has entrusted to us the ministry of reconciliation" (2 Cor 5:18); in the Sermon on the Mount, we learn that, in God's kingdom, peacemakers are truly blessed. The challenge of peace is also our response to God's promises.

Jesus clarified the intent and importance of the law when He highlighted two of its commands – love God, love your neighbor as you love yourself. In other words, love is the key to right relationships. The task of living justly, of making peace, is awesome and arduous. But it is also a possible mission to carry out because God continues to walk with us. He gives us all the resources we need to engage in this ministry. Jesus shares His Spirit with us, empowering us to continue His mission and ministry of setting things right, of making peace. We have much to do because the fullness of eschatological peace still lies before us in hope. Nonetheless, the gift of peace is already ours because of the reconciling, saving deeds of Jesus.

True Peace

The desire for peace is found in the hearts of all people; it is born in each of us. It is a gift given to each of us – a gift that challenges all of us to transform our world and to give it a new heart.

"Since wars begin in the minds of men, it is in the minds of men that the defences of peace must be constructed." Cardinal Bernardin borrows these words of the UNESCO Constitution to describe aptly the framework of peacemaking. Today we also recognize the role of the heart in making peace and accordingly the necessity to stimulate both heart and mind. True peace is more than the mere absence of war. There can be no peace, for example, when injustice oppresses innocent people. There is no real peace when the dignity of the human person is ignored or trampled upon. There is no peace when life, from conception to natural death, is not seen as sacred.

Moreover, people do not experience true peace when they live under the constant threat of destruction; nor is there peace when mothers and fathers hear the cries from their hungry children but have no food to give them. Peace cannot survive when mere survival leads people to desperation. Authentic peace can be found only when there is an acknowledgement that we are all God's children. It is rooted in the dignity and worth of each person. It is daily nourished by just and loving deeds. Peace demands that we acknowledge the rights of all people from conception to natural death. Unless we address all human rights issues with consistency, no right will be secure.

Receiving and nourishing this gift of peace is what life's journey is all about, and this journey takes us both inside and outside ourselves. It is, first of all, a journey within ourselves. This calls for a candid and honest evaluation of our attitudes and opinions; it demands a fresh approach, a new appraisal of things. But the search for peace also requires that we look beyond ourselves – to others. We are called to work for forgiveness and healing in our families and in our communities. If we really want to find peace, we must develop a keen sense of compassion and generosity toward the poor and those who live on the margin of society, in a highly interdependent world. True peace, therefore, leads us inward and outward. It is rooted in our hearts, but it must reach out to embrace all our brothers and sisters.

The Nuclear Danger

A quantitatively new characteristic of today's world has been the pervasive threat of nuclear war. The nuclear context of our age brings sharply into focus the problem of keeping the peace in an interdependent world governed by independent states.

For centuries nations have considered resort to force a tragic, but still necessary, means of defending basic interests and preserving key values. In the nuclear age, however, the linkage between politics and war has been broken. Nuclear war threatens to destroy the very political values which once justified resort to force.

More than 40 years ago the world became familiar with a new type of cloud. It rose over Hiroshima and three days later over Nagasaki, drawing worldwide attention to events described by Pope Paul VI as "butchery of untold magnitude." It is ultimately the manifestation of human intelligence and failure, the turning of human genius and creativity to the service of death.

Speaking at Hiroshima in 1981, Pope John Paul II alluded to this fact and specified the moral challenge of our age when he declared, "In the past, it was possible to destroy a village, a town, a region, even a country. Now it is the whole planet that has come under threat." A former U.S. General of the Army, Omar Bradley, summarized the global situation many years ago, on Armistice Day, 1948. He said:

> We have grasped the mystery of the atom and rejected the Sermon on the Mount. The world has achieved brilliance without conscience. Ours is a world of nuclear giants and ethical infants. We know more about war than we do about peace. We know more about killing than we do about living. The eerie brightness of the cloud which overshadowed Hiroshima four decades ago continues to this day. As Pope John Paul said: "To remember Hiroshima is to commit oneself to peace."

Thus our ongoing goal must be the elimination of nuclear weapons. We must emphasize the need for decisive political action to move world politics away from a fascination with the means of destruction, and toward a world order in which war will be consigned to history as a method of settling disputes. Our efforts must engage all the actors; they cannot be unilateral. These are the challenges which confront us and which must be addressed seriously by all who wish to build a peaceful world. We live in an age of danger but also of opportunity, a time of anxiety and fear, and, also, one of hope.

The Genesis of the Pastoral Letter on War and Peace

The decision to write a pastoral letter on the morality of war in the nuclear age was taken at the 1980 General Meeting of the U.S. National Conference of Catholic Bishops. The vote followed an extensive and wide-ranging discussion among the bishops, in which a number of them expressed concern about the direction of the arms race and a conviction that the Church had something valuable to say about the fate and future of the United States and the world.

One question that commentators inside and outside the Church often raise is why the bishops came to the decision to move into the public debate on war and peace in the 1980s. Behind this question there is usually a lurking suspicion that the decision was a narrowly political concern directed against one party or specific individuals. Such suspicion ignores, for example, the fact that the U.S. bishops' conference has been addressing a wide range of foreign policy issues for a number of years, including the role of human rights in U.S. foreign policy, the posture of the United States on issues of international economic justice, U.S. policy in Latin America and the Middle East, and, in a special way, the problem of the nuclear arms race.

In Cardinal Bernardin's view, three distinct forces were important in the 1980 decision to proceed with a pastoral letter. First, the U.S. bishops have been profoundly influenced by the teaching of recent popes on the issues of war and peace, particularly Pope John Paul II. This influence has been rooted first, in the intrinsic religious and moral power of the teaching itself, and second, in the particular pastoral responsibility the bishops feel in the United States to make the papal teaching applicable to the policies of what was then one of the two nuclear superpowers.

A second motivating force for the U.S. episcopacy has been its experience in opposing abortion in the United States. No institution in the country has been as vocal, as visible, or as persistent in its opposition to abortion as the Catholic bishops. On the one hand, this opposition has led the bishops to experience sustained involvement in a public policy debate at the center of U.S. political life. On the other hand, it has reinforced their opinion that there is a direct parallel between the protection of human life in the womb and the preservation of human life in the face of the nuclear threat. In both cases the bishops believe they have a pastoral responsibility to stand for the sanctity of life in the face of two menacing "signs of the times."

The third motivating force was a sense among many of the bishops that the nuclear arms race, in particular, was heading in an ever more dangerous direction, quantitatively and qualitatively, as we entered the 1980s. The bishops became convinced that a clear moral voice was needed in the United States calling for a drastic change in the nation's definitions of security. Thus, the bishops began the preparation of the pastoral letter.

The first step was the appointment of a special committee to draft the letter for consideration by all the bishops. This committee, of which Cardinal Bernardin was chairman, began its work in July, 1981, and met at least monthly and often weekly for two years, completing its task at a specially convened meeting of the bishop's conference in Chicago on May 2–3, 1983.

Two particular aspects of the drafting of the pastoral letter should be noted: the hearings the bishop held and the circulation of three drafts of the document to the general public. During the hearings, testimony was received from 35 witnesses who represented a great diversity of expertise and a broad spectrum of view on the moral and strategic questions of the nuclear age. The hearings were very valuable to the committee, for they immersed the bishops in the political, strategic, and moral debate. These personal witnesses gave a very profound and wide-ranging sense of the complexity, the danger, and the urgency of the present phase of the arms race.

While this extensive process of hearings was in progress, the committee was both shaping its views and beginning to write the first draft of the letter, which was completed in May, 1982, and circulated the following month. The first draft generated over 700 pages of written commentary, and the bishops found it necessary to revise the writing schedule, postponing a final vote on the document until the spring of 1983, so that they could give the responses adequate attention. The public response to all three drafts of the letter was extraordinarily helpful to the committee. The second draft, which took all the comments into serious consideration, was ready for circulation in October, 1982. It expanded the scriptural and theological sections of the document and criticized more sharply the direction of the arms race and U.S. nuclear policy. It was reviewed and discussed in detail at the bishop's General Meeting in November, 1982, which was open to the press. This meeting had a decisive influence on the development of the third draft.

During the November 1982 meeting, the Reagan Administration sent an extensive commentary on the second draft to every bishop. Many commentators attributed the changes from the second to the third draft to the very critical response made by the Administration. Yet, a careful reading of both drafts show that the decisive influences on the changes were episcopal, not political.

It was, however, the views of the bishops and the discussion which took place at a consultation held by the Holy See in January 1983 that had the really decisive impact on the third draft. The third draft, made public in April 1983, was sent to the U.S. bishops as the working document for the special General Meeting in May 1983. The public commentary emphasized the differences between the second and third drafts, but it vastly overstated the degree of difference, often by concentrating on symbolic words rather than the main substantive arguments in the third draft. Prior to the Chicago meeting, the bishops submitted over 400 amendments, which the committee had to review and take a position on when presenting the document for adoption. During the two days in Chicago, the bishops considered, through a disciplined and complex parliamentary process, the 400 previously submitted amendaments and some additional ones which were presented during the course of the meeting itself. Then, by a vote of 238 to 9, a final text, which reasserted a sharp detailed critique of the nuclear arms race and the prevailing policies driving the race, was approved.

The Framework of Moral Principle and Essential Meaning of the Pastoral Letter

The pastoral letter, "The Challenge of Peace," builds upon the biblical foundation and expands upon the moral teaching of the Church which derives from it.

The letter devotes over 30 pages to the challenge of constructing peace in an increasingly interdependent world. The political and moral challenge it poses for world politics may be its most significant long-term teaching. It shows why the nuclear issue does not exhaust the challenges of the moment; issues of human rights, economic justice, and respect for the rights of all nations, great and small, are unfinished tasks in the daily business of world affairs today.

The urgent need to build peace does not, however, dispense with the constant effort required to prevent any use of nuclear weapons and to limit other uses of force in international relations. It is this section of the letter which has attracted the most attention – the policy section containing an analysis of the moral problems related to the use of nuclear weapons and the strategy of nuclear deterrence.

The argument of the letter must be understood in the context of Catholic teaching. Its premise is that nuclear weapons and nuclear strategy constitute a qualitatively new moral problem. The nuclear age is not simply an extension of the moral questions on warfare addressed by our ancestors. Albert Einstein, one of the fathers of the nuclear age, said that everything is changed except the way we think. The bishops experienced the meaning of this statement as they struggled with nuclear issues in the development of the pastoral letter. The nuclear era poses a profound – indeed, a revolutionary – challenge. The extreme skepticism of the letter regarding the ability to control any use of nuclear weapons is a pervasive influence throughout the policy analysis of use and deterrence.

The first case is "counter-population" warfare – directly intended attacks on civilian centers qualifies as murder in Catholic moral theology. It is not justified even in retaliation for an attack on one's cities, and no exceptions of the principle are admitted.

The second case is the "initiation of nuclear war." The letter opposes it in these words: "We do not perceive any situation in which the deliberate initiation of nuclear warfare, on however restricted a scale, can be morally justified. Non-nuclear attacks by another state must be resisted by other than nuclear means." The letter explicitly acknowledges that it will take time to implement such a policy, and it also acknowledges certain objections to a "no first use" pledge.

The third case, that of "limited nuclear war," involves an assessment of what the real as opposed to the theoretical meaning of "limited" is. Taking into account the long debate – both strategic and moral – which surrounds this question, the letter argues that the entire burden of proof rests on those who would hold that limited nuclear exchange can indeed be contained within moral limits. The judgement is based on Pope John Paul II's statement to the United Nations in June 1982. The committee took the Holy Father's judgement and applied it to the specific details of U.S. strategic policy. Such an application, of course, is done in the bishops' name. They used the term "strictly conditioned" with reference to deterrence in order to stress that deterrence must be seen as a transitional strategy. The letter seeks to keep deterrence limited to a very specific function. Extending it to war-fighting strategies and a clear fire-break between conventional and nuclear weapons is called for. Finally, the bishops mandate an aggressive pursuit of arms control and disarmament objectives, including a halt to the testing, production, and deployment of nuclear systems.

23

Pornography and Obscenity

A Threat for the Dignity of the Human Person

The impact of pornography on society is progressively increasing. Its effects are threatening life by eroding and destroying the dignity of the human person. The tragic message of pornography, especially when directed towards children, is that people exist for the sexual satisfaction of others. Catholic social doctrine cannot accept this, especially because it disregards fundamental truths about the human person that say human life is sacred and has social value.

Cardinal Bernardin calls us to remember that God has made us in His own image and likeness. Therefore, as a violation of human dignity and a debasement of the human person, pornography is equally a debasement of God. We have the duty to protect human life in all circumstances and at all stages of its development. We are exhorted to face the fact that life-diminishing issues – such as prostitution, pornography, sexism and racism – can become life-threatening and easily lead to violence. Human life is diminished when people, especially children, are exploited to produce pornography.

Violence, degradation, and humiliation are simply not compat-
ible with the true sexual nature of the human being. We need
strong strategies to check the rampant pornography. We need to
understand what laws can prohibit and where morality is neces-
sary. A well-reasoned approach to the problem is needed to
strike a balance between freedom and to restrain uncritical ap-
proaches that run the risk of grossly oversimplifying the prob-
lem. We need to stress that human values consist in more than
physical attractiveness. For example, the value of actors, writers
and film makers is greater than their ability to meet particular
demands of their audience. An integral vision of human sexual-
ity is a gift we can offer our sex-saturated society.

Today, there are many opportunities for people of all ages, from children to the elderly, to view pornography. There are many forms of it, from the printed page to films, and it is abundantly available. In the United States alone, it is more than a $10 billion a year business. Many parents rightly worry about the many, uncontrolled occasions which, in effect, turn their children into prisoners of pornography which has crossed all boundaries. Pornography – together with widespread obscenity and indecency – impacts the whole of society in progressive, alarming life-threatening and life-diminishing ways, eroding and destroying the dignity of the human person.

What is pornography? This is Cardinal Bernardin's definition: "By pornography I mean illegal material that links sex and violence as appropriate partners in human intimacy, that portrays children as suitable sexual partners, that characterizes women as playthings for the sexual whims of others, or that warps men's attitudes toward sexuality and women, thereby undermining the family and our society." He emphasizes his own dismay at the reality and the extent of hard-core and child pornography. Hard-core and child pornography go far beyond the titillation of certain popular magazines. By definition, hard-core pornography features sexual violence – scenes of slavery and torture, portrayals of degradation as sexually exciting, the lie that women welcome rape. The basic message in such pornography is that people (usually women) exist for the sexual satisfaction of others (usually men).

To this we must add the frequent, serious, and tragic cases of child pornography, which depicts children in sexual relationships with one another or with adults. This form of pornography victimizes the children who are photographed or filmed as well as other children who, by accident or cruel intent, are exposed to such material. Pornography, obscenity, and indecency portray a degenerating picture of human dignity. Catholic social doctrine can by no means accept it, especially because it disregards the two fundamental truths about the human person – that human life is sacred and social.

Human, social, moral, religious and legal values, as well as the principle of liberty, must be linked in developing a united front against pornography – in order to protect the human dignity of the individual and the values of society as a whole.

The Dignity of the Human Person

In the October 16, 1987, issue of *The New World*, the archdiocesan newspaper, Cardinal Bernardin published an open letter to the people of the Archdiocese, inviting them to join him in working against pornography. He wrote: "My personal concern about pornography is consistent with other concerns about human dignity and sexual intimacy. Pornography is a moral issue precisely because it violates human dignity." Men are desensitized, women are dehumanized, and children are victimized in both its creation and its consumption. Pornography, then is one issue in a continuum of concerns about human dignity and intimate, joyful sexuality at the service of human love and creativity.

As Cardinal Bernardin points out, the Christian vision of responsible and playful, creative and affirming, self-transcending and mutually-giving sexuality is one against which we must measure the impulses of our times – from sexuality as an advertising "come-on" to promiscuity as an evening's casual entertainment.

As the Cardinal notes, the standards we Christians choose to live by are to be more respectful of ourselves and others than the minimums set by civil law. Nonetheless, on hard-core and child pornography the standards of civil law are very clear – such materials are illegal as well as immoral.

This constitutes an unquestionable condemnation of pornography – an attitude derived from the Cardinal's deep concern to preserve the fundamental values of human dignity, which are based on and encouraged by Catholic doctrine. In dealing with such delicate and serious issues from a Catholic point of view, Cardinal Bernardin looks back at the very first chapter of Genesis, which states unequivocally that humanity represents the summit of the creative process. The Creator places all creation in our hands, giving us the awesome responsibility of stewardship over the earth's resources, including the gift of each human life. There is more to the human story: God makes each human person in his own image and likeness – not exactly a carbon copy, but, at least, a close resemblance. The person is the clearest reflection of the presence of God among us. To lay violent hands on the person is to come as close as we can to laying violent hands on God. To diminish the human person is to come as close as we can to diminishing God. Human dignity derives both from the creative act of God and from the constant care and concern that God shows toward all people.

The Cardinal insists that this is the truth about the human person, a truth that makes us free. Unfortunately, there are many individuals, institutions, and systems in contemporary life which propagate as freedom what, in reality, is slavery. True human freedom is not illusory or superficial; it is found only when we face the truth about human life – the inherent dignity of each human being in all aspects and dimensions, including sexuality.

It is because the Catholic social doctrine esteems human life as sacred, emphasizes the Cardinal, that we have a duty to protect and foster it at all stages of development, from conception to death, and in all its circumstances. "Furthermore, it is precisely because we acknowledge that human life is also social," he adds, that "we must develop the kind of societal environment that protects and fosters its development."

As we can clearly see, his position leads to the conclusion that the mere statement that human life is sacred is clearly inadequate. It is also necessary to examine and respond to the challenges to the unique dignity and sacredness of human life today. Human life has always been sacred, and there have always been threats to it. However, we live in a time in history when we have produced, sometimes with the best of intentions, a technology and a capacity to threaten and diminish human life which previous generations could not even imagine.

Now, there are life-threatening issues such as genetic engineering, abortion, capital punishment, modern warfare, and euthanasia. These are all assaults on life which cannot be collapsed into one problem; they are all distinct, enormously complicated, and deserving of individual treatment. Yet, while no single answer and no simple response will solve them, they must be confronted nevertheless as pieces of a larger pattern. That is why, since 1983, Cardinal Bernardin has frequently argued for the need to develop a "consistent ethic of life." This seeks to build a bridge of common interest and common insight on a range of social and moral questions. Successful resolution of any of these issues is dependent upon the broader attitude within society regarding overall respect for life. Attitude is the place to root a consistent ethic of life. A change of attitude, in turn, can lead to a change of policies and practices in society.

We could sum up Cardinal Bernardin's teaching by saying that, when human life under any circumstance is not held as sacred in a society, all human life in that society is threatened. When it is held as sacred in all circumstances, all human life is protected.

Analyzing life-diminishing issues, such as prostitution, pornography, sexism, and racism, the Cardinal reminds us again, that each is a distinct problem, enormously complex, worthy of individual attention and action. Nonetheless, understanding that they all contribute in some way to a diminishment of human dignity provides a theological foundation for more specific reflection and concrete action. At the same time, he exhorts us to face the fact that life-diminishing issues can become life-threatening. News reports frequently chronicle how prostitution, pornography, sexism, and racism can all too easily lead to violence and death. With regard to pornography, psychological research appears to confirm this assertion. We can say then that, when human life is diminished in any circumstance in a society, it contributes to the devaluing of all human life in that society.

Each human person is a paradox. Each of us has the capacity to seek and express what is true, good, and beautiful. Each of us also has the potential for embracing what is false, evil, and ugly. We can love, and we can hate. We can serve, and we can dominate. We can respect, and we can diminish. We can protect human life, and we can threaten it. We should remember that, when the Cardinal says "we," he does not mean simply each of us acting on his or her own. He also includes local communities, the whole nation, the entire society; every social system – east or west, north or south – should be judged by the way in which it reverences, or fails to reverence, the unique and equal dignity of every person.

In addition, our concern is not simply individual human rights but also the common good. Individual rights are to contribute to the good of society, not infringe upon other people's legitimate rights. Human life is diminished when women or men, and especially children, are exploited in the production of pornography, whether in print, film, or television. A sacrilegious note is added when the sacred persons and symbols of religion are exploited. Diminishment of human dignity also occurs in the lives of those who purchase or use pornography. Even more serious diminishment can occur because pornography is not so much an outlet for the baser instincts of the human person, as it is a stimulant. Violence, degradation, and humilation are simply not compatible with the true sexual nature of the human person.

It is relatively easy to make a case against certain kinds of sexual propaganda as corruptive of human freedom and dignity. They destroy or diminish rational freedom either by damaging the capacity for personal reflection or by exciting the passions to the extent where they interfere with rational control of thought and behavior. They diminish human dignity by reducing human persons to sex objects.

The Cardinal's argumentation on this grave problem does not stop here. His thoughts are broad and take into account all aspects of the issue. For instance, he observes that we must acknowledge that pornography, like prostitution, seems to have a permanent attraction for some people, despite the fact that it perversely and sometimes viciously profanes the sacredness of sex and the dignity of the human person.

Addressing the question of sexual propaganda, he points out that it is on the threshhold of the problem of social freedom, an issue that is as complex as it is essential. Yet, the awareness of these complexities does not stop him from reiterating the need for persistence in working against pornography. Bernardin exhorts us in these terms: "let us be stubborn . . . we may not eradicate pornography everywhere and forever, but we can be the crucial difference in the lives of families and individuals and local communities."

The Shaping of Strategies for Action

In striving to shape strategies for action, three issues are worth considering: a) the distinction between morality and law, b) the importance of striking a balance between freedom and restraint in society, and c) the necessity of being faithful to our vision and values in whatever response we make to obscenity, pornography, and indecency in our society. This is how the Cardinal addresses the three issues.

a. *The Distinction Between Moral Principles and Law*. Morality and law are clearly related but also need to be differentiated. Although the premises of law are found in moral principles, the scope of law is more limited and its purpose is not the moralization of society. Moral principles govern personal and social human conduct and cover as well interior acts and motivation. Civil statutes govern public order and concern only external acts and values that are formally social. It would seem, therefore, that, when we pursue a legal course of action with regard to such matters as sexual morality, our expectations may have to be somewhat more limited than in other areas of human morality.

b. *Striking a Balance Between Freedom and Restraint*. In 1970, a U.S. governmental commission concluded that pornography had no harmful consequences and should be free of any public restrictions. That governmental stance gave police and court officials the message that enforcement and prosecution of obscenity laws were, at best, low priorities. As a consequence, the pornography industry grew. But the Cardinal observes that public concern is also increasing: "We are becoming increasingly sensitive to its [pornography's] degradation of women and men, abuse of children, exploration of the immature, and threat to our Judaeo-Christian understanding of human intimacy and family stability."

Cardinal Bernardin encourages us to search for ways to strike a balance between freedom and restraint in society. This is especially important when the restraint in question involves the area of communication, such as sexual propaganda. In this case, we need to ask ourselves whether the corruption of human freedom is such that it requires attention by organized society. Assuming that public order is the norm whose requirements are to be enforced in this attending to corruptive influences, we have to ask what requirements of public order can be applied validly against the claims of freedom. In fact, we may be taking the risk of damaging freedom in a third domain with the consequences more dangerous to the community. This is an important aspect of Bernardin's thought, and we must be careful. As the recipients of the Judaeo-Christian heritage, we do not condemn every portrayal of vice. As a matter of fact, not infrequently the Bible itself portrays vice and violence; its authors did not avoid depicting the most vicious and violent components of human behavior. Similarly, as Richard Griffiths has pointed out, "a refusal to experience art that often deals with eroticism and violence may be a refusal to face the world as it really is." These observations lead to the conclusion that an attitude of confrontation, when human life and dignity are threatened or diminished, is required.

This does not mean that some pornography is legitimate. It means that we need a well-reasoned approach to the problems we are addressing with the express purpose of striking a balance between freedom and restraint. Only then will we find the broad base of support needed for effective action in the legal sphere. We may not find a simple formula that is applicable to all cases and similar for all segments of society. An uncritical approach runs the risk of grossly oversimplifying the problem; this is inappropriate, given the importance of our primary concern – the worth and dignity of the human person.

Having made these comments about the care with which we must proceed in addressing the problem of obscenity, pornography, and indecency in a society like the United States, the Cardinal emphasizes the need to reaffirm the urgency of the challenge and to face up to it creatively and decisively. His position is clear about the need to take legal action against these corruptive influences in society.

c.   *Fidelity to Vision and Values*. Christian witness includes fidelity to the Catholic vision and values as Catholics carry out their social ministry. Pornography is primarily directed at the weaker members of our society: the immature and the inadequate, frequently children and teenagers. The biblical tradition calls us to defend the rights of the weaker members of society – today's widows, orphans, and resident aliens – who too easily can become the object of oppression, degradation, and de-valuing. The Scriptures also tell us that it is a serious matter indeed to lead the little ones astray. Here are Cardinal Bernardin's words:

> Fidelity to our mission means that we have to be careful that we do not contribute to the diminishment or devaluation of human persons as we combat the corruptive influence of obscenity, pornography, and indecency. Fidelity to our mission means not isolating these problems from other life-threatening or life-diminishing issues in the sense of neglecting anything that threatens human life or diminishes human dignity.

In a further reflection he adds that it is important that we portray beauty and not simply unmask ugliness. It is essential that we promote the truth of human dignity and freedom and not simply attack falsity and illusions. In a consumer-oriented society, we need to remind each person that our worth derives from who we are, rather than what we own. In a society that prizes individualism, we need to promote the common good as well. In a society that is preoccupied with sexuality, we need to stress that human value consists of more than physical attractiveness, that the value of actors and writers and film makers is more than their ability to meet particular public demands. An integral vision of human sexuality is one of the gifts we can offer our sex-saturated society.

Unfortunately, there are many influences in society that seek to corrupt human life and cheapen human dignity. These are complex matters that do not allow for simple solutions. However, the Cardinal is convinced that, by thinking and reflecting and deliberating together, we can arrive at solutions which will improve the societal environment in which we seek to protect and foster human life and dignity in all of its circumstances and in all its stages of development.

24

Vatican II

A Change Rooted in Continuity
Preparing for the Third Millennium

Twenty years after the Second Vatican Council, an extraordinary Synod of Bishops invited the Church to reflect upon the elapsed twenty years. Renewal and reform were the themes analyzed. To-day the Church, as an institution and as a community of faith, is starting a post-counciliar process, to engage the modern world in a dialogue about major social and intellectual questions of the day. The event of the Council follows the law of development in Catho-lic thought, that is, "the grow-ing edge of tradition," but it is a change rooted in continuity.

The principle and practice of collegiality is fundamental to the life of the Church. It can be explained as the collaborative relationship of the Pope with the bishops in teaching and ruling the Church. The Supreme Pontiff, together with the bishops, has supreme and full authority over the universal Church. Of course, a collegial style has several consequences in Catholic policy. First of all, it involves a decentralization of the decisionmaking process. Subsequently it demands an engagement of many people in positions of responsibil-ity within the Church. The Church needs ecclesiastical changes and reform. Relationship with Protestant churches and other relig-ious communities must be increased. Vatican II, with its themes of renewal and reform, has opened a new chapter of dialogue be-tween the Church and contemporary culture. It has ascribed to the Church the task of protecting human rights and fostering peace in

a nuclear age. Two important aspects brought along by Vatican II are
the role of laity in the Church and the renewal of religious life. The
role of laity received its strongest theological affirmation at the Coun-
cil. The meetings of bishops and religious people are another aspect
of the renewal of religious life. This ongoing dialogue can have an
important impact on the Church's ministry and service, and on
society.

To commemorate the closing of the Second Vatican Council (1962–1965), Pope John Paul II called an Extraordinary Synod of Bishops (November 24–December 8, 1985) as an invitation for the whole Church to reflect upon and evaluate the previous twenty years. In his announcement of the Synod designed to evaluate the results of the Council, the Pope said that, "Vatican II . . . is a constant referent of all my pastoral actions." In his first encyclical, *Redemptor Hominis*, the Holy Father encouraged the Church to think of the future in terms of the third millennium of Christianity.

Cardinal Bernardin emphasizes the potential of the new "collegial style," which the Church, as an institution and as a community of faith, is assuming in the post-conciliar process. In the Catholic tradition, the life of faith and the life of the mind are complementary. Faith goes beyond reason, but it never contradicts it. This relationship of faith and reason exists in the personal life of every believer, but it also must take on institutional form. Catholic institutions exist to provide living witness to the complementary character of faith and reason, and to provide a living example of how the Church seeks to engage the modern world in dialogue about the major social and intellectual questions of the day.

Vatican II: An Interpretation of the Event

Ecumenical councils are powerful events in the life of the Church. In its 2,000 year history only a few generations of Christians have experienced such an event, but every generation has been shaped by the twenty ecumenical councils. Cardinal Bernardin emphasizes the importance of interpreting the conciliar event, evaluating its theological content, and recognizing that the implementation of the Council, as complex and even a bit untidy as it may have been, is still a blessing. The event of the Council, he observes, follows the law of development in Catholic thought – that is, the dynamic which Father John Courtney Murray, S.J., used to call "the growing edge of tradition." The Catholic style admits of change – indeed, requires change – but it is change rooted in continuity; and Vatican II was a surprise but not an aberration from the law of development.

The movements (in the field of liturgy, ecumenism, and social action) and the authors (Congar, de Lubac, Chenu, Murray, and Rahner) which prepared for the council had been in the Church before 1960, but not at the center of attention. They had lived on the growing edge, saying and doing things which fascinated some, but made others uncomfortable or even hostile. In light of the history of these movements and authors, Vatican II's significance is not that it said entirely new things, but that it took these ideas from the edge of the Church's life and located them in the center. Precisely because it followed the law of continuity and change, Vatican II was an event which summarized a previous process of development, becoming at the same time the starting point for a new process of growth. Once the growing edge had been taken into the center of Catholic thought, it was time for new growth at the edge. Therefore, Bernardin insists, the teaching of Vatican II did not break with Catholic tradition, but it has profoundly reshaped Catholic thinking and practice, as well as the Church's relationships with other institutions and communities. In particular, it has affected three dimensions of Church life: its polity, its self-perception, and, significantly, its posture in the world.

A "Collegial Style"

Catholic polity – the internal governance of the Church – has been most decisively affected by the principle and practice of collegiality. Strictly speaking, the principle applies to the role of the episcopal college in the Church, and particularly to the relationship of the Pope and the bishops in their responsibility for the universal Church. Vatican II defines collegiality in a key passage of its *Dogmatic Constitution on the Church* as follows:

> Just as, in accordance with the Lord's decree, St. Peter and the rest of the Apostles constitute a unique apostolic college, so in like fashion the Roman Pontiff, Peter's successor, and the bishops, the successors of the apostles, are related with and united to one another . . . Together with their head, the Supreme Pontiff, and never apart from him, they (the bishops) have supreme and full authority over the universal Church; but this power cannot be exercised without the agreement of the Roman Pontiff.

Collegiality – highlights Bernardin – calls attention to the collaborative relationship of the Pope and bishops in teaching and governing the Church. This reality, which goes back to the very founding of the Church, was brought into contemporary prominence by Vatican II. Since then, a number of institutions have been created to put collegiality into practice. These include the Synod of Bishops and the national conferences of bishops; a "collegial style" of ministry now influences national episcopal conferences, dioceses, and parishes.

This style has several distinct consequences in Catholic polity: it involves a decentralization of decisionmaking, an engagement of a wider circle of people – bishops, clergy, religious, and laity – in positions of responsibility on the Church, and a recognition of the diverse charisms needed to carry out the Church's ministry. To understand the scope and significance of the collegial principle requires not only a reading of *The Dogmatic Constitution on the Church*, but also *The Decree on the Laity and The Decree on the Pastoral Office of the Bishops*.

A New Way of Perception

A second consequence of the Council has been a shift in the way the Church perceives itself, again, a shift of degree within a predefined Catholic framework. Cardinal Bernardin notes how it involves the use of metaphors which were not at the center of Catholic thinking at the Councils of Trent or Vatican I. The Vatican II shift of perspective is perhaps best illustrated in the now famous example of placing the chapter on "The People of God" before the chapter on "The Hierarchy" in *The Dogmatic Constitution on the Church*; or the description of the Church as a "pilgrim people," with its implied notion of the need for ecclesiastical change and reform. The reemergence of these themes was critically important as a basis for improving the relationship with Protestant churches, with other faith communities, and with the world. The acceptance of shared responsibility for the events leading to the Reformation, the concept of a Church which both learns from and teaches the world, and the explicit acknowledgement of God's saving action in other ecclesial and faith communities all testify to the impact of the Council on the self-perception of the Church.

A New Approach to the World

Changes both in polity and perception are consequences of the Council which primarily affect the internal life of the Church. A third result has been the posture of the Church in the world. In terms of theological principles, Catholicism has always affirmed a positive relationship between the Church and the world. But much of the post-Reformation and post-Enlightenment ecclesial policy placed the Church in direct opposition to major currents of change. On the contrary, in its *Pastoral Constitution on the Church in the Modern World*, Vatican II established a position for the Church in the world which has had striking consequences in the last twenty and more years. It opened a new chapter of dialogue between the Church and contemporary culture, and it ascribed to the whole Church the task of protecting human dignity, promoting human rights, and fostering the spirit and substance of peace in the nuclear age.

The involvement of the Catholic Church today from Washington to Warsaw, from Soweto to Sao Paolo, in precisely these questions is impossible to explain – emphasizes Bernardin – outside the posture set by Vatican II. But he also emphasizes that these developments were changes rooted in continuity with the past: Vatican II adapted Church thinking and practice to contemporary needs, while remaining faithful to our heritage.

The Post-Conciliar Process: An Evaluation

Interpreting the meaning of Vatican II is not simple: not only are we too close in time to the process to gain a balanced perspective, but we are also intimately and intensely involved in what we are evaluating. Two models were set forth, at the time of the Council itself, to describe the post-conciliar challenge. Each model tells us something about what has occurred since 1965, but neither explains everything.

Renewal and Reform

The first description of the post-conciliar period was that of Pope Paul VI in his closing address to the Council. Essentially, the address predicted a process of orderly change in the Church. The dynamic of the model would be to share with the Church as a whole the spirit and substance of what occurred in the Council. In a sense, Bernardin suggests, it was a "trickle-down" description of change.

Six months after the Council ended, Father John Courtney Murray, S.J., proposed a more complex description of the post-conciliar process. He pointed out that the themes of the Council were "renewal and reform," but our understanding of these terms is often too simple. Renewal is an intellectual notion; it means designing and projecting a vision for the Church, the kind of design reflected in the conciliar documents. Reform, in contrast, refers to changing an institution. Its atmosphere is less serene than that surrounding renewal. The dynamic of the post-conciliar reform, argued Murray, will be the tension between renewal and reform. The tension will exist because our vision of renewal will inevitably be larger and clearer than our ability to reshape institutions in order to meet the design of a renewed theology.

Both orderly change and the tension between renewal and reform have been present in the post-conciliar period. The liturgical changes, for example, fit the notion of orderly change. Without saying that the renewal of liturgical practice has always been peaceful or devoid of disagreement, Bernardin sees a comprehensive reshaping of the Church's sacramental practice and a substantial broadening of access to liturgical ministry for both men and women. There are other examples of orderly changes, but two of the more interesting ones are the role of the laity in the Church and the renewal of religious life.

The lay role in the Church received its strongest theological affirmation at Vatican II. It is a fascinating exercise to pick up Yves Congar's work, *Lay People in the Church*, and to see how both *The Dogmatic Constitution on the Church and The Decree on the Laity* reflect – perhaps even surpass – Congar's hopes of the 1940s. And yet Bernardin does not believe we have as yet created the structures within the Church, nationally or even at the diocesan level, to meet the potential which full-scale lay involvement holds for the Church. This is especially true with regard to the contribution of women. Neither have we yet provided a framework and support system to realize the potential of lay Catholic witness in the larger society. While vigorously fostering and supporting the ministries of lay people, we must at the same time give greater visibility to the truth that all members of the Church have an authentic vocation to apostolate. "We are on the way," Bernardin says, "but the full potential of renewal lies ahead of us."

A New Dialogue with Religious

The renewal of religious life in the United States has been one of the most visible realities of the post-conciliar era. Most religious communities have systematically undertaken and enthusiastically pursued the efforts at renewal and reform. The meetings of bishops and religious, which have occurred in this post-conciliar period as a consequence of the study of religious life initiated by the Holy See have given many bishops a more specific sense of how much has been done in this regard by women and men religious. This ongoing dialogue represents a new dimension in the relationship between bishops and religious. The dialogue promises to be mutually beneficial and can have an important impact on the Church's ministry and service to the larger society.

Now that the constitutions of many religious communities have been reshaped as a result of the processes of renewal and reform, the challenge of the moment is to evaluate what has been accomplished, in order to determine what has truly contributed to the renewal of religious life, and to arrive at a consensus in the broader Church as to the wisdom of the changes made. The ongoing dialogue between religious and bishops provides an appropriate forum in which the positive experience that the renewal of religious life has been for the Church can be brought into clearer focus, as well as those elements which may continue to be problematic. This, in turn, must also be communicated to the universal Church. Neither of these examples is a finished story, says Bernardin; each of them will continue to develop. But the mix of orderly change and the unfinished work of renewal which awaits reform provides a snapshot of the implemantation of the Council in the United States and in other parts of the world.

A Church Situated Within U.S. Culture

*Cardinal Bernardin has often reflected on the relationship be-
tween the Church and the social reality within the United
States. The United States is a nation with a great diversity of
races, religions, and customs. Issues such as AIDS and contraception have caused a number of social tensions. In the past
years Americans grew to believe that the Pope was displeased
with the American Catholic Church. There are many disagreements and tensions in the American Church and the last papal visit could not put an end to every conflict.*

*Joseph Bernardin points out that the American Church boasts
millions of Catholics, and that Catholics support a vast network of church-related institutions and socially helpful programs such as schools and hospitals. Pope John Paul II's
attention to the United States is a sign of the importance of
the Church in the United States. The American church must
maintain positive relations and dialogue with the Holy Father.
Bishops must believe that the Pope is the pastor of the universal Church and that he does have the right and the duty to
oversee the Church's ministry everywhere.*

*In the United States, people feel free to criticize everything,
and many people react negatively when they are told what to
do. Today the main question remains of how to maintain the
unity while affirming the diversity in the local realizations of
the Church, namely how to discern a proper balance between
freedom and order. At times, genuine dialogue between the*

Holy See and some members of the U.S. Church is indeed diffi-
cult. For Joseph Bernardin, it is extremely important that the
whole Church must trust in the promise of a risen Christ to be
present with His Church. It is necessary to speak in complete
candor and without fear. In a mutual exchange, it is possible to
discern what will truly enhance the Church's unity and what
will weaken or destroy it. In conclusion, we must continue to
grow in appreciation of the conciliar vision of collegiality, both
as a principle and a style of leadership in the Church.

I n his role as Archbishop of Chicago, Cardinal Bernardin has reflected upon the specificity of the U.S. social reality and its relation to the universality of the Catholic Church. This is an historical question that the Holy See has faced for many years in its relationship with the numerous local realities in which the Church exists. The conciliar documents, The Pastoral Constitution on the Church in the Modern World (*Gaudium et Spes*) and The Dogmatic Constitution on the Church (*Lumen Gentium*), for example, explicitly address the "Tasks of Individual Faithful and Specific Churches."

A World of Diversities

The U.S. is characterized by the presence of people belonging to a great diversity of races, ethnicities, religions, and customs. After centuries of immigration, the country is made up of very diverse people. Recently, Pope John Paul II has directed his attention to the specific situations that have risen in U.S. society because of this condition. Moreover, issues such as AIDS and contraception have caused a number of social tensions in America.

People from various quarters have intimated that the Holy Father was displeased with the Church in the United States, that he felt the U.S. bishops, while good men, are too permissive, that he was beginning to mandate remedial action for perceived problems and abuses. Cardinal Bernardin gave all this a good deal of thought and was more than a little troubled by it. In 1987, the Holy Father made his second pastoral visit to the country, and, on September 16, in Los Angeles, Cardinal Bernardin spoke to the Pope on behalf of all the U.S. bishops, addressing the particular situation of the country. His presentation, "The Relationship of the Universal Church and the Particular Churches" provided the best contribution to create a new atmosphere for understanding and collaboration on various levels.

At the same time, the Cardinal did not avoid the many disagreements and tensions in the U.S. Church – between some Catholics and the Holy See, between others and their own bishop, and among various formal and informal groups of Catholics. In *The Chicago Catholic*, the archdiocesan newspaper, (September 4, 1987), reflecting on the papal visit in the United

States, he wrote: "It would be naive to imagine that the Holy Father's presence among us will put an end to every conflict or resolve every tension. Nevertheless, it is important to remember that in the Catholic Church the papacy is an important – indeed, indispensable – principle of unity."

The Cardinal faces such problems with serenity and trust, declaring that "This has been – and remains – an extraordinary period in history." In fact, he notes that the rate of religious practice among the 53 million or more Catholics in the United States is commendably high; that the Catholics support a vast network of church-related institutions and programs – schools, hospitals and much else – which serve not only their own needs but also the needs of society at large. Furthermore, he observes that there has been a flowering of vocations to the restored permanent diaconate as well as a notable expansion of lay involvement in church-related activities. And finally he concludes, "most would say that there is a lot that's healthy and dynamic about the Church in this country, and there are many reasons for hopefulness about the future." (March 1988).

And yet, his positive view does not obscure the negative side of this reality. In a note to Bishop James Malone of Youngstown, Ohio, a former president of the National Conference of Catholic Bishops, he acknowledges a substantial amount of internal conflict within the U.S. Catholic community:

> "Some has been healthy – a refreshing exchange of views among people who care intensely about their religious heritage. But some has weakened the conceptual and functional unity of the Catholic community."

A Spiritual Reawakening: Great Promise for the Future

Cardinal Bernardin examines the problems in the U.S. more thoroughly and observes that "for a long time . . . it has been customary to sing the praises of pluralism in the Church. But pluralism often means polarization and disregard of essentials. Moreover, one must not forget that the cultural assimilation of U.S. Catholics has taken place in the last 25 years. Therefore, assimilation has conferred many socioeconomic benefits on Catholics at the price of imposing on them the dominant secular culture."

As a consequence, dissent has seemed to supply a rationale for accepting the moral revolution urged upon Catholics by the secular culture into which they were being assimilated. The situation today is marked by some confusion over what it means to be a Catholic in the United States. The Cardinal states emphatically his hope for the Church in the U.S., saying that "a spiritual reawakening is taking place whose dynamism holds great promise for the future." He does not think – as some maintain – that the

Pope is really displeased with the performance of the U.S. bishops or that he has lost confidence in them.

He calls Pope John Paul II's attention to the U.S. as more of a sign of the importance of the Church in the United States. In fact, the Cardinal thinks: "Just as the actions of our government in the economic and political spheres have an impact on the rest of the world, so does the life of the Church in the United States influence the Church elsewhere."

Constructive Relations between the Local Church and the Holy See

In order to encourage constructive relations between the local church and the Holy See, in a context which must be characterized by collegiality of all bishops and clergy with the Pope, Cardinal Bernardin believes that some conditions need to be fulfilled. For instance:

a) The relations and dialogue with the Holy Father must be positive and candid, not defensive and equivocal. The bishops accurately reflect their experience and then listen to his perspective. In other words, collaboration, not confrontation, must be the name of the game.

b) At the same time, the bishops must truly believe that the Pope is the pastor of the universal Church and that he does have the right and duty to oversee the Church's ministry everywhere – both affirming and supporting, and also correcting whenever necessary.

An Open Society with Guaranteed Freedom

The United States are an open society where everyone prizes the freedom to speak his or her mind. Many tend to question things, especially those matters which are important to them, as religion is. They want to know the reason why certain decisions are made, and they feel free to criticize if they do not agree or are not satisfied with the explanations. They see this as an integral part of the call to live their lives as responsible, educated adults. It is also important to know that many Americans, given the freedom they have enjoyed for more than two centuries, almost instinctively react negatively when they are told what to do. However, the majority of the Catholics in the United States have a deep faith and accept the Church as described in the conciliar documents. They contribute to the life of their parish and diocese, as well as the broader Church. In a special way, they support the Pope and want to be united with him as pastor of the universal Church.

Maintaining the Unity While Affirming the Diversity

The practical question that must be addressed today, states Cardinal Bernardin, is how to maintain unity while affirming the diversity in the local realizations of the Church; how to discern a proper balance between freedom and order. He observes that the Second Vatican Council invited Catholics to engage in a discernment which identifies and confirms the elements of truth and grace found in their respective cultures, purifying them of what is evil, and elevating them by restoring them to Christ.

Both the Holy See and some members of the Church in the U.S. are sometimes locked into what seem to be adversarial positions. Genuine dialogue becomes almost impossible. This is, of course, a great concern of the Holy Father. But it is also painful for the bishops, as the shepherds of their particular churches, when they are cast in an adversarial position with the Holy See, or with certain groups within their dioceses.

In this context, within a Church that is one but diverse, the Cardinal offers four brief reflections which are helpful to understand better the framework in which many factors act. First, there has to be in the whole body of the Church a much greater trust in the promise of the risen Christ to be present with his Church and in the living action of the Holy Spirit. The human family is part of a mystery, a unique convergence of the divine and human. For this reason it is wrong to rely only on secular models, although we can surely learn from them. Second, it is necessary to speak with one another in complete candor, without fear. Even if the exchange is characterized by some as confrontational, one must remain calm and not become the captive of those who would use the clergy to accomplish their own ends. Third, in such a mutual exchange – conducted with objectivity, honesty, and openness – it is possible to discern what will truly enhance the Church's unity and what will weaken or destroy it. Sometimes, the outcome of our endeavors will not be immediately evident, but this in itself should not deter us, because we must allow for growth and development in certain areas of the Church's life and ministry. Fourth, one must affirm and continue to grow in appreciation of the conciliar vision of collegiality as both a principle and a style of leadership in the Church. In the United States the episcopal conference has been a visible expression of that collegiality, enhancing the pastoral role of each bishop precisely because it provides a framework and a forum for the sharing of ideas, for teaching and elucidating sound Catholic doctrine, setting pastoral directions, and developing policy positions on contemporary social issues.

These reflections lead Cardinal Bernardin to believe in complete candor that the Church in the United States has always been and will always be "one, holy, Catholic, and apostolic." Moreover, although the Catholic community in the United States is facing many problems, the U.S. society – assures Cardinal Bernardin – has in its own rich tradition the intellectual and spiritual resources necessary to solve them.

26

Religion and Politics

The themes of religion and politics and their relation in human societies have been a major subject for Cardinal Bernardin. He discussed them widely as a bishop and as a citizen, in the Conference of American Bishops, at universities – where he delivered speeches – among the believers of his archdiocese. As people of faith and citizens of all countries, we find that his questions are our questions too, his analysis is worth reading and studying. Does a separation of Church and State – as it can be seen in our Western culture – offer better ground to carry on two-level policies, or is it better to have them both administered by a same body, as it happens in Muslim countries? In which ways can church and state cooperate and help each other? What is the role that we have to perform as Christians when called to give our contribution in the political life? This and much more finds extensive explanation in Bernardin's approach.

The theme of religion and politics has been part of Western culture since Christianity first appeared in the Roman world. "Separation of Church and State" is the phrase often invoked to explain the relationship between religion and politics in the United States.

The problem of such separation often concerns that fine line which delineates the boundaries of religion and politics, as well as the difference between "public" and "private" morality. In the context of his "delicate situation that is both universal, yet, uniquely Chicago," Cardinal Bernardin speaks in practical terms of the problem: "How do I carry out my responsibilities as a religious leader in the real world, while respecting the appropriate boundaries of religion and politics?"

However, he insists on the following point as a necessary condition for examining the question of the relationship between religion and politics:

> "The place of the Church is separate from society. In society, churches are voluntary associations, free to address the public agenda of the nation. More specifically, they are voluntary associations with a disciplined capacity to analyze the moral-religious significance of public issues. That, at least, is how the Catholic bishops see their place in the public policy debate."

Religion and Politics: Continuity and Change

The First Amendment of the U.S. Constitution, part of the "Bill of Rights," begins with the statement that, "Congress shall make no law respecting an establishment of religion, or prohibiting the free exercise thereof . . . "

The interpretation and legal application of the First Amendment have been widely debated and their discussion is not over yet. Father John Courtney Murray, S.J., for example, took on the task of being the "theologian of the First Amendment."

The separation clause has a crucial but limited meaning: it holds that religious institutions are to expect neither discrimination nor favoritism in the exercise of their civic and religious responsibilities. Father Murray believed deeply in the political wisdom of the separation clause, but he resisted all efforts to transform the separation of Church and State into the division of religion and politics.

"The purpose of the First Amendment of the U.S. Constitution," highlights Cardinal Bernardin, "was not to silence the religious voice, but to free religion from State control so that moral/religious values and principles could be taught and cultivated in the wider society. This left religious institutions with the kind of moral influence they should have in civil society. The Church is not to be seen as one more interest group, but it is free to teach and preach a moral vision designed to influence the laws and institutions of society. The First Amendment guarantees religious institutions the right to be heard in the public debate. Their influence in the public arena would depend upon the quality of their contributions to the wider civil conversation."

In the United States civil discourse is certainly structured by religious pluralism. The condition of pluralism, wrote Murray, is the coexistence in one society of groups holding divergent and incompatible views with regard to religious questions. The genius of American pluralism was that it provided for the religious freedom of each citizen and every faith. However, it did not purchase tolerance at the price of expelling religious and moral values from public life and the nation.

What, then, is the goal of the U.S. system vis-à-vis religion? Cardinal Bernardin has no doubt about it: "to provide space for a religious substance in society, but not for a religious State." And he continues: "There is a legitimate secularity of the political process, and there is a legitimate role for religious and moral discourse in the U.S. life. The dialogue which keeps both alive must be a careful conversation which seeks neither to transform secularity into secularism nor to change the religious role into religiously dominated public discourse."

Murray spent a substantial amount of time and effort defending the Church's right to speak in the public arena, as well as stressing the limits of the religious role in that arena. While defending the right of the Religious Right (e.g., Baptists, fundamentalists) to speak, all of us in the religious community need also to be tested and to test each other on how we address public questions.

Complexity is a test we all must face; it is a test the Religious Left (e.g., mainline Protestants) has often failed, thereby paving the way for the Religious Right. From issues of defense policy through questions of medical ethics to issues of social policy, the moral dimensions of public life are interwoven with empirical judgments. Yet, empirical complexity should not silence or paralyze religious/moral analysis and advocacy of issues.

Cardinal Bernardin stands with Murray in attributing a public role to religion and morality in the national life. But he also agrees with Murray that religiously rooted positions must somehow be translated into language, arguments, and categories which a religiously pluralistic society can agree on as the moral foundation of key policy positions.

The Religious Right, at times, fails to address the complexity of the policy agenda and the legitimate secular quality of public discourse. Even when Catholics come to a conclusion similar to that of the Religious Right – such as opposition to abortion – their moral vision is encompassed by a different framework. Catholics situate a firm, unyielding opposition to abortion within a wider framework of respect for life on many fronts. This broader moral argument is different in tone, scope, and substance from the Religious Right's approach to public policy.

From Theology to Policy: The Logic of the Life Issues

Thus far we have principally concentrated on how religion and politics should be related. But the issues of a religiously pluralistic society go beyond procedural questions. The substance of the religious/moral vision which the Church brings to the policy debate ultimately determines its impact in the public arena.

The source of the contemporary interest in religion, morality, and politics lies in substantive questions. As a society, we are increasingly confronted by a range of issues with undeniable moral dimensions. They span the spectrum of life from conception to natural death, and they bear upon major segments of domestic and foreign policy.

Two characteristics of U.S. society intensify the moral urgency. The role of human rights in its foreign policy, for example, has specific consequences each day for people all around the world. But the formulation of a human rights policy is not a purely political or technical question. It requires sustained moral analysis from case to case. Even more striking is the pervasive influence of technological change: in the last two generations we have cracked the genetic code and smashed the atom. These events cannot be fully understood apart from moral analysis. The interaction of technology, politics, and ethics has driven the question of religion and politics to the forefront of discussion, as Pope John Paul II's approach well shows. These themes have been forced upon us by the actual circumstances. It has become clear that human life can be increasingly threatened or enhanced along a broad spectrum of human life issues.

This consciousness moved Cardinal Bernardin, in 1983 at Fordham University, to call for a "consistent ethic of life" as a framework for dialogue within the Church and the wider society.

A key concept in the formulation of a consistent ethic is the analogical understanding of issues. Such a vision pushes the moral, legal, and political debate beyond an "ad hoc" or "single issue" focus, setting the moral discussion in a broader context of concern for human life in all its circumstances.

The consistent ethic can provide the framework of Catholic moral teaching in light of which discussion about priorities, policies, and cases can occur. A consistent moral vision should begin with the initiation of life. Protecting innocent life from direct attack is a fundamental human and moral imperative, not an exclusively Catholic belief. War and abortion are linked at the level of moral principle. They are also comparable questions in terms of national policy. The Cardinal concludes his argument by recalling that U.S. citizens face the responsibility of a policy of abortion on demand, and also the reality of living in a nation which can initiate a nuclear cataclysm and, perhaps, a nuclear winter.

Moreover, the Catholic position on abortion requires "by the law of logic and the law of love" a social vision which joins the right to life to the promotion of a range of other rights: nutrition, health care, employment, and housing. The defense of human life leads inexorably to the respect for human rights, domestically and internationally.

Finally a consistent ethic is a social ethic; it joins the need for personal moral vision to the need for a just and compassionate social policy. A compassionate society must be capable of caring for the human person before and after birth. The State has responsibility both to protect human life and to promote the dignity of each citizen, especially the most vulnerable. We will not be a just society until civil law protects the right to life of each person, particularly of the unborn child. We will not be a compassionate society until public policy and the private sector bridge the dangerous chasm separating the rich from the poor.

The Moral Implication of Public Policy

In Cardinal Bernardin's view, two popular misconceptions tend to derail the discussion about Church participation in public policy development: the notion that morality is limited to personal matters and the belief that public policy is a purely secular endeavour. He insists, on the contrary, that religious values are not limited to personal morality, and that the founding principle of U.S. society is the dignity and worth of every individual.

Precisely because we esteem human life as sacred, we have a duty to protect and foster it at all stages of development from conception to natural death and in all its circumstances. In addition, because we acknowledge that human life is also social, we must develop the kind of societal environment that protects and fosters its development. There are important moral and religious dimensions to each of the problems facing the human community, and these dimensions must be taken into consideration in the development of public policy.

Cardinal Bernardin illustrates clearly how a moral vision seeks to direct the resources of politics, economics, science, and technology to the welfare of the human person and the human community. Perhaps the most significant factor that we have to face in our scientific and technological age is that, for the first time in human history, we have the power to destroy ourselves and our world. A directing vision is needed to bring the technology and the arms race to its appropriate subordinate role. Only people, however, possess moral vision. Our hope for the future is rooted in people who can express such a vision and in those who are willing to implement it.

The Cardinal is also very clear in arguing, even briefly, the case for the necessity and the possibility of constructing a coherent linkage of moral principles and policy choices. The necessity of moral analysis in the policy debate is rooted in the issues we are facing in the last decade of this century. They are not purely technical or tactical in nature; they are fundamental questions in which the moral dimension is a pervasive and persistent factor. We live in a world which is interdependent in character and nuclear in

context. The factual interdependence of the world's economies raises key
questions of access to resources for the industrial nations, but also justice
in the global economic system for the developing nations. The nuclear
context of the age brings sharply into focus the problem of keeping peace
in an interdependent world governed by independent states.

The U.S. Catholic bishops, in their pastoral letter "The Challenge of
Peace: God's Promise and Our Response," spoke of today's dual challenge:
building the peace in an interdependent world and keeping the peace in the
nuclear age. Both tasks exemplify the necessity of shaping a factual view
of the world in terms of the demands of the moral order. "The possibility
of meeting the moral challenge in our conception of policy," argues Cardinal
Bernardin, "is rooted in two resources of the American country and
culture." The U.S. Constitution itself is a bearer of moral values, including
respect for life and reverence for the law, a commitment to freedom and a
desire to relate it to justice. To ignore the moral dimension of public policy
is to forsake the U.S. constitutional heritage. In addition, U.S. society has
the resource of the religiously pluralistic character of the nation. The
purpose of the separation of church and state in U.S. society is not to
exclude the voice of religion from public debate, but to provide a context of
religious freedom where the insights of each religious tradition can be set
forth and tested.

Cardinal Bernardin points out that it is not the function of law to enjoin
or prohibit everything that moral principles enjoin or prohibit. He states:

"No church or religious group should insist that its morality be
translated into civil law if the issue is one of private morality. In such
instances, we cannot place legal constraints on the freedom of others.
Rather, we must seek to promote what we consider to be morally good
through persuasion and example."

The Cardinal is in full agreement with Pope John Paul II's thinking in
his "World Day of Peace Message," 1982, where he said that: "Peace cannot
be built by the power of rulers alone. Peace can be firmly constructed only
if it corresponds to the resolute determination of all people of good will.
Rulers must be supported and enlightened by a public opinion that encourages them or, where necessary, expresses disapproval."

In this perspective, the public plays both a positive and a restraining role.
One of the hallmarks of U.S. democracy is that individuals and groups are
free to participate in any dimension of the public debate. However, they
must also earn the right to be heard by the quality and consistency of their
arguments.

On October 31, 1986, a few days before the U.S. Congressional elections,
Cardinal Bernardin wrote in his weekly column: "It is a privilege to live in

a democratic society where we have a voice in how our nation will be run and what policy will be followed. There is a corresponding responsibility to participate in the public forum, especially by voting." He then continues by focusing on the role of the Church, which is "to bring its distinguished heritage of moral analysis to bear on the issues which confront our society. Each of us has a responsibility to evaluate the candidates and their positions, taking into consideration the moral dimensions of the issues which confront us as a society."

Finally, he encourages everybody to participate. Even though, he says, "some may see themselves as outsiders to the political process because of poverty and isolation from the mainstream of American society," and "some try to excuse themselves on the dubious premises that the election is dull or that they are too busy to vote," citizens should not "give in to the temptation to leave the political process to others."

Public Morality and Personal Choice: Connection and Complexity

The phrase "public morality" is at the centre of the debate on religion and politics, but it is a concept surrounded by a distressing degree of confusion. The problem is partially due to the collapsing of two distinct questions into one argument: how we determine which issues are issues of public or private morality, and how a public official should relate personal convictions about religion and moral truths to the fulfillment of public duty. Murray offered some essential ideas on the first question, but did not address the second.

Today, in the U.S., there is a public consensus in law and policy which clearly defines civil rights as issues of public morality and the decision to drink alcoholic beverages as clearly one of private morality. Neither decision was reached without struggle. The fact that a spontaneous public consensus is lacking at a given moment does not prohibit its being created. When he was told that the law could not make people love their neighbours, Dr. Martin Luther King, Jr., replied that it could stop their lynching them. Law and policy can also be instruments of shaping a public consensus; they are not simply the product of consensus.

The debate about public morality is inherent in a pluralistic society; it will never end. Today people in the U.S. struggle about the status of abortion. The U.S. Supreme Court decisions and their supporters have relegated abortion to the status of private morality. The Catholic bishops have consistently held that abortion, like war and poverty, is without question an issue of public morality because the unborn child's right to life is at stake.

Summarizing, Cardinal Bernardin insists on the fact that we can relate the best of religion to the best of politics in the service of each other and the wider society, nation and human, to which we are bound in hope and love.

The Role of the Church in Development of Public Policy

Recently, Pope John Paul II has widely and thoroughly dealt with the question of the role of the Christian in the political community. In *Christi fideles laici*, signed on January 30th, 1989, he writes: "A charity that loves and serves the person is never able to be separated from justice. Each in its own way demands the full, effective acknowledgement of the rights of the individual, to which society is ordered in all its structures and institutions. In order to achieve their task directed to the Christian animation of the temporal order, in the sense of serving persons and society, the lay faithful are never to relinquish their participation in 'public life,' that is, in the many different economic, social, legislative, administrative and cultural areas, which are intended to promote organically and institutionally the common good. The Synod fathers have repeatedly affirmed that every person has a right and duty to participate in public life, albeit in a diversity and complementary of forms, levels, tasks and responsibilities."

"The participation of the Catholic Bishops in public policy discussion," underlines Cardinal Bernardin, "is rooted in our conviction that moral values and principles relate to public policy as well as to personal choices. It is also rooted in a belief that we honor our constitutional tradition of religious freedon precisely by exercising our right to participate in the public life of the nation." To explain the Church's role in the development of public policy, the Cardinal clarifies three basic issues: the place of the Church in the public arena, the posture the Church assumes, and the perspective it uses to guide its participation in the public debate.

"To put it succinctly, the separation of Church and State means that religious communities should expect neither favoritism nor discrimination in the exercise of their religious and civic functions," argues the Cardinal. They are free to participate in any dimension of the public debate, but they must earn the right to be heard by the quality of their arguments. Therefore, the challenge is how to speak as a Church to a public issue; how to speak from a tradition of faith in a language which is open to public acceptance by citizens of several faiths or no faith.

The U.S. bishops' pastoral letter on war and peace has two stated basic purposes: helping Catholics form their conscience on the issues under discussion and contributing to the public policy debate about the morality of war. The Cardinal makes a case for an activism based on the extremity of present-day problems. He cites two cases. First, the pastoral letter provides a framework within which we can make a moral analysis of the critical issues facing us in the nuclear age: If nuclear weapons are used, we all will lose. Second, the U.S. Catholic bishops have chosen to be equally visible in their opposition to abortion. That is why one cannot, with consistency, claim to be truly pro-life if one applies the principle of the sanctity of life to other issues, but rejects it in the case of abortion. To fail to stand for this principle is to make a fundamental error. But the moral principle does not stand alone; it is related to other dimensions of the Church's social teaching.

These themes drawn from Catholic theology are not restricted in their application to the community of faith. These are truths of the moral and political order which are also fundamental to the Western constitutional heritage. The opposition to abortion, properly stated, is not a sectarian claim but a reflective, rational position which any person of good will may be invited to consider.

The appeal to a higher moral law to reform and refashion existing civil law was the central idea that Dr. Martin Luther King Jr. brought to the U.S. civil rights movement of the 1960's. The pro-life movement of the 1980's and 1990's is based on the same appeal. Pro-life advocacy today should be seen as an extension of the spirit of the civil rights movement. "If we can demonstrate how a moral vision enriches the choices and the challenges which confront us as a nation," concludes Cardinal Bernardin, "then the consideration will be given to the moral factor in every policy debate."

The Role of the Religious Leader in Public Policy Development

From Cardinal Bernardin's position illustrated above, it should be clear that the Catholic bishop's role in the development of public policy is an extension of his teaching role in the Church, always within the framework of Catholic tradition and in union with the Pope and other bishops. Because of differences in other ecclesial structures, the role of other religious leaders may take a somewhat different shape.

One of the first problems that religious leaders have to face continually is the question of credibility. Some people perceive them as operating outside their own area of expertise, when they make statements regarding public policy. "In this regard," the Cardinal replies, "we do bring a dimension to the discussion that is proper to our competence, however. We merely ask that people evaluate our arguments on their merits."

A further problem is their personal limitations as they attempt to develop the moral dimension of any issue. At this point, Cardinal Bernardin is very clear and humble: "I am simply Joseph Bernardin - nothing less, nothing more. I have my own blind spots. I have my own doubts. At times I lack the courage to set forth my convictions clearly and without hesitation. Sometimes I simply do not know what to do." His solution is to engage in frequent dialogue with others. The pastoral letter on peace and war - he observes - was conceived and brought to full term in a process of dialogue. Bishops' collaboration with others helps ensure the quality of a moral vision for the nation and makes it both credible and worthy of implementation.

The third problem that religious leaders have to face when they engage in public policy development is the pressure that special interest groups bring to bear on the process. Cardinal Bernardin has great respect for people who commit their talents and energies to a specific project that significantly impacts public policy discussions. But as a religious leader, he finds that he has to keep within his perspective the whole range of issues that affect the quality of human life.

In this regard, as noted above, he has called for a consistent ethic of life; he argues that such moral issues as genetics, abortion, capital punishment, modern warfare and the care of the terminally ill are each distinct, but they are also linked. He points out that success on any one of the issues threatening life requires a concern for the broader attitude in society about respect for human life from conception to natural death and in all its circumstances.

A final point, which is so central to Bernardin personally and to his ministry, is prayer. "In prayer," he says, "we discover not only God, but our own true selves and one another as well. Through prayer and reflection on the Scriptures, we come to know God as one who cares about this world and about each of us. We come to know and appreciate his plan for us: that we live in peace, harmony, and unity with one another. We come to understand more deeply how all the inhabitants of this planet are our sisters and brothers, including in a special way the poor, the needy, and the oppressed."

He insists that: "Our best efforts – no matter how well thought out and brilliantly executed – will not quite reach the mark unless they flow from minds and hearts that are at peace with themselves."

A Society Without Religion is Doomed to Create a Poor Culture

On September 9, 1996 Joseph Bernardin spoke at Georgetown University. He gave students his reflections on the public life and witness of the Catholic Church in the context of U.S. society and culture. His argument again supported the clear distinction between church and state, opposed all exclusion of religion from civil society, and advocated a broad, deep, activist role for religious institutions in shaping our public life. As he had already done previously, he used the Vatican II's Declaration on Religious Liberty for religion and politics as teaching instruments. He restated the central role of religion in society as important. The quality and character of civil society demands that religious institutions exercise the full range of their ministries of teaching and service in order to cope with today's troubling issues, since a society without religion is doomed to create a poor culture. Throughout the centuries and even more in the present, the task of religion has always been that of giving a vision to society. Where there is no vision, people perish. The convergence of forces arising from contemporary society and threatening human life and sacredness create a new context in which the ancient themes of an ethic of stewardship of life take on new relevance. This must be addressed by building within civil society a shared vision of what human sacredness demands, and how we instill binding principles of restraint and respect in our both our personal codes of conduct and our public policies. Religious participation, and general standards of civility have concentrated attention on the quality and character of our own civil society. Religious communities flourish in the fabric of civil society. In terms of the U.S. political tradition, the logic of church-state relations, which stresses legitimate separation of secular and sacral institutions, should not govern the logic of civil society. The logic of this relationship is engagement, not separation. Another crucial contribution that religion can make to civil society is through the ministry and work of religious institutions of education, health care, family service, and direct outreach to the poorest parts of our society. The web of religious institutions is a pervasive aspect of the U.S. social support system.

Cardinal Bernardin firmly believed that the time was ripe to think about how a more extensive public-private pattern of collaboration could serve to extend the range of effectiveness of religious institutions and at the same time use scarce public resources more efficiently in support of human needs. But perhaps the most effective, long-term contribution that religious communities can make to civil society is the kind of citizens who are shaped, often decisively, by participation in a religious tradition.

27

International Relations in a Highly Interdependent World

We live in a highly interdependent world, and more often than in the past human relations have repercussions on everyday life. This has always been a permanent concern for Cardinal Bernardin. He emphasizes that in the modern world, where international relations are becoming increasingly global, a country must pay attention to the effects its decisions have, or could have, on communities in other parts of the globe, especially people of poor countries.

In his interpretation of the world's interdependence, the Archbishop of Chicago has been ahead of his time in understanding major social changes. His voice has overtaken U.S. borders, crossing the national boundaries and reached other continents. With reference to the Second Vatican Council's Pastoral Constitution on the Church in the Modern World, *which calls the Church "to read the signs of the times," the archbishops point out many aspects of the nations' activities that can negatively affect other countries. The nuclear danger, a deep concern highlighted in the collegial pastoral letter "The Challenge of Peace" (issued in 1983 by an ad hoc committee of the National Conference of the U.S. Catholic Bishops and chaired by the archbishops of Chicago), is one of the major elements that brings the issue of interdependence to the forefront.*

Cardinal Bernardin points out three categories that better de-
scribe this context: the fact of interdependence as the steadily
growing number of bonds that tie nations and people even more
closely together, the meaning of interdependence as the direct
and decisive way in which states and other key actors in the in-
ternational system act beyond national borders, and the chal-
lenge lying in the fact that in this materially interdependent
world there is not yet a way to shape moral interdependence.
Furthermore, the relations between economic development and
the poor is a major concern related to interdependence today.
And what is the role of the Churches in this emergence of
global interdependence? The Cardinal is very clear in his re-
sponse – they should participate, along with many other institu-
tions and actors, in shaping public opinion and in bringing to
debate specific assets which derive from the nature of an eccle-
sial entity.

Today, socioeconomic relations have a much more direct reper-
cussion on everyday life and the development of the human
family than in the past. Such influence, moreover, is no longer
restricted to a national scale – indeed, its scope is international
and simultaneously so. For instance, if the United States follows a certain
economic trend, the effects of such a decision immediately materialize in
Africa, Central America, and on other continents. We generally refer to this
new phenomenon as "interdependence."

Back in 1984, John Paul II, in his exhortation answering the 63 "propositions" relating to the sixth general Synod of Bishops on "Reconciliation
and Penance in the Mission of the Church," warned that: "Each person's
sin will reflect somehow on the others." The "interdependence between
people and nations," the fact that "men and women in various parts of the
world" feel strongly about the "injustice committed in far away countries"
is a constant preoccupation of the Pope in his encyclical, *Sollicitudo rei
socialis* ("The Social Concern of the Church"), of December 30, 1987.

The effects and consequences of the interdependence of events in the world
today are also one of the most important concerns of Cardinal Bernardin. In
almost all his major addresses he underlines the necessity for action, for taking
care of the consequences of every private or public decision.

He raises three questions about interdependence: first, in regard to the
character of international relations today, what are the dominant features
of our world? Second, in terms of the assets which the Church brings to
international relations, what can it offer the world? Third, in regard to the
relationship between the Church and the U.S. political system, is it possible
to influence the public debate?

In his interpretation of the word "interdependence" – "the interlocking
relations among regions, people, and nations" – Cardinal Bernardin has

been ahead of his times in comprehending the major social changes and new international relations. Above all, he has fully understood the importance of interdependence vis-à-vis the issue of nuclear danger and social emargination. His voice too has crossed national boundaries and reached other continents.

Jnterdependence and Nuclear Threat Jn The Contemporary Scene

It is one of the major documents of the second Vatican Council, "The Pastoral Constitution on the Church in the Modern World," that inspires Cardinal Bernardin's reflections on the role of the Church, which is called "to read the signs of the times" as part of its social teaching and ministry. This directive has been interpreted to mean that, prior to making moral judgments on secular events, the Church must draw upon the work of various disciplines – particularly the social and physical sciences – to grasp the empirical content of problems. That is why, in writing the pastoral letter on peace, the U.S. bishops interviewed a broad spectrum of people with expertise in the political, military and scientific dimensions of the nuclear question before they began their specific moral analysis.

Following that same logic, Cardinal Bernardin directs his attention to the international system today and asserts that the Church's primary role in the foreign policy debate is its ability to bring moral analysis to bear upon policy decisions. He has no doubts as to which are the most salient dimensions of the world today: its interdependent character and its nuclear danger.

Raymond Aron has pointed out that a key characteristic of the postwar international system is constituted by its being a single system. In the last twenty-five years, such a system has manifested a steadily increasing degree of interdependence. This is best described by the three following categories:

The fact of interdependence is the steadily growing number of bonds which tie nations and people ever more closely together, from increased communication to a more integrated international economy.

The meaning of interdependence is the direct and decisive way in which states and other key actors in the international system act beyond national borders, at a speed and frequency which link states and peoples today in a qualitatively different way from the past. Its effect has been to blur the distinction between foreign and domestic policy. For instance, in 1984, interest rates in the United States had a decisive and damaging effect on the debt-ridden nations of Latin America. Therefore, under contemporary conditions of interdependence, even interest rates are a key foreign policy decision.

The challenge of interdependence lies in recognizing the fact that, while we live in a materially interdependent world, we have not yet found a way to shape moral interdependence among nations. The move from material to moral interdependence will require the establishment of rules and relations which channel our growing interaction toward the goals of a more equitable international system.

And yet Cardinal Bernard wisely warns us that the agenda of international relations cannot be limited to the positive challenges we face. Unfortunately, the present international system is also characterized by an all-pervasive threat of nuclear war. We have lived with the danger for two generations and may even have grown too familiar with it. However, familiarity should not blunt our sense of the qualitatively new reality which nuclear weapons pose for world politics.

What are the new features of world politics? Cardinal Bernardin observes that for centuries nations have considered resort to force a tragic but still minimally rational means of defending basic interests and preserving key values. In the nuclear age – he argues – the linkage between politics and war has been broken: nuclear war threatens to destroy the key political values which once justified resort to force. Therefore, the world which we face today is interdependent in its political-economic dimensions, and nuclear in its political-strategic aspects. This is why the Church's role in international relations has to be assessed in terms of its ability to provide direction, meaning and guidance for a foreign policy capable of grasping the potential of interdependence and reducing the danger of the nuclear arms race.

In another context, the Cardinal has elaborated on this point, stressing that interdependence means we are locked together in a limited world. The factual interdependence of our economies raises key questions of access to resources for the industrial nations, but also justice in the economic system for the developing nations. The nuclear context of the age brings sharply into focus the problem of keeping the peace in an interdependent world governed by independent states. Both tasks exemplify the necessity of shaping our factual view of the world in terms of the demands of the moral order. Also Pope John Paul II specified the moral challenge of the nuclear age when he stood before the monument at Hiroshima and declared: "In the past it was possible to destroy a village, a town, a region, even a country. Now it is the whole planet that has come under threat." By way of this powerful quotation, cardinal Bernardin contends that all our political assumptions, as well as our moral judgments about war, are faced with a qualitatively new challenge today.

The Role of the Church in International Relations

Therefore, the truth of our age is: if nuclear weapons are used, we all lose. There will be no victors, only the vanquished; there will be no calculation of costs and benefits because the costs will run beyond our ability to calculate. There is no policy which can substitute for this basic goal: the prevention of any use of nuclear weapons under any conditions. And nuclear prevention, as we have already shown, goes together with interdependence.

In the context of the emergence of global interdependence, than, what is the role of the churches? From Cardinal Bernardin's perspective, they should participate, along with many other institutions and actors, in shaping public opinion. This, in turn, should act as a directive force for policy. In this view, the churches become part of a larger process. Nevertheless, they should still bring to the wider debate some specific assets which derive from the nature of an ecclesial entity.

With regard to the Catholic Church, the Cardinal states that it brings two distinctive gifts to the policy debate: a transnational perspective and a tradition of moral analysis. In fact, the Church has thought and acted in a transnational fashion from its very beginnings. Although theologians do not often speak of the Church as "transnational" – this being the vocabulary of political analysts they have always been convinced of its universality. Hence the "transnationality," as it were, of the Church is one of its principal contributions to the present political system.

As a corollary of this shrewd analysis, Cardinal Bernardin insists that transnational actors are powerful forces of influence in an interdependent world. They all share, in different ways, certain key characteristics: they are based in one place, are active in several nations, possess a trained corps of personnel, have a single guiding philosophy and a sophisticated communications system. He observes that the description fits perfectly the reality of IBM, GM and GE in the postwar world, as well as the structure of the Catholic Church since the fourth century. "We have been a transnational actor for a millennium and a half!" is his final comment.

One example, drawn from the experience of the U.S. bishops in the Central America debate, will suffice to highlight the issue. The contacts they have had with the Church in central America have provided a distinctive perspective on the U.S. policy debate, and have often influenced a multiplicity of concrete choices. The U.S. bishops have argued for the need to recognize the primacy of the local roots of the problems. This perspective has allowed them to see the fundamental issue clearly without looking exclusively at it through the lenses of superpower politics. In this regard – underlines the Cardinal – the bishops of the United States have been instrumental in helping to resist the imposition of a purely East-West framework on such a complex reality.

Moreover, the Church brings to the foreign policy debate a tradition of moral analysis. Cardinal Bernardin distinguishes two elements in the contemporary foreign policy debate, which give particular relevance to the Church's tradition of moral analysis: The combination of global interdependence and nuclear danger gives an increasing number of policy problems an irreducible moral character. Hence, we cannot deal with an empirical policy problem without addressing its moral dimensions. In addition, it becomes evident that we must employ a disciplined analysis of how to relate the ethical to the empirical aspects of policy. The cardinal's contention is that it is precisely at this intersection of ethics and policy that the Church has something to offer.

The U.S. Political System and the Churches

Cardinal Bernardin sees a real possibility of meeting the moral challenge in two resources of the U.S. nation and culture. The first is its religiously pluralist character. The separation of church and state in American society does not exclude the voice of religion from public debate. On the contrary, it provides a context of religious freedom where the insights of each religious tradition can be set forth and tested. This opens the public debate to assessment by moral criteria.

The second resource is part of the U.S. constitutional tradition, itself a bearer of moral values including respect for life and reverence for the law, a commitment to freedom and a desire to relate it to justice. Hence, to ignore the moral dimension of foreign policy is to erode both a religious and a constitutional heritage, as the Cardinal points out.

In the foreign policy debate of the 1980's, he detects two causes for testing the U.S. capacity to use the moral resources of culture and church in determining both the ends and means of policy: nuclear arms and Central American policy. In particular, he insists that the perspective we bring to an issue is as pertinent to shaping a morally responsible policy as the values and principles we use to analyze specific policy choices. This is why, on both the nuclear question and Central America, U.S. policy would benefit from a change of perspective.

In underlining the role of the churches in the policy debate, the Cardinal refers to Alexis de Tocqueville who long ago elaborated the difficulty of democratic states to maintain a consistent foreign policy. Clearly, these states must deal with the impact of public opinion, whose results on foreign policy, historically, have not always been beneficial for us or for others. The key question, therefore, is how to shape and structure public opinion so that it can exercise a positive role in the larger policy process.

Cardinal Bernardin is aware of the fact that "shaping public opinion" may sound manipulative and arouse suspicion. In this regard, he highlights two of its aspects: First, if it is going to be a significant force in the policy debate, public opinion requires a solid base of knowledge and some channels – above and beyond the electoral process – through which it can express a perspective and position. Second, public opinion is one of the places in the policy debate where the moral arguments and technical elements of policy intersect. The essence of a democratic society is that both political and moral responsibility for the policy of the government is shared by the people.

The issue of moral purpose in U.S. foreign policy has been a persistent topic in American history. Its content has changed over the years – from the idealism of Wilson to the realism of Morganthau – but the need to provide moral purpose for the direction of U.S. power has been a continuing thread of the country's history. There have always been critics, but they have never won the day. Indeed, the 1970's saw a resurgence of the relevance of moral argument in the foreign policy debate when the human rights policy of the U.S. government sparked new interest in moral and political questions. The 1980's have focused the moral argument on a different dimension of policy – the threat of nuclear war.

It is in the context of this historical perspective that Cardinal Bernardin sees the role of the church in helping to restructure the foreign policy debate as directly tied to its potential to influence public opinion. In the United States, the Church is both a broadly-based community and a social institution capable of projecting a policy position in the public arena. All religious institutions share this twofold character of community and organization to some degree. As a community, the church has regular access to a wide spectrum of U.S. citizens. As an organization, it can use a series of forums both to foster the discussion of policy questions and to focus specifically on the moral dimensions of policy. Here is the twofold task the churches should fulfill in helping shape foreign policy, the Cardinal concludes.

28

Antisemitism

The Historical Legacy and the Continuing Challenge for Christians

In recent years, Cardinal Bernardin highlighted the Church's strong stand against antisemitism and acknowledged its past wrongdoings, calling antisemitism "the most tragic form that racist ideology has assumed in our century." The Cardinal traces antisemitism back to the Greco-Roman civilization, highlighting events such as the Jewish revolt against the Romans and the destruction of the Temple of Jerusalem, both of which generated tension and alienation of the Jews by the first Christian populations. He underlines that inclusion of this rocky and often painful history is crucial for a present day reconciliation between Christians and Jews. This era also gave birth to the "perpetual wandering" identity attributed to Jews who, according to Christians, were condemned to perpetual statelessness as a punishment for killing Jesus.

Until the twentieth century, Bernardin explains, antisemitism remained a dominant part of Western Christendom, contributing to the development of common Christian attitudes towards the Nazi movement and the party's success.

*As Christians, he advises, we must confront antisemitism by: re-
storing the history of anti-Judaic theology to Catholic teaching
materials; work towards an understanding of the Holocaust by
dealing honestly with the Church's failures, promoting the education of the Holocaust in Catholic education; recognizing
bonds with Jewish people; and above all engaging in public repentance as a Church. Cardinal Bernardin calls us all to reflect
on the legacy of antisemitism and join together to confront any
resurgence that may occur.*

I n an address given at the Hebrew University on March 23, 1995,
Cardinal Bernardin expressed the Church's position on antisemitism,
from the early days of Christianity to the present time. He emphasized
that in recent years the Catholic Church has undertaken important
efforts to acknowledge its guilt for the legacy of antisemitism and to
repudiate as sinful any remaining vestiges of that legacy in its contemporary
teaching and practice. In 1989, he recalls, the Pontifical Commission for
Peace and Justice issued a strong declaration on racism, which had an
international impact. The document – whose title was "The Church and
Racism: Towards a More Fraternal Society," insisted that "Harboring racist
thoughts and entertaining racist attitudes is a sin." The Church calls
antisemitism "the most tragic form that racist ideology has assumed in our
century."

Pope John Paul II has taken up the challenge of antisemitism, put forth
by the Pontifical Commission. During a visit to Hungary in 1991, the Pope
spoke of the urgent task of repentance and reconciliation, stating: "In face
of a risk of a resurgence and spread of anti-Semitic feelings, attitudes, and
initiatives . . . we must teach consciences to consider antisemitism, and
all forms of racism, as sins against God and humanity."

Origins of Antisemitism

Cardinal Bernardin calls to our attention that antisemitism has deep roots
in Christian history, roots that go back to the earliest days of the Church.
As Father Edward Flannery has shown in his classic work on antisemitism,
The Anguish of the Jews, the early Christian community inherited a
cultural tradition from the Greco-Roman civilization that included a
prejudicial outlook towards Jews. Bernardin underlines that Jews were
disliked in pre-Christian Greece and Rome for their general unwillingness
to conform with prevailing social habits. It is regrettable, he continues, that
this long history of antisemitism has been virtually eliminated from our
textbooks. Inclusion of it, as painful as it is for us to hear today, is essential
for authentic reconciliation between Christians and Jews in our time.

Other factors, Cardinal Bernardin notes, contributed to the growth of anti-Jewish feelings among Christians in the first centuries of the Church's existence. The gradual tendency towards separation from anything Jewish was further enhanced by the desire to avoid any linkage between the Church and the Jewish community after the disastrous Jewish revolt against the Roman imperial authorities (66–70 C.E.). Aside from the destruction of the Temple in Jerusalem, this attitude generated continued post-war pressure and Rome retributed all actions undertaken against the Jewish community.

Anti-Judaic interpretations of the New Testament which emerged in the first centuries of Christian history, he continues, only represented the beginning of difficulties for the Jewish community. Unfortunately, a strong tendency to regard Jews as entirely displaced from the covenantal relationship because of their unwillingness to accept Jesus as the Messiah soon developed in the teachings of the early Fathers of the Church, despite St. Paul clearly taught the contrary.

The belief that the Jews had been totally rejected by God and replaced in the covenantal relationship by the "New Israel," clarifies Bernardin, led to the emergence of the so-called "perpetual wandering" theology which consigned the Jews to a condition of permanent statelessness as a consequence of their displacement from the covenant, and as a punishment for murdering the Messiah.

Although the patristic writings were far more than an extended anti-Jewish treatise, Cardinal Bernardin stresses that Christians cannot ignore this "shadow side" of patristic theology, which in other aspects remains a continuing source of profound spiritual enrichment. The "shadow side" of this theology, he notes, has unfortunately been omitted from basic Christian texts far too often. Yet, we cannot understand the treatment of Jews in subsequent centuries without some grasp of this theology. The history that it deeply influenced is characterized by persistent forms of social and religious discrimination and persecution, which brought continual humiliation as well as political and civil inequality upon the Jewish community.

This legacy of antisemitism – with its deeply negative social consequences for Jews as individuals and for the Jewish community as a whole – remained the dominant social pattern in Western Christendom until the twentieth century, and continued to exercise a decisive role in shaping Catholicism's initial reactions. The proposal to restore a Jewish national homeland in Palestine is but an example of this new attitude. Its central importance in shaping popular Christian attitudes towards the Nazis and their stated goal of eliminating all Jews from Europe and beyond is often stated by the Archbishop of Chicago. Little doubt remains that this persistent tradition provided a seedbed for the Nazis' ability to succeed.

Contemporary Developments

Cardinal Bernardin maps out that in the three decades or so since the beginning of the Second Vatican Council, the negative theology of the Jewish people has lost its theological foundations. In chapter four of *Nostra Aetate*, the Council clearly asserted that a valid basis never existed neither for the charge of collective guilt against the Jewish community for supposedly "murdering the Messiah" nor for the consequent theology of permanent Jewish suffering and displacement.

The Holy See's 1985 *Notes on the Correct Way to Present the Jews and Judaism in Preaching and Catechesis in the Roman Catholic Church* (issued to commemorate the twentieth anniversary of *Nostra Aetate*) clearly repudiated a "displacement" theology, maintaining that "the history of Israel did not end in 70 A.D. (i.e., with the destruction of the Temple of Jerusalem by the Romans)" and that "the permanence of Israel . . . is a historic fact and a sign to be interpreted within God's design."

Other recent documents of the Holy See further seal the coffin on the biblically unfounded "displacement" theology, as the Cardinal makes known. The *New Catechism of the Catholic Church* rejects the notion of Jewish responsibility for the death of Christ, reminding Christians that Jesus died on the cross for their sins. Further, in the Holy See-Israel Agreements, the Vatican not only recognizes Israel's right to existence, but unequivocally condemns all forms of racism, including antisemitism. Pope John Paul II, who has contributed significantly to the development of the Church's new theological outlook on Jews and Judaism, has affirmed the right to security and tranquillity – the prerogative of every nation – for the Jewish people living in the State of Israel.

Cardinal Bernardin emphasizes the need for continued scholarship and theological reflection, especially on those texts of the New Testament considered by many as problematic. Although none of these texts can be really listed as "anti-Semitic" or even as "anti-Judaic," the question of their classification is an open matter between scholars. Different poitions are held on this point and will likely remain as such for the foreseeable future. Other tanslations or interpretations, the Archbishop of Chicago points out, certainly are to be included among the goals we must pursue in the effort to eradicate antisemitism. Bernardin strongly advises the Church to adopt a pastoral approach while waiting for a scholarly resolution of the question of antisemitism in the New Testament. Today, Christians must realize previous negative teachings on the Jews as an acknowledged part of their biblical heritage. This interpretationt can no longer be regarded as definitive in the light of our improved understanding of developments in the relationship between early Christianity and the Jewish community.

Nazism and Antisemitism

Considering again today's longly debated issue of Nazism and antisemitism, Cardinal Bernardin recalls that during the past several decades scholars throughout the world have put forward various perspectives on the relationship between the rise of Nazism and traditional Christian hatred against the Jews. Hitler's often-quoted remark to Church leaders, who came to see him to protest his treatment of Jews, is an argument they often point out. On that occasion, the Nazi leader said he was merely putting into practice what the Christian churches had preached for nearly two thousand years. These perspectives, the Cardinal adds, also highlight the close similarity between much of Nazi anti-Jewish legislation and laws against Jews in earlier Christian-dominated societies.

Furthermore, many Christians found a main motivation for their active or tacit support to the Nazi movement in the Church's traditional beliefs about Jews and Judaism. Some even went so far as to define the Nazi struggle against the Jews in explicitly religious and theological terms. In this context, Cardinal Bernardin affirms that today both the Church and the believers must not minimize the extent of Christian collaboration with Hitler and his associates. A constant confrontation with past actions is our deep moral challenge to maintain our own integrity as religious community, he adds.

The Archbishop of Chicago backs the perspective of scholars such as Yosef Yerushalmi who have insisted that "the Holocaust was the work of a thoroughly modern, neopagan state," not merely a "transformed" medieval antisemitism rooted in Christian teachings. The Cardinal concludes: The Shoah cannot be simply seen as the final and most gruesome chapter in the long history of Christian antisemitism. It was rather a plan for the mass destruction of human lives, supposedly undertaken with the excuse of "healing" humanity, as the psychologist Robert J. Lifton has put it. Rooted in modern theories of inherent biological and racial inferiority, this plan coupled with the escalation of bureaucratic and technological capacities. At its depths, it was anti-Christian as much as anti-Jewish. One of its theoreticians even attempted to rewrite the New Testament on totally based Nazi concepts. It coalesced several important modern strains of thought into its master plan for human extermination.

To bring this plan to its required realization, the Nazis envisioned the elimination of the "dregs" of society. The Jewish people were the first and foremost samples of such "dregs." This category also embraced Gypsies, the disabled, the Polish leadership, homosexuals, and certain other designated groups. Proper distinctions need to be maintained between the wholesale attack on the Jewish people – for whom there was absolutely no escape from Nazi fury – and on the other categories in the Nazi list. A linking can be detected between the Nazi attack on Jews and the victimization of these other groups – whose suffering and death were integral part of the overall Nazi plan.

Hope for the Future

Leaving back "the horrors of the past" and looking at "the possibilities of the future," it is clear that our confrontation with "the legacy of antisemitism" will not be an easy task. "But confront it we must," Cardinal Bernardin says. Here follow several ways in which this can be done :

"1. The history of antisemitism and of anti-Judaic theology must be restored to our Catholic teaching materials. Innocence or ignorance is not a pathway to authentic virtue in this regard; courageous honesty is. In our religious education programs we should be prepared to tell the full story of the Church's treatment of Jews over the centuries, ending with a rejection of the shadow side of that history and theology at the Second Vatican Council. We can and must highlight moments of relative tranquillity and constructive interaction when they occurred in such countries as Poland, Spain, and the United States. However, these stories should never obscure the more pronounced history of hostility and subjection.

2. We also need an integral understanding of the Holocaust. In developing such an understanding, it's our duty to speak against unwarranted and generalized accusations directed at the Church and Church leaders. We need to reemphasize protests and oppositions made by Christian leaders, grassroot groups and individuals: the Fulda Declaration of the German Catholic Bishops, the Barmen Declaration of the German Evangelical Church (Lutheran), the encyclical letter 'Mit Brennender Sorge' issued in German by Pope Pius XI, the efforts of Archbishops Angelo Roncalli and Angelo Rotta, the Zegota movement in Poland, the many Catholic religious women whose communities protected Jews, the men and women of Le Chambon in France, Jan Karski of the Polish government-in-exile, the Austrian peasant Franz Jagerstatter – and many more could be added. However, all this didn't suffice. But these Christians preserved a measure of moral integrity in the Church during the years of Nazi darkness.

Nevertheless, the witnessing of these courageous Christian leaders, groups, and individuals should never be used to argue against the need for a full scrutiny of Church activities by reputable scholars. We must be prepared to deal honestly with the genuine failures of some in the Christian churches during that critical period. The Catholic Church must be prepared to submit its World War II record to a thorough scrutiny by respected scholars.

3. Education about the Holocaust should become a prominent feature in Catholic education at every level. To assist in realizing this goal, Seton Hill College near Pittsburgh has established a program explicitly designed for Catholic teachers that works closely with both Yad VaShem and the U.S. Holocaust Memorial Museum.

4. But we must go beyond merely teaching the failures of the past, as crucial as that task remains. *Nostra Aetate* and subsequent documents from the Holy See, as well as Pope John Paul II, have not merely removed the classical prejudices against Jews and Judaism from Catholic teaching. They have laid out the basis for a positive theology of reconciliation and bonding. This, too, must become a part of our current effort in education.

5. Liturgy and preaching are additional areas that require constant attention by the Church. In 1988, the U.S. Bishops' Committee on the Liturgy released a set of guidelines for the presentation of Jews and Judaism in Catholic preaching. They offer directions for implementing the vision of *Nostra Aetate* and subsequent documents of the Holy See in the Church's ministry of the Word during the various liturgical seasons. The seasons of Lent/Holy Week and Easter – whose texts can serve to strengthen traditional Christian stereotypes of Jews and Judaism if not interpreted carefully – are highlighted in particular way. The great challenge of these liturgical seasons is that they become times for reconciliation – not for conflict and division as in past centuries – between Jews and Christians. During these central periods of the liturgical year, Christians need to recognize their bonds with the Jewish people in agreement with the vision expressed by the Second Vatican Council and by Pope John Paul II.

6. Education and preaching will not prove completely effective unless we also have women and men of vision and recon-

ciliation who embody the new spirit of Jewish-Christian
bonding. Above all, in the light of the history of antisemitism
and the Holocaust, the Church needs to engage in public
repentance." In conclusion, the Cardinal is strongly convinced
that "as we reflect today on the legacy of antisemitism, Jews and
Christians need to recommit themselves to counter its
disturbing resurgence in North America, Latin America, and
Europe, together with other forms of racism and intergroup
violence."

29

The Sacredness of Life

Religion, Culture, and Politics

Each human must be committed to preserving life. Each Christian should, likewise, protect life against today's social challenges. Cardinal Bernardin gently reminds us of our commitment to life, against all odds. A gift as rich as life itself that comes from a generous donor has to be cared for as sacred. We must do this both for ourselves and on behalf of those who cannot speak for themselves – i.e., all unborn children threatened with abortion. We must stand up to society when roles and rules are made for the good of selfish and elitist groups who want to do away with the old and the sick – i.e., our commitment against euthanasia. Once again, Cardinal Bernardin shows us the way to a Christian-shaped society.

In addressing important themes as religion, justice, economy, politics, health care, among others, Cardinal Bernardin always provides an encompassing framework for them – i.e. an ethically lived life. Caring for life, supporting it, and responding to basic human needs of nutrition, health care, housing, and education are essential aspects of a consistent ethical life. But caring for life does not exhaust our moral obligations as Christians, since we are witnessing public issues and cases where life is being taken without moral justification.

Care for Life and Defend It

Modern society poses a full range of threats to life. We not only have to care for life, but we also have to defend it. In his encyclical, "The Gospel of Life," John Paul II has identified three issues – abortion, capital punishment, and euthanasia – as the banners of what he described a creeping "culture of death." In past Catholic tradition, capital punishment has not been regarded as "unjust killing" in the way abortion and euthanasia have been. But today, different types of life taking should be systematically related. The US society today sustains nearly 1.5 million abortions annually, is overwhelmingly in favor of capital punishment, and is now moving rapidly toward acceptance of assisted suicide. Although these problems have to be treated separately, there is also a truth to be learned in relating these three issues.

The truth – Cardinal Bernardin points out – is that respect for life will cost us something. To move beyond solutions and problems, often solved by taking life, will require a more expansive care for life – at its beginning and its end. In both the abortion and assisted-suicide debates, the basic picture one has of the social fabric of life is crucial in passing a moral judgment on these specific issues. Both abortion and assisted suicide have been defined as "private choices". This means that both cases are not taking into account possible social consequences.

Assisted suicide, for instance, can be considered a deeply personal issue, but it also directly affects the doctor-patient relationship and,therefore, the wider role of doctors in society. It introduces a deep ambiguity into the very definition of medical care, since medical care always signified the search for remedies to make life last longer, and now it involves killing. Cardinal Bernardin assessed that our witness would be more effective and persuasive to face present-day challenges if we viewed life across the spectrum, from conception until natural death, calling our society to see the connection between caring for life and defending it. In this, of course, there are implications for the internal life of the Church. It has to remain a voice for life – vigorous, strong, consistent, as it did in the recent case of partial birth abortion.

The Christian conception of caring for life, embodied in the daily witnessing and commitment of each one of us, must invite the wider society to see the linkage between care for and defense of life. These efforts from within the Church are essential to match the public witness of the Church in society.

An Appeal of a Dying Cardinal: Assisted Suicide is Still Unethical

The meaning of life and the fact that no reason can justify its elimination have been deeply rooted in the conscience of the Cardinal until the last minutes and hours of his earthly life. In a letter reflecting his own impending death, Cardinal Bernardin told US Supreme Court Justices there "can be no such thing as a 'right to assisted suicide. '" No such right can exist, he added, "because there can be no legal and moral order that tolerates the killing of innocent human life, even if the agent of death is self-administered." The Cardinal continues his forceful and heartfelt appeal saying : "I am at the end of my earthly life – there is much that I have contemplated these last few months of my illness, but as one who is dying I have especially come to appreciate the gift of life."

"Physician-assisted suicide is decidedly a public method," he said. "It is not simply a decision made between patient and physician. Because life affects every person, it is of primary public concern." And furthermore, he asserts that "Creating a new 'right' to assisted suicide will endanger society and send a false signal that a less than 'perfect' life is not worth living."

30

Healthcare

A Point of View from a Cardinal Diagnosed with Cancer

No other subject can be of greater interest in a world that val-
ues people for their money and not for their human qualities.
Cardinal Bernardin analyzes today's situation in the field of
the healthcare system while detecting possible areas of inter-
vention. He shows us the biblical way of providing care and its
possible modern applications. He examines it as a Christian
and as a patient, since he has experienced healthcare systems
as a result of his illness. Following him in this analysis, we also
learn how precious human life is and from which perspective
it should be lived. An incumbent death can be faced with dig-
nity and hope, Bernardin teaches us. A healthcare system wor-
thy of human society must be designed on human and
religious values.

During his whole ministry as a bishop, Cardinal Bernardin in-
vested considerable time and energy on issues related to Catholic health care. When, in 1994 health care reform became part
of the public policy debate, he made several contributions to
that discussion. He both underlined the importance of the not-for-profit
status of Catholic health care institutions and expressed his appreciation
for the dedication to, and service in, the ministry of Catholic health care

by religious women and men. In 1995 he wrote the Pastoral Letter "A Sign of Hope" on the meaning of Catholic health care ministry to gather several of his concerns and to give direction to health care ministry in the Archdiocese of Chicago. Before beginning the project, however, he was diagnosed with pancreatic cancer and had to undergo surgery with radiation therapy and chemotherapy treatments. He then faced the health care problem both as a bishop and as a patient.

Being at Home

His diagnosis, surgery, and post-operative radiation and chemotherapy led him into a new dimension of his life-long journey of faith, as he recently recalled : "For the first time in my life I truly had to look death in the face. In one brief moment, all my personal dreams and pastoral plans for the future had to be put on hold. Everything in my personal life and pastoral ministry had to be re-evaluated from a new perspective. My initial experience was of disorientation, isolation, a feeling of not being 'at home' anymore", were his words on the subject. Like all other cancer patients, he faced anguishes, fears and pain, but relying trustfully in Jesus he journeyed from a former way of life into a new manner of living.

Then came the impulse of writing a pastoral letter, with his reflections on his own illness as well as on the state and future of Catholic health care. This work was Bernardin's attempt to define more clearly what is distinctive about Christian health care ministry.

In a simple but effective way, he offered his reflections on the Christian value and social aim of health care, the roots of which must be traced back to the Bible and the Babylonian captivity of the Hebrew people. Their sufferings, always put in God's hands, are an important lesson for those of us who live in a world where disease and tragedy can shake the foundations of our faith and of our very being. In its own way, illness is a kind of human exile, a feeling of not being "at home," and of being cut off from our former way of life.

Never Give Up Hope

In moments of sickness, a Christian must never give up hope. Trusting in God's inseparable love, we are confident in the possibility to continue living despite the chaos we encounter along our pilgrim journey. However, this hope is not a hope for something ; it is not the expectation that something will happen. Even when a cure is unlikely, one can still hope. Cardinal Bernardin speaks of an attitude about life and living in God's loving care. Jesus cured people of their illness, and it is certainly appropriate for us to hope and pray for cures. However, the fuller meaning of Jesus' healing miracles was the strengthening of people's faith so that they could live as a people of hope. As Christians, we are called and empowered to comfort others in the midst of their suffering by giving them a reason to hope. We are called to help them experience God's enduring love for them. This is what makes Christian health care truly distinctive.

Many External Challenges

A Christian must seek to do more than merely cure a physical illness. Like Jesus, a Christian must heal the whole person. The heart of Christian health care is indeed in caring for people in such a way that they have hope. In an environment that is evolving rapidly as a result of technological change and institutional forces, health care delivery is no longer centered in the free-standing, acute care hospital. It is increasingly focused not only on curing illness but also on preventing illness and building "wellness." It is no longer focused solely on the patient but also attends to the overall health of the community.

Health care has experienced many external challenges, for example, people have attempted to curb its escalating cost. A national discussion on the possibility of systemic reform of American health care , i.e., how it is provided and financed has been raised.

The U.S. Catholic bishops participated in that debate and articulated several principles that should guide health care reform. Cardinal Bernardin developed a Protocol to inform and guide the making of important decisions by Catholic health care institutions in the Archdiocese of Chicago. Central to that Protocol (issued in August, 1994) is the Cardinal's belief that health care is an essential ministry of the entire community of faith, the Church. Therefore, it should be seen as part of the whole Church and available especially to the poor and marginalized, women and children, the aged and the disabled.

In the future, health care will increasingly be provided in the context of what is often described as "integrated delivery." As a result, Cardinal Bernardin suggested that Catholic health care enter into relationships with organizations, systems, and businesses that may share some but not all of our Christian values.

As it has already been pointed out, Cardinal Bernardin had the experience of health care system as a patient, since he had been diagnosed a cancer. Beyond human suffering, life and death for a Christian of Bernardin's level have the same deep value.

Death as a Friend and Not an Enemy

Speaking as a terminal patient and as a bishop and man of faith, Cardinal Bernardin delivered a speech at the Georgetown University. In his concluding words we can read a testament of faith, a message of hope for all sick people, an invitation to a stronger support and commitment for the protection of life. The beauty of its meaning is here entirely left to his own words pronounced on that occasion.

"I now face a very different horizon. In human terms, I have been advised my life span is now quite limited. This fact does not change any of the moral or social analyses that I have used in this address. But it does shape one's perspective decisively. I have already said that, as a person of faith - of resurrection faith – I see death as a friend not a foe, and the experience of death is, I am convinced, a transition from earthly life to eternal life -from grace to glory, as St. Augustine said.

These are my deepest convictions of faith, which have been rooted in God's word and confirmed by the sacraments of the Church. But the experience I am now going through sheds new light on the moral order also. As a bishop, I have tried, in season and out of season, to shape and share a moral message about the unique value of human life and our common responsibilities for it. As my life now slowly ebbs away, as my temporal destiny becomes clearer each hour and each day, I am not anxious, but rather reconfirmed in my conviction about the wonder of human life, a gift that flows from the very being of God and is entrusted to each of us. It is easy in the rush of daily life or in its tedium to lose the sense of wonder that is appropriate to this gift. It is even easier at the level of our societal relations to count some lives as less valuable than others, especially when caring for them costs us – financially, emotionally, or in terms of time, effort, and struggle.

The truth is, of course, that each life is of infinite value. Protecting and promoting life – caring for it and defending it – is a complex task in social and policy terms. I have struggled with the specifics often and have sensed the limits of reason in the struggle to know the good and do the right. My final hope is that my efforts have been faithful to the truth of the gospel of life and that you and others like you will find in this gospel the vision and strength needed to promote and nurture the great gift of life God has shared with us."

Index

223